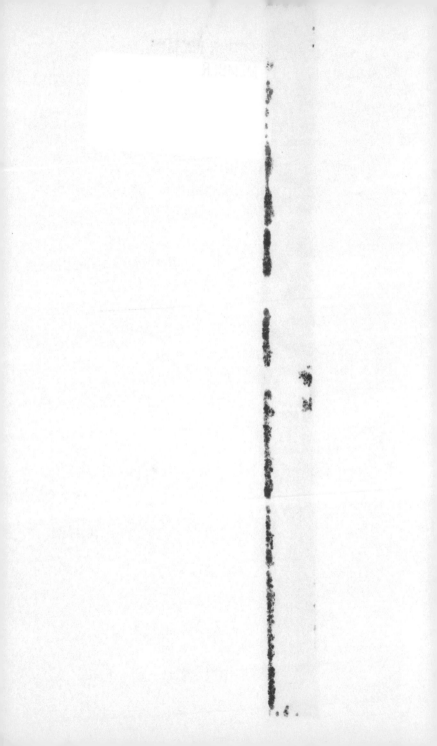

THE SCOTTISH EDUCATIONAL SYSTEM

THE SCOTTISH EDUCATIONAL SYSTEM

by

S. LESLIE HUNTER, M.A., M.Ed.

SENIOR LECTURER IN EDUCATION,
JORDANHILL COLLEGE OF EDUCATION, GLASGOW

1966

PERGAMON PRESS

OXFORD · LONDON · EDINBURGH · NEW YORK
TORONTO · SYDNEY · PARIS · BRAUNSCHWEIG

PERGAMON PRESS LTD.,
Headington Hill Hall, Oxford
4 & 5 Fitzroy Square, London W.1

PERGAMON PRESS (SCOTLAND) LTD.,
2 & 3 Teviot Place, Edinburgh 1

PERGAMON PRESS INC.,
Maxwell House, Fairview Park, Elmsford, New York 10523

PERGAMON OF CANADA LTD.,
207 Queen's Quay West, Toronto 1

PERGAMON PRESS (AUST.) PTY. LTD.,
19a Boundary Street, Rushcutters Bay, N.S.W. 2011, Australia

PERGAMON PRESS S.A.R.L.,
24 rue des Écoles, Paris 5ᵉ

VIEWEG & SOHN GMBH,
Burgplatz 1, Braunschweig

First edition 1968

Reprinted 1969

Library of Congress Catalog Card No. 67-24310

Printed in Great Britain by A. Wheaton & Co., Exeter

08 012494 1 (flexicover)
08 012495 x (hard cover)

Contents

Foreword and Acknowledgements

THIS book originated as a response to the needs of students in colleges of education and university departments of education in Scotland. It provides an overall view of the Scottish educational system as it exists today, and brings together in one volume material which is scattered throughout various acts, regulations, reports and other official publications. References at the end of each chapter are planned to direct students requiring additional information to relevant sources.

It is hoped that the book will also be of value as a textbook in courses of comparative education. For students in colleges of education and university departments of education in England, it provides a basis for accurate and informed comparison of the systems of education north and south of the Border. For students abroad, it contributes towards filling the gap which exists in published material on the Scottish system. Since most of the material on British education refers to England, with few references to Scottish sources, there is a danger that the two systems may be regarded as the same. The present work aims at highlighting those elements of structure, tradition, and outlook which are distinctive of Scottish education.

The author is indebted to various members of staff at Jordanhill College of Education for providing facilities, information, and advice: H. P. Wood, Principal; J. Gibb, Assistant Principal; L. A. Stenhouse, Principal Lecturer in Education; T. D. Morrow, Lecturer in Education (now Principal Lecturer in Education, Callendar Park College of Education, Falkirk); W. M. T. Mason, Principal Lecturer in Further Education; A. S. Duncan, Principal Lecturer in Commerce; J. P. H. Round, Tutor in Youth Leadership.

At Glasgow University the following have been particularly helpful: S. D. Nisbet, Professor of Education; T. R. Bone, Lecturer in Education; N. Dees, Director of Extra-Mural Education.

J. T. Wilson, Headmaster of Mossbank School, Glasgow, provided useful insights into the work of approved schools; and P. Milne, Assistant Director of Education, Ayrshire, helped to unravel some of the complexities of local administration.

Special reference must be made to various officers of the Scottish Education Department, who gave generously of their time and knowledge; their help has been invaluable.

Notwithstanding the indebtedness acknowledged above, the author is entirely responsible for any errors of fact or of judgement which this book may contain.

Glasgow   S. LESLIE HUNTER

October 1966

CHAPTER 1

Historical Development

THE purpose of this chapter is to provide a general outline of the historical development of Scottish education, with particular reference to those features which may lead to a deeper understanding and appreciation of the present educational system. Thus a comprehensive coverage is not attempted and there are no detailed references to sources.

A list of some useful general and local histories is given at the end of the chapter.

BEFORE THE REFORMATION

Scots are traditionally proud of their educational system, which has a very long history. The date of origin is generally accepted as A.D. 563, the year in which Columba landed in Iona. The Celtic Church established monasteries in many parts of Scotland, and to at least some of these monasteries seminaries were attached, their function being to prepare young monks for the Church. Later, from about the seventh century, lay scholars were admitted, and boys came, for example to Iona, from England, Ireland and Scandinavia, as well as from the mainland of Scotland.

From the eighth to the eleventh centuries, however, the history of Scottish education is virtually a blank, although it seems that these schools were conducted by three types of official: the master or rector, who was in charge of the educational work at each monastery, and who was a man of importance and dignity; the scoloc, who was a young student assistant to the master; and the ferleighinn (or ferleyn) who appointed the rector and lectured in theology to advanced students. The curriculum can only be con-jectural: religion; Latin and Greek; the study of sacred manu-scripts, poetic metre and astronomy; the learning of psalms. But very little is known about Scottish education under the Columban Church.

With the spread of Roman Christianity the picture becomes clearer, and there are reliable documents from the twelfth century on. David I took over the Celtic monasteries as they stood for the Roman Church, which was the national church of Scotland for four centuries. The monasteries and abbeys of the Roman Church had usually schools within their precincts, and also main-tained schools in neighbouring burghs, towns and parishes. Thus there developed cathedral schools, abbey schools, collegiate schools, parish schools and song schools—the latter originally teaching music, "manners and virtue" to choirboys. In addition many schools conducted by the Church in the neighbourhood of abbeys and cathedrals became schools of the burghs in which they were situated, with the town councils gradually taking over control from the Church. By the end of the fifteenth century every principal town in Scotland had its grammar or burgh school which taught mainly Latin.

The fifteenth century was marked by the founding of three universities—St. Andrews in 1411, Glasgow in 1450, Aberdeen in 1494—and by the passing in 1496 of an Act which stated that barons and freeholders of substance were to put their eldest sons to school from the age of 6 or 9 until they had "perfite latyne". Although this Act seems to have had little effect, it is of interest as being the first Act in Europe which attempted to introduce some element of compulsory education.

THE REFORMATION AND THE FIRST BOOK
OF DISCIPLINE

The Reformation reached its height in Scotland in the mid-sixteenth century, and in the tearing down of many of the religious institutions of the Roman Church many schools were destroyed.

However, the Reformers showed an immense interest in education. In 1560 John Knox and his colleagues produced the *First Book of Discipline* in which the chapter on education set out a scheme for a national system of education. There were to be elementary schools in country parishes in which the 5–8 year olds would be taught reading and the elements of the Catechism by the reader or minister of the parish; grammar schools in towns of "any repute" in which the 8–12 year olds would study Latin grammar; high schools in important towns in which selected pupils of 12–16 would study Latin, Greek, logic and rhetoric; and universities in which the most able scholars would pursue a 3-year Arts course followed by a 5-year course in medicine, law or divinity. It was a compulsory scheme for rich and poor, promotion from one stage to another depending on ability; the stated aim was the moral culture of every child and the highest good of the community.

This remarkable scheme came to naught. Parliament rejected it; moreover money for its financing was to come from the confiscation of the lands of the Old Faith, and these were seized by the nobles. But the importance of the scheme need hardly be emphasized; it served as a standard and an ideal towards which to strive, an ideal only realized in Scotland some 300 years later.

SCHOOLS IN THE SEVENTEENTH TO NINETEENTH CENTURIES

Throughout this period, although Scotland remained a poor country, there was a considerable expansion in the provision of education, both in the form of the traditional parish and burgh schools and in the form of schools provided by various voluntary agencies.

Parish Schools

In the seventeenth century progress was gradually made towards the ideal of a school in every parish. While Acts of 1616,

1633 and 1646 achieved little, the 1696 *Act for Settling of Schools* had a fair measure of success. The Act decreed that in every parish a school should be established and a schoolmaster appointed on the advice of the heritors and minister of the parish, and required the heritors to provide a house for the school and to settle a salary of approximately £5 10s. to £11 per annum for the schoolmaster. The story throughout the eighteenth century is generally one of reluctant heritors being prodded by local presbyteries to fulfil their obligations. Often the building eventually provided consisted of two rooms, or even one room in which the master lived and taught his pupils; it was frequently dilapidated, badly lit and inadequately ventilated; it was sometimes in a church, a stable or a barn.

In large parishes one school was quite inadequate, and the 1803 Act empowered heritors to establish in these areas additional schools which became known as "side schools"; but many parishes were without a school even in the nineteenth century, when provision fell to be made increasingly by the churches and various voluntary organizations.

The curriculum of parish schools consisted mainly of reading, writing, reckoning and religion; some schools taught Latin and enabled poor but talented youths to proceed from parish school to university; some schools added subjects like geography, bookkeeping, navigation. Conditions of work were rarely good; classes were often large, methods mechanical and discipline strict.

Some of the teachers in parish schools were scholarly, dedicated men, but in general there were wide variations with regard to intellectual ability, professional competence and personal qualities. The teacher was appointed, usually *ad vitam aut culpam*, by heritors and minister, and until 1861 was examined by the presbytery with regard to ability and character and obliged to sign the Confession of Faith. The salary was usually inadequate—in 1800 it fell below the wage of a casual labourer. The 1803 Act fixed a range of approximately £16 10s. to £23; the Act of 1861, £35 to £70. There was also income from fees, and in many cases from undertaking other offices such as heritors' clerk or session clerk. In 1800 one teacher acted as dominie, parish clerk, leader of the choir, beadle and gravedigger—all for £8 a year.

In spite of its various shortcomings the parish school system was in advance of the educational facilities provided in other European countries during this period, and served Scotland well until 1872, when it was incorporated in a more comprehensive national system of schools.

Burgh Schools

The significance of the Reformation for grammar or burgh schools was that control passed increasingly from the church to the town councils, although the church retained until 1861 the right of supervision, which extended to the religious orthodoxy of the master. The school was generally maintained by town assessments or grants from the "common good" of the burgh.

In the smaller burghs the grammar school provided elementary as well as secondary education, that is English, writing and arithmetic as well as the classics. In the larger burghs the grammar school was almost exclusively devoted to the classics, chiefly Latin, elementary subjects being taught in Lecture or English schools which taught mainly reading and writing to children up to the age of 8 or 9. Subjects such as French and mathematics were not common until the nineteenth century, when most schools regarded Latin, Greek and mathematics as "the university subjects". Some of the smaller grammar schools further from university influence added, like some of the parish schools, geography, book-keeping or navigation. Social and recreational education tended to be neglected in favour of academic work, a tendency typical of Scottish secondary education. From earliest times religious instruction was regarded as essential.

Most schools were not large and internal organization varied considerably, but from the 1830's it became the custom to organize schools in departments under separate masters, with or without a rector in control. Conditions were not always good, work was hard and discipline strict. A day of 10 hours was not uncommon in the seventeenth century, and one of 6 hours was usual in the nineteenth century.

Masters in the grammar schools were usually more highly qualified and better paid than dominies in parish schools. By the mid-nineteenth century approximately 70% had had some university education and 40% were graduates. Income, which varied from place to place, was in the form of salaries paid by the town councils, and pupils' fees, a separate fee generally being paid for each subject. Appointment was by the town councils, the issue of church approval being solved in 1861 when the examination of masters passed to a panel of six professors from the nearest university. Tenure was usually for a stated period, rather than *ad vitam aut culpam* as in the parish schools.

Although some parish schools provided education beyond the elementary stage, and although the smaller burgh schools provided elementary as well as secondary education, the parish schools are usually regarded as forerunners of today's primary schools, and the burgh schools as forerunners of today's secondary schools.

Academies

In the mid-eighteenth century a reaction to the exclusively classical curriculum of the larger grammar schools found its main expression in the development of "academies". In spite of this title these institutions arose to meet the demand for certain scientific, commercial and practical subjects. The first academy was opened at Perth in 1761, and between that date and 1830, sixteen academies were established, generally by public subscription. These schools were usually superior to grammar schools in buildings, staffing and organization. Many, however, soon lost their non-academic bias, but not before their presence had exerted a liberalizing influence on the grammar school curriculum. In some cases grammar schools thus reformed adopted the title "high school"; in others the two types of institution amalgamated, usually under the title of "academy".

Academies constituted another important forerunner of present-day secondary schools. They were doubly important as marking a recognition of the need for changes in secondary education to accompany changes in social, economic and industrial conditions, a need which Scottish secondary education has constantly been slow to recognize, even in the twentieth century.

SSPCK Schools

The deficiencies of the parish system were partly repaired by the Society in Scotland for Propagating Christian Knowledge, founded in 1709, which raised voluntary contributions in order to establish schools, especially in highland areas "where error, idolatry, superstition and ignorance do most abound, by reason of the largeness of parishes and scarcity of schools". (As late as 1758, 175 highland parishes were without a school.) The Society provided the teacher, the local heritors provided the building, and the curriculum consisted mainly of religion plus the three R's.

The Society later experimented with technical education, mainly in the form of spinning schools for girls, and by 1795 had over 300 ordinary schools and over ninety spinning schools. It is estimated that in the first 100 years of its existence the Society was responsible for the education of some 300,000 children, mostly in areas where no other school was provided. When the 1872 Act put an end to its activities the Society had over 200 schools, but the standard in buildings and instruction had fallen considerably below the original aims of the Society.

Church Schools

The historical connection of the Church with education has already been noted; perhaps the most effective work of the main denominations was done in the nineteenth century.

From 1824 the Education Committee of the General Assembly of the Church of Scotland established "assembly schools", particularly in the Highlands and Islands, thus complementing the parochial system and the work of the SSPCK. Although instruction was denominational the schools were not exclusive, and the curriculum was similar to that of the parish schools. In towns the Church of Scotland also established "sessional schools", so called because the kirk session provided the accommodation and the teacher, supplied books and equipment, established a set of rules, and superintended and maintained the schools. In the 1860's there were 120 sessional schools, of which the forty-six in Glasgow dealt with 36% of the school population of the city. By helping to provide elementary education in towns where the population was growing rapidly (Glasgow's population rose from 77,385 in 1801 to 395,000 in 1861) sessional schools played a major part in Scottish education between 1813 and 1872.

The Free Church after the Disruption of 1843, the Roman Catholic Church, and the Scottish Episcopal Church established their own schools. The extent of church provision was revealed in the Second Report of the Argyll Commission in 1867: 519 Church of Scotland schools; 617 Free Church schools; 74 Episcopal schools; and 61 Roman Catholic schools. At that date there were 202 SSPCK schools, over 1100 parish schools, over 50 burgh schools, and 23 academies.

Private Adventure Schools

Private adventure schools, many of them of doubtful educational value, existed in Scotland from an early date. Although the nineteenth century saw the development of some excellent private schools for the highest social classes, it also saw the proliferation of adventure schools run for profit by teachers of questionable qualifications. In 1866 there were eighty-eight such schools in Glasgow alone, with nearly 7000 children on the rolls. The Argyll Commissioners found colliery clerks, labourers, herring-fishers, weavers, an overseer and a staff sergeant in the militia running adventure schools as a sideline. The conditions were usually uniformly bad, and the curriculum little more than reading, spelling, and "moral lessons". In 1867 there were over 900 private adventure schools in Scotland, and although the 1872 Act did not put an end to such schools, it cut down on the number of children attending them.

Other Types of School

Throughout the nineteenth century the general pattern of schools became increasingly complex. There were endowed institutions, the earliest "hospitals" dating from the seventeenth century. There were works schools run by some factories, the most famous being that of Robert Owen at his model factory at New Lanark. There were schools of industry which gave girls vocational instruction in knitting, needlework, cookery and housework. There were industrial schools to cater for children aged 7–14 who were vagrants, beggars, or the associates of criminals. There were subscription schools, parents clubbing together to pay for a teacher in a locality where there was no other educational provision. There were infant schools stemming from the pioneer work of men such as Owen, Buchanan and Stow. There were schools provided in the Highlands and Islands by three Gaelic Societies.

By the 1860's the situation was chaotic. There was no coherent system of schools; there was no central control and organization; there was wide variation in the standards of the different types of school; and about one-fifth of Scottish children still attended no school at all. There was a demand for an effective national system of education. A Royal Commission under the chairmanship of the Duke of Argyll was appointed in 1864 to investigate the state of education in the country and the result of its reports was the passing of the Education (Scotland) Act, 1872, one of the major landmarks in the history of Scottish education.

THE 1872 ACT AND ELEMENTARY EDUCATION

The 1872 Act established a national system of public elementary schools, and made education compulsory between the ages of 5 and 13. Parochial and burgh schools formed the nucleus, and denominational schools might be transferred voluntarily to the national system; many of the voluntary schools were so transferred within a few years, although Roman Catholic and Episcopal schools remained independent until 1918.

Public schools were open to children of all denominations and were subject to inspection, but not with regard to religious instruction. Religious instruction was safeguarded and a conscience clause gave authority to any parent to withdraw his child from such instruction.

Local management of schools was vested in school boards, which consisted of five to fifteen elected members. To begin with there were 984 school boards, one for every parish or burgh in Scotland. School boards were required to maintain and keep efficient the schools under their management, to provide the additional accommodation necessary, to enforce attendance at school, and to fix school fees, the system being financed by means of government grants, local rates and fees. The boards were given the right of appointing teachers who held office during the pleasure of the particular board; existing teachers were confirmed in their appointments.

Finally, a central controlling and co-ordinating body, the Scotch Education Department, was established.

The 1872 Act was the most important and ambitious measure affecting education in Scotland before the twentieth century, and marks the start of the modern era in Scottish education. The system of public elementary schools established by the Act was to develop into the present system of primary schools covering the length and breadth of the land.

SECONDARY EDUCATION AFTER 1872

A major deficiency of the 1872 Act was its virtual neglect of secondary education, although this is hardly surprising, since the aim behind the Act was to provide universal elementary education. After 1872 secondary education developed along three main lines.

The first line of development was in "higher class" schools. Under the Act the management of burgh schools was transferred from the town councils and magistrates to the new school boards, so that these schools became public schools. Those burgh schools in which the education given was not chiefly in the three R's, but rather in the higher branches of knowledge such as the classics, modern languages, mathematics, science, were designated "higher class" public schools; eleven were so specified in the Act, and school boards were allowed to upgrade other public schools to this status. This process was hindered by the fact that such schools to begin with were not eligible for state grants or a share in the local school-rate. Secondary schools which were not legally burgh schools—certain academies, endowed institutions and private schools—were not affected by the Act, became known as higher class schools, and continued to develop purely secondary education.

Secondary education was advanced by certain important developments in the latter part of the nineteenth century—for example, a complete reorganization of endowments in the 1880's; the statutory annual inspection of all higher class public schools from 1886 and the voluntary inspection of other similar schools; the institution in 1888 of the Leaving Certificate examination which, adopted by almost all the higher class schools, both public and private, gave a clear goal and raised and equated standards among schools; the setting up in 1892 on a county basis of secondary education committees to plan for the expansion of secondary education, including the handling of its finance, for which grants had been made available under a number of statutes. This last was important as marking a move towards the county as the unit of educational administration.

After the Education (Scotland) Act, 1908, the higher class schools, both public and private, came to be known as "secondary schools"; such schools developed during the twentieth century into the 5- and 6-year secondary schools of the present day.

The second main line of development of secondary education was in Higher Grade Schools or Departments set up as a result of the Code of 1899. These schools were originally planned to give a

3-year secondary course with a vocational bias towards a science or commercial side. However, when Supplementary Courses were introduced (see below) offering vocational opportunities similar to those in Higher Grade Schools, the latter were made more liberal in approach and the curriculum was broadened and directed towards the Intermediate Certificate introduced in 1902 for pupils aged not less than 15 who passed in four or more subjects in the Leaving Certificate examination. Many of these schools eventually developed 5-year courses and took their pupils up to the full Leaving Certificate. In 1920, when there were about 200 Higher Grade Schools, those with 5-year courses were fully recognized as secondary schools by the Scottish Education Department. Some of today's well-known Scottish secondary schools had their origin as Higher Grade Schools.

The third line of development, that of secondary education of up to 3 years' duration, was in courses originally closely tied to the elementary schools. There were various systems of courses and a confusing terminology. First of all, from 1873 to 1899 was the system of "specific subjects", under which pupils in the later years of the elementary school might study one, two, or three from a list of subjects, each subject arranged in three grades or stages. In 1892 a Merit Certificate was introduced, open to pupils over age 13 in elementary schools, who satisfied H.M. Inspectors in certain subjects. In towns some of the school boards organized the specific subjects in such a way as to develop higher departments at the top of the elementary school; but in the country as a whole only a fraction of children studied specific subjects, most children and parents in the nineteenth century being content with a purely elementary education.

In 1899 the system of specific subjects was replaced by that of Advanced Departments, and the function of the Merit Certificate was changed to that of marking the satisfactory completion at about age 12 of a course of elementary education, before entry to any form of post-elementary work. The basic curriculum of Advanced Departments was prescribed by the Scottish Education Department, and the course, usually of two years' duration, was intended for pupils likely to leave at the end of compulsory schooling. This system only operated until 1903, although some of the larger and better-organized Advanced Departments developed into Higher Grade Schools.

In 1903 the qualifying examination replaced the Merit Certificate as a determinant of which children were to proceed to post-elementary education, and the Advanced Departments were replaced by Supplementary Courses. The curriculum of Supplementary Courses, although partly general, introduced a new vocational bias—commercial, industrial, rural, or domestic. The Merit Certificate was now used to mark the satisfactory completion of a Supplementary Course of not less than one year. In some of the larger burghs these courses were provided in separate central schools which took pupils from neighbouring elementary schools. Supplementary Courses, although criticized for their early vocational bias, survived for 20 years, and were the only provision for the majority of pupils; those who failed the qualifying examination did not receive any recognized form of secondary education.

In 1923 the qualifying examination ceased to be the concern of the Scottish Education Department, and its place was taken by local control examinations conducted by the education authorities set up by the Education (Scotland) Act, 1918, and Advanced Divisions replaced Supplementary Courses. The curriculum of Advanced Divisions was broader, with a less specialized vocational bias, and led to the award of the Day School Certificate (Lower) after a 2-year course, and the Day School Certificate (Higher) after a 3-year course. These Certificates replaced the Merit and Intermediate Certificates respectively. In the 1930's, about one-quarter of all recognized secondary schools offered Advanced Division courses; some courses were provided in the separate central schools mentioned above; but most Advanced Divisions were still just "tops" to primary schools. Moreover, over 10% of all children did not get the length of Advanced Divisions, and of those who did, only about one in six reached the third year of the course.

By the Education (Scotland) Act, 1936, the distinction between secondary education and Advanced Divisions was removed, and all post-primary education was designated
"secondary". The school-leaving age was to be raised to 15 on
1st September, 1939, but this did not come into effect because of
the outbreak of war. The Code of 1939 abolished the Day School
Certificate (Lower) and replaced the Day School Certificate
(Higher) by a new Junior Leaving Certificate. The operation of
this Certificate was, however, suspended because of wartime
conditions, and after the war no national certificate was reintroduced to mark the end of a 3-year course of secondary
education.

After the Education (Scotland) Act, 1946, and the raising of the
school-leaving age to 15 in 1947, secondary courses of 5 or 6
years' duration became generally known as "senior secondary"
courses, and those of 3 years' duration as "junior secondary"
courses. A classification in these terms forms the starting-point
for the description of present-day secondary education given in
Chapter 5.

FURTHER EDUCATION

Technical education in Scotland had its origin in evening classes
for the instruction of working mechanics instituted in Glasgow in
1800. These classes led to the establishing in 1823 of "The Mechanics Institution". Similar developments led to the establishing in
Edinburgh in 1821 of "The School of Arts", for the purpose of
giving workmen education in scientific principles. These two institutions, from which have sprung what are now Strathclyde
University and Heriot-Watt University, were the forerunners of
the mechanics' institutes which developed in many towns in
Scotland and England, and made an important contribution
towards establishing the modern system of technical education.

From the mid-nineteenth century certain government grants
were available for technical education; for example, from 1859
the Department of Science and Art instituted a system of grants

to establishments providing training in branches of science related to industrial occupations. The administration of these grants was transferred to the Scotch Education Department in 1897, and in 1901 the Department issued a Code of Regulations for Continuation Classes in Scotland which organized post-school education into four divisions: classes for the completion of elementary education; elementary classes in technical subjects; organized courses in technical education lasting 3 years or more; non-vocational classes. It was to an exception in this Code that Scotland owes its most important line of development in technical education; certain established and successful institutions situated at important centres of population were allowed to develop on lines of their own. These exempted institutions became known as "central institutions", and have been responsible for the development of advanced courses in various branches of technical education.

Work at less advanced levels has traditionally been the sphere of evening classes or "night school" in Scotland. There were comparatively few before 1872, and the instruction they gave was of a very elementary character. The 1872 Act empowered school boards to provide evening classes for pupils over age 13, and the Code of 1901 introduced the reorganization mentioned above.

The 1908 Act laid upon school boards the duty of providing continuation classes for the further instruction of young people above the age of 14 with reference to the crafts and industries practised in the district. Such courses had also to include English language and literature, the laws of health, and opportunity for physical training. The 1918 Act gave education authorities power to require the compulsory part-time attendance—up to age 16 and later to age 18—at day continuation classes of those who left school at the minimum age. This provision was not put into effect. The relevant provisions were replaced by provisions of the 1946 Act for the compulsory attendance of young persons who had left school and were under the age of 18, on one day a week at "junior colleges" (the equivalent of the county colleges envisaged for England), but this provision likewise was not put into operation.

Although attendance at courses of further education thus remains voluntary, there has been a tremendous expansion in the provision of such courses in the mid-twentieth century. The whole field of present-day further education, including the work of central institutions and further education centres (or colleges of further education), is the subject matter of Chapter 10.

THE TRAINING OF TEACHERS

There was no professional training of teachers in Scotland before the nineteenth century. In 1828 David Stow, a Glasgow philanthropist, began in a model infant school the training of teachers to implement his educational ideals, and the Glasgow Educational Society, of which Stow was secretary, opened a "normal seminary" or training college in Dundas Vale in 1837. This was in effect the first teacher training college in the British Isles.

The direction taken by subsequent events led to the development of training colleges under the control of the main religious denominations; for example, both the Church of Scotland and the Free Church established one college each in Glasgow and Edinburgh in the 1840's, and one each in Aberdeen in the 1870's. For over 60 years the training of teachers was carried out almost entirely by the Education Committees of the Churches.

The pupil-teacher system, which was also to last for 60 years, was introduced in 1846. Under this system certain pupils were selected at about age 13 for a 5-year apprenticeship, during which they helped with the work of teaching, being paid a small salary, and continuing their own education. Thereafter they were eligible to compete for Queen's Scholarships tenable at training colleges. Provision was also made for allowances to be paid to teachers so trained, and this accelerated the move towards a trained profession; nevertheless by 1867 only a third of Scottish teachers held certificates.

After 1872 the majority of entrants to the profession, except graduates, went through the colleges; for example, in 1877 the three Church of Scotland colleges were providing 2-year courses for about 500 students, almost all of whom had been pupil-teachers, the brightest having been awarded Queen's Scholarships.

The Code of 1873 allowed Queen's Scholars to take certain university classes concurrently with college training, and some responsibility for the training of teachers was shifted from the churches to the universities by the Code of 1895 which authorized each university to set up a local committee to be responsible for the professional training of students who received their academic education in university classes. This situation only lasted until 1905, however, and it is true to say that Scottish universities have never been closely involved with teacher training. For the whole of the nineteenth century, moreover, the great majority of university graduates who entered teaching were untrained.

By the beginning of the twentieth century there was a need to combine the existing training facilities into a national system, and in 1905 Provincial Committees for the Training of Teachers were established in each of four university areas called "provinces" to train both primary and secondary teachers. From 1906 these Committees took over the work of the former university local committees, and in 1907 assumed responsibility for the Church of Scotland and Free Church training colleges in Edinburgh, Glasgow and Aberdeen. In each case the double provision was reduced to a single training centre, and the nucleus of the present system of colleges was established as follows: Moray House, Edinburgh, 1913; Aberdeen 1919; Dundee 1920; Jordanhill, Glasgow, 1921.

In 1920 a co-ordinating National Committee for the Training of Teachers, composed of representatives of education authorities, was set up with responsibility for training policy; the four Provincial Committees were reconstituted; and separate Committees of Management were authorized for one Episcopal college, two Roman Catholic colleges, and one college of Physical Education—all four being women's residential colleges. The day-to-day business of the National Committee was carried on by a Central Executive Committee representative of the National Committee and other interests. This remained the administrative machinery for teacher-training until 1958, when new Regulations introduced the present system described in Chapter 12.

The twentieth century brought many important developments in actual training. Regulations of 1906 introduced the principle of professional training for all teachers. The qualification for teaching in primary schools was the Teacher's General Certificate, awarded after a 2-year training college course or a 1-year postgraduate course at a training college. Certain ordinary graduates could also take an endorsement which enabled them to teach the secondary level Supplementary Courses. Intending teachers of higher classes in secondary schools had to be honours graduates, for whom a training course leading to the Teacher's Special Certificate was provided. A course of training leading to the award of the Teacher's Technical Certificate was also provided for holders of diplomas in recognized specialist subjects such as art, music, domestic science. The same Regulations replaced the pupil-teacher system with the more satisfactory junior student system. Junior students were given 3 years of professional training and general education in certain recognized secondary schools from ages 15–18; those successful in obtaining certain Leaving Certificate passes were awarded the Junior Student Certificate and could proceed as "senior students" to the 2-year training college course.

Of modifications introduced by the 1924 Regulations, two were of far-reaching importance. In the first place, all men candidates for the Teacher's General Certificate were required to be university graduates. This virtually eliminated the male nongraduate teacher in Scotland, a situation hardly paralleled elsewhere in the world, and certainly not in England. In the second place, the junior student system was abolished, since the combination of academic work plus practical teaching overburdened the students and led to their early segregation from other secondary pupils. Henceforth all non-graduate women candidates for training had to have the Leaving Certificate. In addition, requirements for the Teacher's Special Certificate and the Teacher's Technical Certificate were given in greater detail.

The position described above was modified in certain respects by the 1931 Regulations—for example, the course for non-graduate women was extended to 3 years. These Regulations, with amendments, governed teacher-training until 1965. Details of present entry requirements, courses and certificates are given in Chapter 12, along with information with regard to salaries, superannuation, professional organizations and status.

ADMINISTRATION

In the years following the 1872 Act many school boards did excellent work, taking over existing schools, building new schools, and enforcing attendance. For example, in Glasgow in 1874 there were twenty-seven schools with accommodation for just under 10,000 pupils; by 1883 there were sixty-two schools, thirty-one of them newly built, with accommodation for 44,000 pupils. But there were too many boards and the areas they administered were too small for efficiency. The Act of 1918 ended their existence, established the county as the unit of local administration, and laid the basis for the development of the modern system of local administration of education which is described in detail in Chapter 2.

The Scotch Education Department established in 1872 had its headquarters in London, and was assisted until 1878 by a Board of Education sitting in Edinburgh. The Department was formally a Committee of the Privy Council, but in practice a separate government department. It had the same President and Vice-President as the English Committee of the Privy Council on Education, and shared its Permanent Secretary. Thus from 1872 to 1885 the Vice-President of this Committee was in effect Minister of Education for Great Britain. However, when a Secretary for Scotland was appointed in 1885, part of his work was to be Vice-President of the Scotch Education Department, and a separate Permanent Secretary was appointed.

The Secretary for Scotland officially remained Vice-President of the Committee of the Privy Council until 1939, although the Committee did not meet after 1913, the Department being conducted by the authority of the Vice-President alone from 1914. The position of Secretary for Scotland was given the status of Secretary of State in 1926, and in 1939 the Department's functions were vested directly in the Secretary of State for Scotland. The title of the Department was changed to Scottish Education Department by the 1918 Act, and the transfer of the Department to Edinburgh was completed by 1939.

The powers of the Secretary of State with regard to Scottish education, and the present structure and functioning of the Scottish Education Department are explained in Chapter 2.

FINANCE

Education in Scotland was financed almost entirely by voluntary effort till well into the nineteenth century. The first parliamentary grants for Scottish education were sums of £10,000, paid in 1834, 1836, 1837 and 1838, towards the cost of new buildings. The scope of the grant was soon widened, and a Committee of the Privy Council on Education was set up to control expenditure. Schools which availed themselves of grants were open to inspection, and in 1840 the first Inspector of Schools in Scotland was appointed.

In 1862 the system of "payment by results" was introduced by a Revised Code of the Committee of Council. Under this system grants were paid on a capitation basis, and were dependent partly on the pupil's attendance, and partly on his performance in reading, writing and arithmetic, as judged by the Inspector. This system of individual examination applied to children over the age of 6 for whom specified tests in the three R's were laid down in six grades of difficulty known as "standards". This system of awarding grants was postponed in Scotland, eventually operating only from 1873 to 1890; in a modified form, based on the performance of classes rather than individual pupils, it continued until 1899, when grants came to be paid almost entirely on average attendance.

The finance of Scottish secondary education became complex and confusing in the last two decades of the nineteenth century. Money might be provided by fees, endowments, rates, a grant from a secondary education committee or a town or county council, or by government subsidy under five statutes passed between 1887 and 1898. By the 1908 Act various grants, including those by which secondary education had previously been financed, were consolidated in a central fund, the Education (Scotland) Fund, placed under the control of the Scotch Education Department. The 1918 Act extended the functions of the Education (Scotland) Fund to include the distribution of all monies voted by Parliament for education in Scotland, and laid down principles to determine the amount of the sums to be paid into the Fund. The Education (Scotland) Fund continued to be the main channel through which parliamentary grants were paid to Scottish education until the Fund was abolished by the Local Government and Miscellaneous Financial Provisions (Scotland) Act, 1958, which introduced the present system of finance described in the next chapter.

GENERAL DEVELOPMENTS

Twin trends in the twentieth century have been towards an expansion and improvement of educational provision, and towards a new, broader concept of the term "education", a concept which is far removed from instruction in the three R's, which was a main concern of the 1872 Act. These trends, first clearly apparent in the 1908 Act, were advanced by the Acts of 1918 and 1945 and embodied in the consolidating Acts of 1946 and 1962.

Thus there has been a gradual increase in the time spent at school. The official school-leaving age was raised to 14 in 1901, 15 in 1947, and is to be raised to 16 in 1970. Linked with this compulsory attendance is the trend towards voluntary staying on at school, which became marked in the 1960's.

Education is now free. Elementary education was free for children aged between 5 and 14 by 1891. The abolition of fees in secondary education was a longer process, and the first statute to provide for free secondary education was the Act of 1945. By the 1930's, "free education" was generally taken to include the provision of books, writing material and equipment, and the 1945 Act made this practice compulsory.

Social and welfare facilities gradually expanded during the century. For example, the 1908 Act authorized school boards to institute medical examination and supervision of the pupils in their districts, although in many areas compulsory medical inspection did not become the rule until the 1930's. The 1945 Act made such inspection one of the duties of education authorities, and since then the School Health Service has grown into a complex and important organization. The provision of school meals for pupils, first mentioned in the 1908 Act, is now a duty of education authorities, as is the provision of free milk each day. In a similar way the provision of bursaries for pupils attending secondary schools and students attending colleges and universities has been greatly extended.

Various other aspects of educational legislation since the Second World War show clearly the twin trends mentioned above—for example: the organization of the system in the three progressive stages of primary, secondary and further education; the references to the criteria of "age, ability and aptitude"; the clear statutory recognition given to the youth service; the guiding principle of educating pupils, as far as possible, in accordance with the wishes of their parents; the laying on education authorities of duties and powers with regard to handicapped children, child guidance clinics, the provision of milk, meals, clothing, hostels, transport—all the various activities of education authorities which are more closely examined in the next chapter.

As a result of an early start and fairly rapid progress, Scottish education, by the nineteenth century, had earned for itself a considerable reputation throughout the world. There are those who doubt whether this reputation has been maintained in the twentieth century. For example, on the final page of his book *Two Hundred and Fifty Years of Scottish Education*, published in 1953, H. M. Knox, after making an interesting comparison of advances in Scottish and English education, comments: "It would appear that Scotland, which had a national system of education when England was merely groping in the dark, has been marking time or even falling behind."

The question arises as to whether this statement, a fair and balanced comment at the time, still holds true. The chapters which follow present the evidence on which a judgement may be made.

SELECTED READING IN THE HISTORY OF SCOTTISH EDUCATION

General

EDGAR, J., *History of Early Scottish Education*, Edinburgh, James Thin, 1893.

KERR, J., *Scottish Education: School and University*, Cambridge University Press, 1910.

MORGAN, A., *Rise and Progress of Scottish Education*, Edinburgh, Oliver & Boyd, 1927.

GRANT, J., *History of the Burgh Schools of Scotland*, Glasgow, Collins, 1876.

KNOX, H. M., *Two Hundred and Fifty Years of Scottish Education*, Edinburgh, Oliver & Boyd, 1953.

Local Histories

BOYD, W., *Education in Ayrshire Through Seven Centuries*, London, University of London Press, 1961.

BAIN, A., *Education in Stirlingshire from the Reformation to the Act of 1872*, London, University of London Press, 1965.

LAW, A., *Education in Edinburgh in the Eighteenth Century*. London, University of London Press, 1965.

JESSUP, J. C., *Education in Angus*, London, University of London Press, 1931.

SIMPSON, I. J., *Education in Aberdeenshire Before 1872*, London, University of London Press, 1947.

CHAPTER 2

The Administration of
Scottish Education

SCOTTISH education, apart from the universities and independent schools, is administered centrally by the Scottish Education Department and locally by education authorities.

CENTRAL ADMINISTRATION

The arrangements made for the central administration of Scottish education are shown in diagram form in Fig. 1.

The Scottish Office

The Secretary of State for Scotland is responsible to Parliament for the work of the Scottish Office, which consists of four major Departments: the Department of Agriculture and Fisheries for Scotland, the Scottish Home and Health Department, the Scottish Education Department, and the Scottish Development Department, all of which are located at St. Andrew's House, Edinburgh. The Secretary of State also shares with a number of other Ministers responsibilities for the administration of certain services which are organized on a Great Britain basis.

As this is a very broad area of responsibility, the Secretary of State is assisted by a number of government Ministers and senior civil servants. On the ministerial side, there is a Minister of State and three Joint Parliamentary Under Secretaries of State. The Minister of State, as the Secretary of State's deputy, exercises a general oversight of the work of all four Departments. He also has

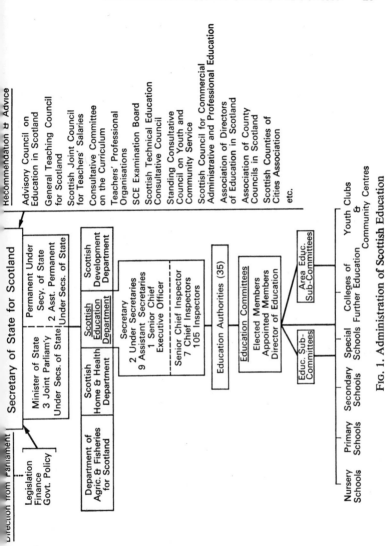

Fig. 1. Administration of Scottish Education

specific functions in connection with one of the Departments, and usually takes a particular interest in Highland affairs. The Joint Parliamentary Under Secretaries have duties in the Scottish Office allocated to them by the Secretary of State; for example, a typical grouping of recent years for one of the Under Secretaries has been: education; child care; recreation; the arts; health and welfare; home safety; food hygiene and composition. The Joint Parliamentary Under Secretaries share with the Secretary of State the handling of Scottish legislation in the House of Commons, and often represent the Scottish Office at meetings with other Departments and outside organizations.

On the official side, there is the Permanent Under Secretary of State, the senior civil servant in the Scottish Office, who acts as personal adviser to the Secretary of State over the whole area of the latter's responsibilities. The Permanent Under Secretary is not burdened with the charge of a particular Department, his concern being with the higher policy of the Scottish Office as a whole, with matters affecting more than one Department, and with the allocation of responsibilities among the various Departments. He is assisted by two Assistant Permanent Under Secretaries of State. In addition, each of the four main Departments has a Secretary responsible to the Secretary of State, and a civil service staff.

The Scottish Education Department

The Secretary of State discharges his functions with regard to education primarily through the Scottish Education Department, the present organization of which is shown in Fig. 2.

The Secretary of the Department is responsible to the Secretary of State for the work of the entire Department; one of the two Under Secretaries is in charge of Divisions I-IV, which are concerned broadly with the organization and content of education. The other Under Secretary is in charge of Divisions V-VIII, which are concerned broadly with the real resources—teachers and buildings—and with child care. Division IX (Finance) and Division X (Establishment and Organization) report to the

Secretary

Under-Secretary

Assist. Secretary: Div. I *Primary and Secondary Education.*
 (Provision; curricula; development; examinations.)
Assist. Secretary: Div. II *Formal Further Education.*
 (Education authority level; links with industrial training.)
Assist. Secretary: Div. III *Formal Further Education (Higher).*
 (Central Institutions; matters concerning universities; research; visual aids; students' awards; endowment schemes.)
Assist. Secretary: Div. IV *Informal Further Education.*
 (Youth and Community; sport; the arts; libraries; National Institutions and museums.)

Under-Secretary

Assist. Secretary: Div. V *Supply and Training of Teachers.*
 (Recruitment, supply and distribution; training; colleges of education; General Teaching Council; Commonwealth education.)
Senior Chief Executive Officer: Div. VI *Teachers' Service.*
 (Teachers' salaries, superannuation and records.)
Assist. Secretary: Div. VII *Building.*
 (Educational building; capital investment.)
Assist. Secretary: Div. VIII *Children and Special Services.*
 (Approved schools; child care, adoption; special education; employment of children.)

Assist. Secretary: Div. IX *Finance.*
 (Accounting; audit; financial budgeting and cost control; statistics; school meals and milk.)

Assist. Secretary: Div. X *Establishment and Organization.*
 (Staff recruitment, training and welfare; Annual Report; Dept.'s interest in legislation.)

H.M. Senior Chief Inspector of Schools

H.M. Chief Inspectors—H.M. Inspectors (Higher Grade)—H.M. Inspectors.

Fig. 2. Scottish Education Department: Organization

Secretary of the Department. Each Division, apart from Division VI, is the responsibility of an Assistant Secretary, and is divided into a number of Branches. Branches are headed by civil servants of either Principal or Chief/Senior Executive Officer grades. The thirteen officers who form the Secretariat are responsible for decisions on broad issues of policy and also for the more important executive decisions, while heads of Branches are responsible for the day-to-day work of their respective Branches. The total civil service staff of the Department, including staff of the Inspectorate and of the Royal Scottish Museum, numbers over 700.

It may be useful to classify broadly the various functions of the Secretary of State with regard to Scottish education, whether these functions are discharged through the Scottish Education Department or otherwise.

First of all, the Secretary of State has certain legislative functions. For example, he may issue regulations[1] on diverse aspects of the educational system—teachers' salaries, school meals, grant-aided schools, students' bursaries, and so on. There is a standard procedure for making regulations whereby they are issued in draft in the first instance, and education authorities and other interested persons have not less than 40 days in which to make representations on what is proposed in them. These representations are then considered and the regulations are made in final form; this may be the same as the draft version or may differ from it. After being made in final form the regulations are laid before Parliament and come into operation, though for 40 days thereafter it is open to Members of Parliament to move that they be annulled. In cases of urgency the Secretary of State has the power to issue provisional regulations without going through the draft procedure. These provisional regulations come into immediate operation but last only for a limited, stated period; they too may be annulled by a resolution passed by Parliament.

Secondly, the Secretary of State has functions which may be classed, perhaps rather loosely, as "judicial" functions. For example, he may cause a local inquiry to be held for the purpose of the exercise of any of his functions under the Education (Scotland) Act, 1962.[2] He is also usually the final court of appeal in disputes arising within the education service. For instance, a teacher dismissed by an education authority may ask the Secretary of State for an inquiry into the reasons for the dismissal. If as the result of any such inquiry the Secretary of State is of the opinion that the dismissal is not reasonably justifiable, he so informs the education authority with a view to reconsideration of the resolution for dismissal. If the education authority does not accept the Secretary of State's opinion, the Secretary of State has powers to require the authority to pay to the dismissed teacher an amount up to one year's salary.[3] In this and in various other cases, the decision of the Secretary of State is final.

In the third place, the Secretary of State has certain financial functions. For example, the central government's financial support for Scottish education is provided mainly in the form of general grants allocated to local authorities by the Scottish Development Department, and specific grants allocated by the Scottish Education Department. The Department pays grants to certain central institutions, to teacher training authorities, to grant-aided schools, and to various other institutions and organizations, and awards bursaries to students in higher education. The Secretary of State prescribes teachers' salaries, and approves schemes of expenditure submitted by education authorities. It should be noted that although the Secretary of State has these and other financial functions, the actual accounting for what is done is the province of the Department; it is the Secretary of the Department who is the accounting officer responsible to Parliament.

Fourthly, the Secretary of State has administrative and executive functions. This is the largest category and covers the day-to-day work of the Scottish Education Department which, as the central supervising authority, guides the development of Scottish education in almost all its aspects. For example, the Department supervises the provision by education authorities of primary, secondary, and further education; approves various education

authority schemes—building projects, plans for further education, schemes for the transfer of pupils from primary to secondary
education, and so on; maintains a general oversight of staffing,
curricula and methods; supervises the development of the school
meals service, though not the school health service, which is the
responsibility of the Scottish Home and Health Department; and
is responsible for the certification and superannuation of teachers. [4]
The Department also has responsibilities with regard to provision
for deprived and homeless children, the work of remand homes
and approved schools, responsibilities which are the province of
the Home Secretary in England but of the Secretary of State in
Scotland. The Secretary of State has also certain responsibilities
in relation to the Scottish universities, although they do not come
under the jurisdiction of the Scottish Education Department.

Much of the Department's executive work is effected by means
of statutory instruments—for example regulations, rules, codes—
which have the force of law; and by circulars and memoranda,
which do not have the force of law. Circulars serve various functions—for example, elucidation of a statutory instrument, an
intimation of Departmental policy, a request for information;
memoranda in general give advice and guidance about some aspect
of education, and some of the Department's memoranda, such as
Junior Secondary Education published in 1955 and *Primary Education in Scotland* published in 1965, are justly famous in Scottish
education.

It should be stressed that constitutionally government departments are instruments of Ministers of the Crown, who are per-
sonally answerable to Parliament for the conduct of affairs.
Consequently the executive action taken by any department is
subject to parliamentary scrutiny, and each department must
ensure that any action it takes on its Minister's behalf and in his
name actually accords with his policy and directions. Thus all
action of the Scottish Education Department is taken in the name
of the Secretary of State for Scotland, but in practice circulars and
memoranda are usually signed by the Secretary, or other officer,
of the Department.

One of the Department's functions merits separate consideration, namely, the inspection of schools and educational establishments by Her Majesty's Inspectors of Schools.

The Inspectorate

The organization of the Inspectorate is shown in Fig. 3. There are at present 113 Inspectors in Scottish education, including a Senior Chief Inspector who is responsible for co-ordinating the work of the entire Inspectorate, and seven Chief Inspectors. For the purposes of inspection the country is divided into three Divisions, an Eastern Division, a Western Division, and a North and Highland Division, each in the charge of a Chief Inspector. Each Division is further subdivided into a number of Districts, each in the charge of a District Inspector who is usually assisted by a number of Inspectors, the number varying according to the size of the District. Each Division also has a Divisional staff, who work mainly but not exclusively in secondary schools. These Divisional Inspectors total twenty-eight, and there are nine others who operate on a national basis, as shown in the footnote to Fig. 3.

There is a Chief Inspector with special responsibility for the whole field of primary education, and a Chief Inspector responsible for the whole field of secondary education; each is assisted by a team of Inspectors, who also have attachments to District or Divisional staffs. The inspection of secondary schools, where teaching is usually given by specialist teachers, is largely done by Inspectors who are specialists in their respective subjects.

In addition to these arrangements for the inspection of primary and secondary schools, there are two Chief Inspectors responsible for the field of further education; they are assisted by seventeen Inspectors, plus a few who have responsibilities in both secondary and further education.

The Inspectorate is one of the most important links in Scottish education,[5] as it prevents the central administration, the local administration, and the schools from working in isolation.

H.M. Senior Chief Inspector

H.M. Chief Inspector	H.M. Chief Inspector	H.M. Chief Inspector	H.M. Chief Inspector	H.M. Chief Inspector	H.M. Chief Inspector (2)
Eastern Div.	Western Div.	North and Highland Division	Primary Education	Secondary Education	Further Education

Districts (Eastern Div.)

1. Edinburgh
2. E. Lothian
   Midlothian
   W. Lothian
3. Peebles
   Selkirk
   Roxburgh
   Berwick
4. Fife
   Clackmannan
5. Stirling
   Perth and
   Kinross

(14 Inspectors)

Districts (Western Div.)

6. Glasgow
7. Dunbarton
   Argyll
8. Lanark
9. Renfrew
10. Ayr
    Bute
11. Dumfries
    Kirkcudbright
    Wigtown

(24 Inspectors)

Districts (North and Highland Division)

12. Dundee
    Angus
13. Kincardine
    Zetland
    Aberdeen
14. Aberdeenshire
    Banff
15. Moray and Nairn
    Inverness
16. Ross and
    Cromarty
17. Sutherland
    Caithness
    Orkney

(13 Inspectors)

Primary Education: Team of 7 Inspectors from various districts

Secondary Education: Team of 9 Inspectors from Divisional Staffs

Further Education: 17 Inspectors, plus assistance from 5 Inspectors from Divisional Staffs

Fig. 3. Organization of the Inspectorate

Note. Each Division has a Divisional Staff; total number of Inspectors on Divisional Staffs—28. There are also 9 specialist Inspectors who operate on a national rather than Divisional basis—2 in Music, 2 in Commerce, 2 in Approved Schools, 2 in Special Education, and 1 in School Meals.

Inspectors inspect schools at appropriate intervals with regard to premises, staff, equipment, curricula and teaching methods. They may examine and approve schemes of work. They make recommendations for the award of final certificates of competence to teach to young teachers who have served a 2-year probationary period. They advise teachers—this is the new concept of the Inspector as an educational consultant. District Inspectors discuss with Directors of Education various aspects of Departmental policy, and keep Directors informed of the work of the schools in their areas. They feed back information to the Department, thus acting as a two-way link between the central authority and the schools.

The power of the Inspectorate lies in the influence which individual Inspectors exert. In general they do not order; rather do they strongly advise. If strong resistance to this advice means that the education being provided is less than efficient, then the Inspector will say so—for example, to the relevant headmaster or Director of Education.

Inspectors frequently serve on panels dealing with primary, secondary, or further education, or with individual subjects of the secondary curriculum. These panels advise the Department and prepare memoranda for the guidance of teachers. In recent developments in the curricula of primary and secondary schools a strong lead has been given from the central authority through the Inspectorate. Inspectors also take part in local teachers' conferences and in the work of bodies concerned with such aspects of education as school broadcasting, school libraries, visual aids and programmed learning.

Comment

Within the educational system from time to time are heard various criticisms of the machinery outlined above for the central administration of Scottish education.

First of all, there is the criticism that the Secretary of State has too broad an administrative responsibility, is considerably overworked, and consequently has insufficient time to devote to the problems of Scottish education. This criticism tends to be made by those who regard the Secretary of State as a kind of "one-man-band". In actual fact, as shown at the beginning of this chapter, there is considerable assistance provided on both the ministerial and civil service sides. In making a major decision regarding education the Secretary of State has at his disposal the technical knowledge and accumulated wisdom of experienced civil servants such as the Secretary of the Department and the Senior Chief Inspector of Schools. Moreover, he has consultations on general educational issues with a number of statutory and non-statutory bodies, some of which are indicated on the right-hand side of Fig. 1. Thus the facilities are there for keeping the Secretary of State informed; his burden, though formidable, is bearable.

In the second place, complaints are occasionally heard of pressures exerted on the Secretary of State from outside Scotland, and lack of attention paid to Scottish education at Westminster. It is certainly true that pressures are exerted on the Secretary of State by the Cabinet and the Treasury, and that attendances at debates on Scottish education in the House of Commons tend to be small; but in spite of these alleged pressures Scotland has succeeded in maintaining its own distinctive educational system, with its own Act, Code, Regulations, Inspectorate, system of schools, pattern of examinations and so on. Moreover, facilities are provided, in the form of the Scottish Grand Committee, for Scottish matters to receive full discussion without involving Members of Parliament whose knowledge of Scottish affairs is slight. A striking illustration of this was the enlightened discussion in 1965 of the Bill to establish the General Teaching Council for Scotland.

In the third place, concern is occasionally expressed about the dangers of bureaucracy and centralized control. As shown above, the powers of the Secretary of State are extensive; but there are checks on this power. For example, before statutory instruments become law there is opportunity for representation, discussion, and debate; under the Education (Scotland) Act, 1962, the

Secretary of State must each year present to Parliament a report of his proceedings under the Act during the preceding year;[6] and there is constant press publicity for actions taken by the Secretary of State, a publicity which has been known to alter or postpone some particular development in education unacceptable to Scottish opinion in general or to the teaching profession in particular. Moreover, there is evidence to show that the Scottish Education Department, although accepting a moral responsibility to give a lead in Scottish education, welcomes developments being initiated in other areas of the system. There is more than a gentle rebuke in this statement by the present Secretary of the Department: "there is still a disquieting tendency in the Scottish educational world to look to the Department to take the initiative in far too many things . . . it is really remarkable that people should expect so little to come from the periphery and so much from the centre."[7]

A final comment concerns the Inspectorate. Since the class teacher's most important personal contact with the central authority is usually with H.M. Inspectors, a vital factor in such contact is the general attitude obtaining in the profession towards the Inspectorate. There are some teachers, a minority, who object on principle to inspection, claiming that it is not compatible with the integrity and standing of a profession. The majority accept the institution of the Inspectorate, though some object to individual Inspectors. Perhaps the title "Inspector" has unfortunate connotations, and may even be misleading. Certainly the historical association of inspection with the award of government grant, particularly under the system of payment by results,[8] was hardly calculated to promote the friendliest of relations between teachers and Inspectors; and today, there may still be a few Inspectors who by and large do nothing more than inspect schools and write reports. But this is a narrow and outmoded view of a modern Inspector's function; an Inspector still inspects, but today he is just as likely to be found leading an experiment in teaching reading, speaking at a conference on history teaching by the "patch" method, or consulting with a director of education on the siting of a new secondary school. Furthermore, the idea of the Inspector in the role of consultant is gaining ground. As he visits the schools in his District an Inspector builds up a knowledge of curriculum planning, teaching methods, experimental approaches, laboratory layout, textbooks used and so on. All this information is at the disposal of headmasters and teachers, and is particularly useful for young inexperienced teachers, and those working in the remoter parts of the country. It goes part of the way—although perhaps only a small part of the way—to meet one of the difficulties found in most educational systems, namely that the teacher, once qualified, rarely sees other teachers teach.

The changing role of the Inspectorate was well expressed by the Advisory Council as long ago as 1947 in its report, *Secondary Education*: "To stimulate by discussion and suggestion, to spread ideas and be a link between school and school, to provoke the unreflective to thought and to awaken healthy doubts as to the sufficiency of familiar routines—in such services lies the most valuable function of the Inspectorate. . . ."[9]

Scotland, then, has a national system of state-supported schools, centrally controlled by the Scottish Education Department in St. Andrew's House, Edinburgh. In no sense is this control a stranglehold. Teachers in Scottish schools do not teach with the feeling that "Big Brother" in the form of the Scottish Education Department or its Inspectorate is watching them. There are large areas of freedom for teachers in the classroom situation; the Department interferes little in the day-to-day running of the schools; its directions concerning curricula are not over-precise;[10] textbooks are not centrally prescribed; the tone from St. Andrew's House is one of recommendation, suggestion, advice.

The Scottish system is far removed from the extreme centralization of the Soviet Union, or even France; on the other hand, it does not suffer from the variation and inequality of provision of such a decentralized system as that of the U.S.A. The situation is an interesting one. From a psychological standpoint it may be seen as a manifestation of the much vaunted British achievement of compromise solutions; from an historical point of view, it developed gradually from the 1860's and 1870's, often by force of circumstance; and from a pragmatic standpoint, it works.

LOCAL ADMINISTRATION
Education Authorities

The local administration of Scottish education is the responsibility of thirty-five education authorities. These education authorities are: the county councils of twenty-nine counties; two joint county councils (Moray and Nairn, Perth and Kinross); and the town councils of the four cities (Aberdeen, Dundee, Edinburgh, Glasgow).

Statute requires each council which is an education authority to have an administrative scheme setting out the arrangements made by the council for discharging its functions with regard to education in its area. What follows describes the general position.[11]

Each education authority must appoint an education committee, to which it must delegate all its functions with regard to education, with the following exceptions: the raising of money by rate or loan; the approval of the estimates of capital and revenue expenditure and the authorization of the expenditure included therein; the power to incur expenditure not previously authorized by the council. Certain other functions may also be excluded from the delegation.

The education committee appointed by each council consists of two categories of member: elected members, that is, members of the council, who must constitute a majority of the committee; and appointed members, that is "persons of experience in education and . . . persons acquainted with the needs of the various kinds of schools in the area". The appointed element must include at least two persons nominated by representatives of the churches or denominational bodies in the area, and at least one person nominated to represent any denominational schools managed by the education authority. The education committee must include women as well as men.

Education committees vary in size from one education authority to another. The range is from fifteen to over seventy, but only four have a membership of more than forty. The appointed element varies from one-tenth to one-third of the whole education committee; in about half of the areas it comprises at least one-quarter of the whole committee.

Sub-committees of the education committee are set up to deal with such matters as teaching and staffing, primary and secondary schools, further education, property and supplies, and so on; the numbers, titles and functions of these sub-committees vary among the various education authorities. At least half of the members of any sub-committee must be members of the council.

In addition, unless the Secretary of State agrees otherwise in some particular case, each education authority must provide for the constitution of local area education sub-committees, representative of appropriate interests—for example, parents, teachers, industry and commerce, the education committee itself, and certain local bodies.[12] These area education sub-committees have certain minor functions of management and supervision of local educational establishments—for example, functions concerning the letting of schools, janitation and cleaning, absenteeism, exemptions from school attendance, and the fixing of local day holidays.

Directors of Education

Each education authority must employ a director of education[13] to be the chief education officer of the authority, and every administrative scheme relating to education must set forth the functions to be assigned to the director of education.[14] Broadly speaking these functions may be summarized as follows: to give expert educational advice to the education authority; to carry out the decisions of the authority; to be the official correspondent of the authority; to be in control of teaching and ancillary staff. Thus the director of education advises and guides the education authority, which makes decisions on educational policy, decisions which the director of education must then put into effect.

The education authority may provide the director with a deputy and perhaps one or more assistant directors, depending on the size of the area to be administered.

The influence of the director of education depends to a large extent on the director himself. An energetic and skilful director may carry his education committee with him, arouse local interest in education, and mould the educational traditions of a county for a generation or more.

Powers and Duties of Education Authorities

Education authorities have conferred on them by statute a range of powers and duties, of which the following are important examples: the adequate and efficient provision of all forms of primary, secondary, and further education; the provision of adequate facilities for recreation and social and physical training; the provision of special education for handicapped pupils; the provision of a child guidance service; provision for religious observance and instruction in schools; provision, free of charge, of books, writing materials, stationery, mathematical instruments and other necessary articles; the enforcement of attendance at school; provision, in the case of a county, of books for general reading; provision and maintenance of hostels for pupils attending day schools; the payment of bursaries and other allowances to persons over age 15 attending schools and further education centres; the granting in certain cases of exemption from the obligation to attend school to pupils over 14 years of age; the payment of fees of pupils attending schools at which fees are payable; the provision of transport or payment of travelling expenses; provision of milk and a midday meal; provision of clothing for pupils inadequately clad; provision for the medical inspection and treatment of pupils; the appointment and dismissal of teachers; the making of by-laws with regard to the employment of children.

It will be seen from the above that education authorities have wide responsibilities with regard to ensuring the adequate and efficient provision of education in their particular areas. Details with regard to specific functions are published in regulations issued from time to time in connection with buildings, bursaries, health, school meals, and so on.

It may be useful to state again the relationship between central and local administration: it is the education authorities which *provide*; the Scottish Education Department regulates and supervises this provision.

Comment

The arrangements outlined above for the local administration of Scottish education are sharply criticized from time to time. Criticisms tend to be on three broad lines: firstly, that the local administration of education is too important a matter to be included among the various functions of a county council; secondly, that the elected members on the education committee may not be particularly well qualified to deal with educational issues; and thirdly, that teachers themselves do not have an adequate say in the local administration of education.

To view these criticisms in perspective it is necessary to understand how the present position arose.

It must be noted, first of all, that the tradition of local management of local affairs is well established in Scottish history. The parish was one of the earliest units of administration, civil, religious, and educational, and from the Reformation on, attempts were made to establish a system of parish schools which would be the responsibility of ministers, heritors (local landowners) and parishioners. When the state began effectively to take over the task of providing for education from 1872, the parish was retained as the unit of administration, and about 1000 school boards were set up to manage schools locally. Time proved that there were too many school boards, and that the areas they administered were too small to be economic or efficient. Hence the Education (Scotland) Act, 1918 adopted the county as the unit, and provided for the election of "education authorities".

These authorities were not yet the county councils. The intention was that they should be so, but there was opposition to this on the ground that the provision of education should be the responsibility of people specially elected for the purpose. Thus the 1918 education authorities, elected every three years, had an existence separate from that of the county councils, and thirty-eight education authorities took the place of 947 school boards. By the Local Government (Scotland) Act, 1929 these *ad hoc* authorities were discontinued, and the responsibility for the local administration of education was vested in the *ad omnia* county councils.

The tendency throughout has been to reduce the number of administering units, with a consequent increase in the size of the area administered, and it has been suggested frequently that the present total of thirty-five authorities might be considerably reduced. The most recent suggestions were contained in a White Paper published in 1963, where it is stated: "the evolution of local government in Scotland has now reached a stage where boundaries are becoming increasingly artificial and where areas of many individual authorities are too small. The problem is to continue the process of evolution and provide a structure which will allow local authorities to cope at one level with truly local services, and on a wider plane with those services which need a broader basis for the most effective administration."[15] The White Paper went on to suggest that the areas of existing authorities be enlarged by a process of combining counties, so that a reduced number of councils could exercise certain major functions throughout a wider area, and that within these enlarged counties new authorities be created to be responsible for areas formed by combining existing burghs with neighbouring landward areas. These new authorities, which might be designated "burgh councils" or "rural councils" depending on the circumstances of each area, would be responsible for essentially local services. There might be some fifty burgh or rural councils, and perhaps only ten to fifteen county councils.

These proposals were closely examined and widely discussed until early 1966, when events were given a new turn by a government announcement that a Royal Commission was to be set up to carry out a comprehensive review of local government in Scotland.

The White Paper envisaged education as remaining a function of *ad omnia* bodies, the new county councils, but in the ensuing discussions certain educational interests expressed regret that the opportunity was not being taken to consider seriously a return to the former *ad hoc* education authorities. In May 1964, for instance, a committee of the Educational Institute of Scotland recommended: "that the Institute's ultimate aim should be the establishment of *ad hoc* education committees and that this aim should be adopted as long-term policy."[16] There is certainly a strong enough case for *ad hoc* authorities to justify public and professional debate about the form of local control of education which will accord best with modern conditions.

What the Royal Commission will make of the situation remains to be seen. Although many engaged in the education service accept the validity of the criticism that education is too important to be one of the various functions of a county council, it is rather unlikely that the near future will see any major change in the existing situation.

If this is so, then the problem is that of ensuring the efficiency of the existing arrangements for the local administration of Scottish education. This leads to a consideration of the two remaining criticisms.

There is no doubt that many teachers in Scotland are worried by the fact that local administration is largely the responsibility of councillors who may not be particularly well qualified to deal with education. A leading Scottish newspaper commented thus: "In some authorities the education committee is not treated as something essentially different from the committees on markets or cleansing. It is not thought to demand any greater interest or devotion. Sometimes the choice of convener shows more concern for rotation than education."[17] And the committee of the Educational Institute of Scotland already quoted, further recommended: "That the type of representative on education committees be reviewed to ensure that members will have a direct interest in and knowledge of educational matters."[18]

While there are grounds for statements such as these, it should be noted that the position has in general changed for the better in the past 10 years or so, with increased public interest in education. Moreover, it is the isolated case of folly or injustice which tends to be highlighted; many education authorities in Scotland have an enviable reputation for the enlightened provision of educational facilities in their areas.

A further development in 1963, as a result of which teacher representatives may now serve on education committees, went some way towards meeting the criticism that teachers themselves do not have an adequate say in the local administration of education. By the Local Government (Scotland) Act, 1947, teachers in the employment of an education authority were disqualified from being members of that authority or of its education committee.[19] A Working Party set up by the Secretary of State in 1961 recommended[20] that it should be made possible for serving teachers to be included, at the discretion of the education authority, among the appointed members of the authority's education committee. This recommendation was officially accepted, the 1963 Act gave the necessary legal sanction,[21] and by 1966 twenty-four education authorities had appointed teacher representatives. Another Working Party appointed at the same time examined relations in general between teachers and education authorities, and suggested improvements in the machinery for the appointment, promotion, transfer and dismissal of teachers.[22]

It seems likely that it will be in relatively small ways such as these that changes in the local administration of Scottish education will be effected. Any far-reaching reorganization, with the establishment of *ad hoc* bodies of benevolent educational experts is likely to remain a utopian dream.

FINANCE

Scottish education is financed from two main sources: Exchequer grants and local rates. The money from these sources constitutes the financial basis on which education authorities maintain schools, provide equipment, pay teachers, and carry out various duties laid on them by the Education (Scotland) Act, 1962, and other relevant statutory instruments.

The Exchequer's main contribution is provided through general grants paid to local authorities by the Scottish Development Department in accordance with the provisions of the Local Government and Miscellaneous Financial Provisions (Scotland) Act, 1958; and through specific grants paid by the Scottish Education Department to education authorities and managers of other educational establishments.

The aggregate amount of general grant—£82,070,000 for the year beginning 16th May 1965[23]—is fixed by the Secretary of State in relation to the expenditure by local authorities on twelve services including education, and apportioned to the authorities on a basis of weighted population, a principle which takes account of the fact that scattered population makes the provision of essential services more expensive.[24] At the present time general grant amounts to about 60% of total estimated relevant expenditure. In addition the Exchequer contributes, in the form of equalization grant, about 19% of expenditure which would otherwise be borne by local rates.

It should be noted that, since general grant relates to expenditure on twelve services, no part of the grant is identifiable as specifically for education, although education is the largest single element. This system contrasts with the former percentage grant system for education, in which the distinctive feature was the granting of 60% of the "net recognizable expenditure" of the authority on education. This meant in practice that a progressive authority, willing to spend money on education, was assured of substantial help. Under the present system, since the distribution of grant depends only on weighted population, the amount of

grant received by such a progressive authority is not commensur-
ate with its expenditure. This fact led to the charge that the
introduction of the general grant, allegedly to give greater freedom
to local authorities to determine priorities among the services
concerned, was in fact an economic measure, and that education,
as the largest item of relevant expenditure, would suffer. In
fact this has not happened; indeed the evidence shows that
the rate of growth has been greater under the general grant
system.

There is at present discussion as to the desirability of a shift in
the balance between central and local sources in the finance of
Scottish education. Few would claim that the local contribution
to education should be dispensed with; experience in Britain,
the U.S.A. and Commonwealth countries shows that reliance on
some measure of locally obtained revenue is in the best interests
of the education service. But expansion of the scale and cost of
provision necessary at the present day has led to the suggestion
that the central government should bear an increased share of the
financial burden; one suggestion has been that teachers' salaries,
which constitute approximately 50% of current expenditure by
education authorities, might be made a direct charge on the
Treasury.

An overall picture of the finance of Scottish education is given
in diagram form in Fig. 4.[25] On the left of the diagram are the
main sources of income of education authorities and a note of the
direct expenditure of the Scottish Education Department, which
amounted to an estimated £19·1 million in 1964–5. In the centre
of the diagram is an analysis of the expenditure by education
authorities of a total sum of £133·4 million. On the right of the
diagram is a breakdown of the current expenditure by education
authorities of £107·2 million.

It will be seen that the combined expenditure of education
authorities and the Scottish Education Department in 1964–5 was
estimated at £152·5 million.[26] The figure for 1960–1 was just over
£103·2 million. There was thus a rise of almost 50% in 4 years.
This process is likely to continue as a result firstly of rising costs,

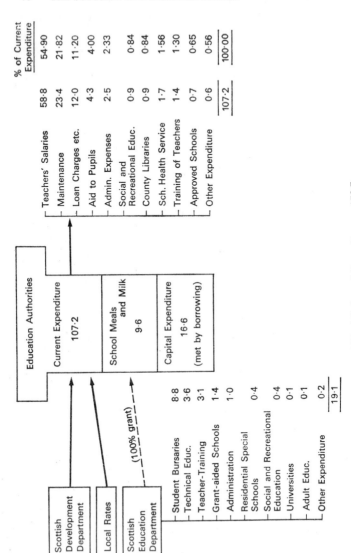

		% of Current Expenditure
Teachers' Salaries	58·8	54·90
Maintenance	23·4	21·82
Loan Charges etc.	12·0	11·20
Aid to Pupils	4·3	4·00
Admin. Expenses	2·5	2·33
Social and Recreational Educ.	0·9	0·84
County Libraries	0·9	0·84
Sch. Health Service	1·7	1·56
Training of Teachers	1·4	1·30
Approved Schools	0·7	0·65
Other Expenditure	0·6	0·56
	107·2	100·00

Education Authorities

Current Expenditure 107·2

School Meals and Milk 9·6

Capital Expenditure 16·6 (met by borrowing)

Scottish Development Department

Local Rates

Scottish Education Department

(100% grant)

Student Bursaries	8·8
Technical Educ.	3·6
Teacher-Training	3·1
Grant-aided Schools	1·4
Administration	1·0
Residential Special Schools	0·4
Social and Recreational Education	0·4
Universities	0·1
Adult Educ.	0·1
Other Expenditure	0·2
	19·1

Total Estimated Expenditure = 152·5

Fig. 4. Estimated Public Expenditure on Scottish Education, 1964–5 (Figures in £ million)

and secondly of various developments in education, a number of which will be described in subsequent chapters.*

REFERENCES AND NOTES

1. Education (Scotland) Act, 1962, Section 144.
2. *Ibid.*, Section 68 and First Schedule.
3. *Ibid.*, Section 85.
4. Functions with regard to the certification of teachers are being transferred to the General Teaching Council. See Chapter 12.
5. For a detailed account see Bone, T. R., *School Inspection in Scotland, 1840–1966*, Ph.D. thesis, University of Glasgow, 1966.
6. Education (Scotland) Act, 1962, Section 72.
7. Graham, N. W., The administration of education in Scotland, *Public Administration, Journal of the Royal Institute of Public Administration*, Autumn 1965, Vol. 43, p. 303.
8. See pp. 20–1.
9. Scottish Education Department: *Secondary Education*. A Report of the Advisory Council on Education in Scotland, Cmd. 7005, Edinburgh, H.M.S.O., 1947, Para. 656.
10. For example, the acceptance by the Secretary of State of most of the suggestions in the *Report of the Working Party on the Curriculum of the Senior Secondary School* (Edinburgh, H.M.S.O., 1959) means that headmasters now have greater freedom than ever before in planning Certificate courses.
11. For details see Local Government (Scotland) Act, 1947, Sections 105–6, 108–9.
12. *Ibid.*, Section 109.
13. Education (Scotland) Act, 1962, Section 86 (1).
14. Local Government (Scotland) Act, 1947, Section 106 (5).
15. Scottish Development Department: *The Modernisation of Local Government in Scotland*, Cmnd. 2067, Edinburgh, H.M.S.O., 1963, p. 5.
16. *The Scottish Educational Journal*, 22nd May 1964.
17. *The Glasgow Herald*, 3rd Feb. 1964.
18. *The Scottish Educational Journal*, 22nd May 1964.
19. Local Government (Scotland) Act, 1947, Sections 52 and 125.

---

* The Local Government (Scotland) Act, 1966 has now introduced changes in the system of Exchequer grants to local authorities in Scotland. General grants and exchequer equalization grants will be discontinued from 1967–8 and replaced by "rate support grants". These will consist of three parts: a needs element based on population and other objective factors; a resources element payable to local authorities with low rate resources; and a domestic element. Certain changes in specific grants will mean that the grant for school milk and meals will no longer be distributed in this way.

20. Scottish Education Department: *Appointment of Teachers to Education Committees*, Edinburgh, H.M.S.O., 1962, p. 13.
21. Education (Scotland) Act, 1963, Section 4.
22. Scottish Education Department: *Relations between Education Authorities and Teachers*, Edinburgh, H.M.S.O., 1962.
23. *The General Grant (Increase) (Scotland) Order 1965*.
24. The basis of calculation of weighted population is given in the Second Schedule to the 1958 Act.
25. This figure is based on Scottish Education Department: *Education in Scotland in 1964*, Cmnd. 2600, Edinburgh, H.M.S.O., 1965, Appendixes 1 and 2; and on information kindly supplied by the Scottish Education Department.
26. In fact, the figures given in the diagram for current and capital expenditure of education authorities proved to be under-estimates. Total expenditure on education in 1964–5 was £160 million. See Scottish Education Department: *Education in Scotland in 1965*, Cmnd. 2914, Edinburgh, H.M.S.O., 1966. Appendixes 1 and 2.

CHAPTER 3

The Educational System: Structure and Traditions

THIS chapter outlines the general structure of the Scottish educational system, the component parts of which are dealt with in some detail in subsequent chapters. It also describes some of the conditions which obtain in the system, and the main traditions which lie behind it.

STRUCTURE

The general structure of the educational system is shown in Fig. 5. It may be helpful to take a general view of the system, and then to look more closely at the system of schools.

The System in General

Scotland, like England and Wales, differs from most European and Commonwealth countries, the U.S.A. and the U.S.S.R., in that compulsory education starts at age 5. A small percentage of children attend nursery schools for some period between the ages of 2 and 5, but most children have their first experience of the educational system when they enter primary school. Primary education lasts for 7 years, one year longer than in England and Wales. Towards the end of their primary education Scottish children are assessed for transfer to secondary education. Transfer tests were formerly used to determine quite rigidly the nature and type of secondary course for which a pupil was suited. At present, however, the tendency is towards a more flexible approach to transfer procedures, and transfer tests may well be abandoned entirely when a fully comprehensive system of secondary education has been established. Primary education and transfer to secondary education are fully described in Chapter 4.

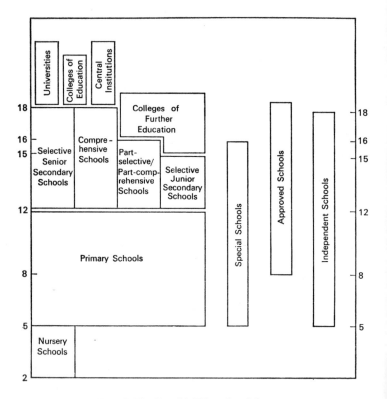

Fig. 5. The Scottish Educational System

It was formerly convenient to classify secondary schools in Scotland as "senior secondary" and "junior secondary". Lest this terminology should mislead it must be stressed that the junior secondary schools in most cases did not "lead in" to senior secondary schools; the two categories were quite distinct. Senior secondary schools were intended to provide 5- and 6-year courses of academic education in preparation for the examinations for the award of the former Scottish Leaving Certificate, the main gateway to higher education. Junior secondary schools were intended to provide 3-year courses of non-academic education for pupils who would leave school at age 15. In the 1950's just under 35% of an age group entered senior secondary schools, and just over 65% entered junior secondary schools.

This simple dichotomy has been gradually rendered outmoded by recent developments in secondary education—for example, the trend towards a system of comprehensive schools; the replacement of the Scottish Leaving Certificate by the Scottish Certificate of Education in 1962, which made it possible for pupils to obtain a certificate after 4 years of secondary schooling instead of 5; the introduction of a more flexible and varied secondary curriculum as a result of the Working Party Report of 1959.[1] One result of the last two developments, for instance, has been that some former junior secondary schools have now "grown" a fourth year, are presenting their ablest pupils for the Ordinary grade of the Scottish Certificate of Education, and have adopted the new prestige name of "high school".

As a result of such developments the most useful classification of secondary schools is a fourfold one as shown in Fig. 5. The selective senior secondary schools take pupils from age 12 to age 18, and provide courses leading to the Scottish Certificate of Education; they do not provide non-certificate courses. At the other extreme the junior secondary schools take pupils from ages 12 to 15, and provide non-certificate courses only. These two categories thus continue as formerly. The "all-through" comprehensive schools take all the pupils of an area for their secondary education, and provide both certificate and non-certificate courses. The part-selective/part-comprehensive schools provide non-certificate courses plus some element of certificate courses; for example, some provide the first 2 years of Higher grade certificate courses and the full 4 years of Ordinary grade certificate courses, in some cases functioning as part of a "two-tier" comprehensive system of junior and senior high schools.

The number of comprehensive schools is increasing and the number of selective schools is decreasing each year. In 1965, 34% of Scottish secondary school children were in schools which were wholly comprehensive, and 24% were in schools which were partly comprehensive. Official policy is to have no secondary schools which provide only non-certificate courses; and 3-year courses of secondary education will automatically disappear when the school-leaving age is raised to 16 in 1970.

The organization of secondary education has thus become increasingly complex; it is described in greater detail in Chapter 5.

After completing 5 or 6 years of secondary education, pupils with the requisite passes in the Scottish Certificate of Education examinations may proceed to higher education. They may enter universities, of which there are eight in Scotland, and study for example arts, science, engineering, medicine, law. They may enter central institutions, of which there are thirteen, for courses in science, technology, commerce, music, art, domestic science, agriculture. Girls from school may enter colleges of education for a 3-year course which will qualify them to teach in primary schools. There are ten colleges of education, of which one is for women teachers of physical education. The major colleges of education also provide 1-year courses of teacher-training for university graduates and holders of certain diplomas and associate-ships of central institutions. The universities are considered in Chapter 11, central institutions in Chapter 10, and colleges of education in Chapter 12.

Pupils who leave school after 3 or 4 years of secondary education generally go straight into employment, and many lose all further contact with the educational system. Some, however, attend colleges of further education for one or other of the variety of courses which such institutions provide—for example, pre-vocational courses, day release courses, evening classes. The system of further education is described in Chapter 10.

What has been outlined so far has been the main "flow" of

pupils and students through the educational system. For children who are handicapped, special schools are provided, in which the education is as far as possible planned to meet particular needs. Provision is made for nine categories of handicap. Children requiring special educational treatment remain of compulsory school age until they are aged 16. Special education forms the subject-matter of Chapter 6.

Approved schools are for the education and training of children and young persons committed to them by the courts. The juveniles in approved schools are usually aged between 10 and 17, although the outside limits are 8 and $19\frac{1}{2}$. The work of approved schools is dealt with in Chapter 7.

Parents who do not wish to take advantage of the state system of education may send their children to independent schools, which are fee-paying. It is also possible for a parent to have his child educated privately at home, provided the education the child is receiving is recognized as efficient.

So far only the general structure of the educational system has been outlined; it is now necessary to examine more closely the system of schools.

The System of Schools

There are three main categories of school in Scotland.

Public schools are managed by education authorities, which receive government grant from the Secretary of State for Scotland. Public schools correspond to local education authority maintained schools in England.

Grant-aided schools are conducted by voluntary managers who receive grant direct from the Scottish Education Department. Grant-aided schools correspond to direct grant schools in England.

Independent schools are conducted by voluntary managers. Such schools, like the corresponding schools in England, are not grant-aided in any way by the Department or by education authorities.

In 1965 there were 140 schools on the Register of Independent Schools; 134 of these had been finally registered, and six provisionally registered. The total roll of independent schools was 18,183. The position with regard to independent schools is considered separately in Chapter 9.

There are twenty-nine grant-aided secondary schools in Scotland, with a total roll in 1965 of just under 19,000 pupils; twenty-eight have primary departments as well as secondary departments, and one is purely a secondary school. Most grant-aided schools are located in the cities: four in Aberdeen, one in Dundee, eight in Edinburgh, ten in or near Glasgow; the remaining six are in the counties—one in Ayrshire, one in Clackmannanshire, two in Dumfriesshire, and two in the joint county area of Perth and Kinross. Table 1 gives separate information about the type and size of grant-aided schools; thereafter such schools are grouped for statistical purposes with public schools.

TABLE 1. GRANT-AIDED SECONDARY SCHOOLS
ANALYSIS BY TYPE AND SIZE

Roll	Residential	Partly residential	Day	Total
1–300	—	9	4	13
301–500	—	2	4	6
501–1000	—	3	7	10
Total	—	14	15	29

There was a total of 3202 public and grant-aided schools in Scotland in 1965. Table 2 gives an analysis of these schools by type and size.[2]

In addition to the schools enumerated in Table 2, there were twenty-six approved schools in Scotland in 1965, with a total roll of over 1500 pupils.

Some interesting facts emerge from Table 2. For example, just over half of all the primary schools in Scotland have rolls of

TABLE 2. PUBLIC AND GRANT-AIDED SCHOOLS
ANALYSIS BY TYPE AND SIZE

Roll	Nursery	Primary	Secondary	Special	Total
1–24	3	526	3	27	559
25–49	47	387	16	47	497
50–99	39	274	40	26	379
100–199	4	208	89	22	323
200–299	—	200	63	7	270
300–399	—	143	72	3	218
400–499	—	155	65	—	220
500–599	—	162	67	—	229
600–799	—	159	110	—	269
800–999	—	47	83	—	130
1000–1199	—	11	57	—	68
1200–1599	—	1	38	—	39
1600–1999	—	—	1	—	1
All sizes	93	2273	704	132	3202

TABLE 3. DISTRIBUTION OF PUPILS IN THE SCHOOL SYSTEM

Part of school system	Numbers of pupils	Percentage
Nursery Schools and Classes (Public and Grant-aided)	6,225	0·68
Primary Schools and Departments (Public and Grant-aided)	594,840	64·84
Secondary Schools (Public and Grant-aided)	284,585	31·02
Special Schools and Classes (Public and Grant-aided)	10,943	1·19
Elsewhere than at School (Provided by education authorities)	1,110	0·12
Independent Schools	18,183	1·98
Approved Schools	1,510	0·17
Total receiving education	917,396	100·00

less than 100 pupils; about two-fifths have rolls of less than fifty pupils; and about one-sixth have rolls of under twenty-five pupils. The very large secondary school is not a feature of Scottish education; only thirty-nine out of a total of 704 secondary schools have rolls of over 1200 pupils.

The distribution of pupils in the various parts of the school system is shown in Table 3.[3] The use of the phrase "Primary Schools and Departments" in this Table is necessitated by the fact that in 1965, 251 of the 704 secondary schools also had primary departments.

The percentages in Table 3 have tended to remain fairly constant over recent years. It is thus a fair generalization to say that out of every 1000 children receiving education in Scotland: 7 are in nursery schools; 648 are in primary schools; 310 are in secondary schools; 12 are in special schools or classes for handicapped children; 1 is receiving education provided by an education authority other than at school, perhaps at home or in hospital; 20 are in independent schools; and 2 are in approved schools.

School Organization

Detailed regulations with regard to the conduct of all public and grant-aided schools are contained in *The Schools* (*Scotland*) *Code, 1956*, which deals with such matters as: the size of classes; accommodation of classrooms; designation of stages and classes; number and duration of school meetings; the keeping of logbook, registers, and pupil's progress records; the qualifications of teachers; and so on. This section is concerned with some of these points of organization.

The yearly stages of primary and secondary courses are designated by letters and numbers from below upwards. The seven yearly stages in the primary school are designated P.I to P.VII; the six yearly stages in the secondary school are designated S.I to S.VI. Where more than one class is formed at any yearly stage, appropriate letters, numbers, or words may be added to the designation in order to distinguish the several classes.

The size of classes is regulated by the Code. The number of pupils in any class in primary departments must not exceed 45, and is further restricted to: 25 in a one-teacher department; 30 in a two-teacher department; 35 in a three-teacher department; 25 in a class for backward or retarded pupils; 20 in a nursery class. The number of pupils in any class in secondary departments must not exceed 40, and is further restricted to: 30 in classes at stages S.IV, S.V, and S.VI; 30 in a class which includes pupils at more than one yearly stage; 20 in a class for certain forms of practical instruction; 25 in a class for backward or retarded pupils.[4] In practice these maxima tend to be exceeded; this was the case with regard to 900 primary classes and 970 secondary classes in Scotland in 1965.[5]

In charge of each primary school is a head teacher; in large schools he may be engaged entirely in administrative duties, and may be assisted by a deputy. Usually one teacher is in charge of one class, although in smaller rural primary schools one teacher may have to teach several stages.

Similarly in secondary schools a head teacher is in charge of the work of the school. In most secondary schools he acts entirely in an administrative capacity, having little time to take part in class teaching; he is often assisted by a deputy head teacher. Teachers in secondary schools tend to be subject specialists, teaching one or two subjects to a number of classes at different stages. The teacher in charge of a subject department is called a principal teacher.

Various regulations in the Code are concerned with the day-to-day conduct of schools. For example, in each school a log book must be kept, and instruction is given as to the kind of entries to be made by the head teacher; registers must be kept in every school in accordance with Rules contained in the First Schedule to the Code; a pupil's progress record in the form prescribed in the Second Schedule to the Code must be kept for every pupil attending a public or grant-aided school; certain duties are laid upon head teachers with regard to schemes of work for their schools, ensuring that records of school work and of homework are kept, and so on.

Additional details of school organization will be given, where relevant, in subsequent chapters.

School Buildings

School buildings in Scotland show a variety of styles and appearances. Much school building took place in the late nineteenth century, when school boards carried out the provisions of the 1872 Act. Schools from this period still exist, with a date around 1876 in the stone above the door, steps hollowed by the feet of generations of school children, rather dull, cheerless rooms, narrow pointed windows, the whole surrounded by prison-like walls.

The early twentieth century saw the vogue of the school planned with classrooms grouped around a central hall. This had distinct advantages; for example, it was economical to build and run; each room had its own door—previously with a system of rooms divided by partitions, one main door might have to serve two or even three classrooms. But the idea of the central hall had severe limitations: frequently it was too small to be of much practical use; it made only a makeshift gymnasium; and noise from the hall penetrated virtually every classroom in the school. This period seemed to establish the traditional decor for classrooms of dark brown varnished wood with dull yellow or fawn walls.

Between the wars the "block" plan was much favoured. The school consisted of one or more blocks, each block containing a row of rooms side by side, all facing out at one side of the block, with a corridor running along the other side. The hall and gymnasium were situated apart from the classrooms, or formed a connection between blocks.

Schools built since the Second World War have looked quite different from schools of any previous period. There has been experiment with new designs and new materials; a new emphasis on light and space; thoughtful positioning of classrooms, cloak-rooms, lavatories, storage space; a genuine concern for what is to happen inside the building. A modern classroom is well lit and adequately ventilated. There is space to move and space for the grouping and regrouping of desks. The desks, or tables and chairs, are the proper size, light in weight, easily moved on rubber feet. There is often a large roller blackboard, adequate storage space, and power points for electrical equipment.

At the present day education authorities are responsible for the provision of new schools and for the alteration of existing schools. Various proposals by education authorities with regard to sites, and plans and estimated costs of building, are submitted to the Secretary of State for approval. Regulations prescribe standards[6] with regard to such items as size of sites for schools and for playing fields, number and size of teaching rooms, ancillary accommodation; and standards with regard to fire precautions, lighting, ventilation, heating, water supply, sanitation and drainage. The introduction in 1965 of simplified approval procedures[7] for certain school projects marked a move towards a less detailed control by the Scottish Education Department, and greater planning freedom for authorities.

The building of educational establishments is a costly process. In 1965 the value of projects started was £21·7 million; of projects completed, £23·4 million; and of work under construction, £55·6 million.[8]

Two comments are worth making at this point. In the first place, although it is true that the most important thing about any school is not the building, but what goes on inside it, nevertheless the former can very often determine the latter. For example, the old "gallery" room of by-gone years, with desks raised on different levels, crowded together and screwed to the floor, left little scope for anything but the mass class teaching which was the order of the day. This kind of room exists only as a curiosity, but its lesson remains. If educators are to experiment with different forms of classroom organization, with group work, with projects, with team teaching, with provision for independent study, with music and movement, they must not be cramped by traditional ideas of what a classroom *ought* to look like. It is the dependence of what can be done on the facilities provided, and not mere status-seeking, which has led teachers to request a larger say in the planning of new school buildings.[9]

There is no doubt that in the more revolutionary aspects of school building a country like the U.S.A. is well ahead of Scotland.[10] One reason for this—apart from the financial one—is that the decentralized system of administration gives freedom to thousands of local school boards to experiment in building the local community's schools. The more centralized system of Scotland tends to ensure equality of provision, uniformity, and economy; but these are bought at a price.

In the second place, although post-war school building in Scotland gives cause for satisfaction, there is another side to the situation: about half of Scotland's school children still attend schools which were built before 1939, and conditions in many of these schools leave much to be desired. Serving teachers have tended to become accustomed to this situation; but too many students emerge from colleges of education to enter schools where conditions practically guarantee that they will be unable to test the educational theories and try the practical techniques which they learned about in college.

TRADITIONS

The traditions which infuse any educational system have positive and negative aspects: positive when they provide stability and security, and constitute the base on which future developments may rest; negative when they turn the attention to the past, generate complacency, and hamper experiment and progress. A harsh critic might claim that Scottish educational traditions, viewed in the light of mid-twentieth-century needs, tend to have negative rather than positive effects.

Certain aspects of the Scottish educational tradition have been touched upon in the two previous chapters. The Scottish people have had, traditionally, a real concern for education and a respect for the educated man. Thus pride is taken in the long and in most respects honourable history of the educational system; in its close connection, in origin and early development, with the church of the day; in the aspiration, dating from the *First Book of Discipline*, towards a national system of education; in the emphasis laid on the importance of local interest and local control, whether on the part of heritors and minister, school board, or education authority.

Of equal importance is the *kind* of education in which pride has been taken, and this has usually been an intellectual, academic education.

The Academic Emphasis

The academic emphasis has been a feature of both primary and secondary education. The parish schools taught the three R's and religion, and earned a reputation for thoroughness which was to stand the system in good stead after 1872 when compulsory education was prescribed for all children. Yet this very attachment to the ideal of a thorough grounding in basic subjects is the source of that suspicion of "frills" which has in the twentieth century kept primary education in Scotland much more formal and much less experimental than primary education in England.

The burgh or grammar schools taught the classics, and established the pattern for a "true secondary education" in the nineteenth century. Although the classics declined in importance during the twentieth century, the ideal of an academic secondary education remained. Although academic, it was not narrow; indeed one of the characteristics of Scottish secondary education has been its breadth. Nevertheless even a broad-based academic education was rather an inappropriate ideal in an era of secondary education for all, and one which even today occasionally hinders the development of the practical and realistic courses which will be essential from 1970, when children of all levels of ability will remain at school until age 16.

Coupled with this emphasis on academic education has gone a great concern for higher education. Scotland had three universities before the Reformation, and in the section on education in the *First Book of Discipline* the space given to universities was twice that given to the system of schools. Even today the university is held almost in awe by many members of the general population, and the title "professor" commands enormous respect.

The Democratic Concept

One important feature of Scottish education is that it has always been noticeably democratic. The scheme propounded by Knox and his colleagues was a democratic scheme; education was regarded as the right of all children, and there were to be bursaries for the poor. The parish schools which spread throughout the country in the next 300 years were open to all; and although the picture of the laird's son and the ploughman's son sitting side-by-side in the parish school can be overdrawn, it is none the less true that there has been, and still is, far less social division and class consciousness in the Scottish educational system than, say, in the English. There are various reasons, social, economic, educational, for this situation. For example, the fact that parish schools often gave a certain amount of secondary education, and that burgh schools especially in smaller burghs provided elementary education as well as secondary education, prevented the strict dichotomy which can lead to the situation in which secondary education is seen as for an *élite*, and elementary education as for the masses. Again, in many parts of Scotland the scattered nature of the population led to the setting up of a secondary school, perhaps in a county town, to take all the pupils of a wide area for their secondary education, thus effecting the social mixing favoured by advocates of today's comprehensive schools.

Co-education

Allied to the democratic concept is the principle of co-education, which has been the rule in most Scottish schools since the Reformation. Independent boarding schools are single-sex establishments, but the majority of Scottish schools are co-educational. The average Scot has viewed with a certain puzzlement the debate on comprehensive education in England, where the protagonists argue in terms of social class, intelligence, mixed ability groups, setting and so on, and yet calmly accept as "comprehensive" a school from which one whole sex has been excluded.

Religion

What is usually called "the religious question" was settled early and amicably in Scotland. The close connection between the Church and the educational system has already been demonstrated in Chapter 1. The 1872 Act provided that voluntary schools might be transferred to the school boards, and many Church of Scotland and Free Church schools took advantage of this provision, thus becoming public or state schools. The preamble to the Act declared that it was expedient that the custom of giving religious instruction in public schools should be continued, and provided in the "conscience clause" that every public school should be open to children of all denominations, and that any child might be withdrawn by his parents from any religious instruction or religious observance in the school, without being placed at any disadvantage with regard to the secular instruction provided.

The 1918 Act which abolished school boards and established *ad hoc* education authorities, provided in section 18 for the transfer of certain voluntary schools to the new education authorities, and schools of the Episcopal and Roman Catholic Churches took advantage of this provision. Existing teachers in transferred schools were taken over by the education authorities, and teachers appointed after the date of transfer had to be approved as regards religious belief and character by representatives of the church or denominational body concerned. It was laid down that, subject to the conscience clause, the time set apart for religious instruction was not to be less than was customary before the transfer, and that a supervisor of religious instruction approved by the Church was to be appointed by the education authority to report to the authority as to the efficiency of the religious instruction given in the school.

A section of the 1918 Act repeated the preamble to the 1872 Act with regard to religious instruction, and provided that education authorities should be at liberty to continue the custom of providing religious instruction in public schools, subject to the provisions of the conscience clause.

The Local Government (Scotland) Act, 1929, which abolished the *ad hoc* education authorities and transferred their functions to the county councils and to the town councils of the four cities, strengthened the section of the 1918 Act with regard to the giving of religious instruction. It provided that it should not be lawful for a council to discontinue the provision of religious instruction unless and until a resolution in favour of such discontinuance, passed by the council, had been submitted to a poll of the local government electors for the area, and had been approved by a majority of electors voting thereat.[11]

Thus the problem of denominational religious instruction has been solved in Scotland without recourse to the system of "dual control" of public education which has characterized the English system.[12] At the same time the traditional association of religion and education has been to a large extent maintained. With regard to schools other than transferred schools, the general practice is for the first 30 minutes of the day in primary schools to be devoted to religious education, and although there is greater diversity among secondary schools, it is fairly general for one or two 40-minute periods per week to be given to the subject. The religious teaching given generally follows the lines laid down in the Syllabus of Religious Education prepared by a Joint Committee on Religious Education, representative of the Scottish churches, teachers, and local authorities. Many schools have an arrangement whereby a minister of religion serves as school chaplain, assists with the religious education given in the school, and conducts school services at such seasons as Christmas and Easter. The practice is growing of appointing to secondary schools specialist teachers of religious education, and although there is at present no Scottish Certificate of Education examination in religion, this is a likely development in the future.

Discipline

Perhaps the most widely known element of the Scottish educational tradition is that of firm, sometimes harsh, discipline. The traditional attitude has been that boys and girls are sent to school to learn their lessons and to do what they are told; if they do not, they are punished. The history of Scottish education affords ample evidence of this. In the seventeenth century the laws of Dundee Grammar School with regard to punishment were characteristic: for a first offence, a public whipping; for a second offence, flogging; and for a third offence, exclusion from the school until a surety was found for the child's good conduct. In parish schools of the eighteenth and nineteenth centuries the disciplinary measure was often a clip on the ear, but sometimes flogging with a cane or "tawse"; the "queelinstane" cooled off offenders in Aberdeen; at Dalkeith a Mr. Barcley made scholars crawl round the floor and beg his pardon; and David Stow's master was known to pierce ears with sharp pointed pens. Selective argument can be used to prove almost anything, but these examples are not grossly atypical, and give some indication of the inheritance of Scottish teachers in this respect.

At the present day the general picture in Scottish schools is one of fair but firm discipline. Although the schools have shared in the changed attitude to authority since the Second World War, boys and girls still address teachers as "sir" or "miss", are expected to be polite and well behaved, and to perform diligently the classwork and homework required by the school. Relationships between teachers and pupils are friendlier and more informal than ever before, but they are still more formal than teacher-pupil relationships in England, and very much more formal than similar relationships in the U.S.A. The general expectation is that the teacher will show ability to "control" the class, and that the pupils will thus be able to "respect" the teacher.

This background perhaps makes more comprehensible a feature of Scottish education which frequently calls forth adverse comment from foreign observers, namely, the retention in the school system of corporal punishment by means of a leather strap or belt. It should be emphasized that for most teachers corporal punishment is a last resort; many schools and individual teachers devise their own systems of deterrents—verbal reprimands, depriving pupils of privileges, sending home an adverse report, summoning parents to see the headmaster, detaining pupils after school hours; but the belt remains the ultimate deterrent.

Many teachers would like to see corporal punishment in schools abolished, but such abolition is a difficult proposition. The difficulty lies precisely in the tradition of the tawse in Scottish education; this has for centuries been the accepted method of punishment in school, and has consequently created the appropriate set of expectations on the part of pupils, parents and teachers. It is certain that an edict at national or even local level for the abolition of corporal punishment in schools would be fraught with the possibility of unfortunate consequences, because such a move is a too sudden change of policy. To maximize success such a move would have to be gradual; for example, a start might be made, quietly, without press publicity, and preferably on the initiative of individual schools, by abolishing corporal punishment in Primary I, and for this class as it moves up through the primary school. A similar policy would be adopted with all subsequent Primary I's. In this way a new tradition gradually replaces an old, until eventually there is a system of primary schools in which there is no corporal punishment. This will not be easy, and in some areas it may not succeed; but it is one of the few approaches which offers the possibility of success.

It is vitally important to keep this matter of corporal punishment in perspective. Thousands of teachers teach from one year to the next either without recourse, or with minimum recourse, to corporal punishment, and then usually in cases of extreme provocation, flagrant breach of rules, or where to fail to take this step would endanger other pupils or undermine the work of the school. The great majority of Scottish teachers operate under a system of discipline which is firm, fair and benevolent; the great majority of Scottish classrooms are pleasant places in which children live and work.

Almost as powerful a force as tradition is attitude to tradition, and the Scottish attitude to tradition is one of respect. Add to this the fact that Scottish teachers tend to be conservative in outlook, and it will be appreciated that change in Scottish education tends to come slowly.

What any individual thinks of the traditions briefly outlined above will be dependent upon individual value judgement. What is important is that these traditions should be borne in mind when evaluating the various parts of the educational system to be described in the chapters which follow.

REFERENCES AND NOTES

1. Scottish Education Department: *Report of the Working Party on the Curriculum of the Senior Secondary School*, Edinburgh, H.M.S.O., 1959.
2. This Table is based on Scottish Education Department: *Education in Scotland in 1965*, Cmnd. 2914, Edinburgh, H.M.S.O., 1966, Table 1, p. 99. Figures are as at 15th Jan. 1965.
3. Table 3 is based on Scottish Education Department: *Education in Scotland in 1965*, Cmnd. 2914, Edinburgh, H.M.S.O., 1966, Table 2, p. 100. Figures are as at 15th Jan. 1965.
4. Details of class size in special schools and classes are given in Chapter 6.
5. Scottish Education Department: *Education in Scotland in 1965*, Cmnd. 2914, Edinburgh, H.M.S.O., 1966, p. 14.
6. *The School Premises* (*Standards and General Requirements*) (*Scotland*) *Regulations, 1959*, and amendments. See also the *School, Etc., Building Code* (3rd ed., 1960) and amendments.
7. Scottish Education Department: Circular No. 593. *School Building Code: Simplification of Procedures*, 23rd Aug. 1965.

8. Scottish Education Department: *Education in Scotland in 1965*, Cmnd. 2914, Edinburgh, H.M.S.O., 1966, p. 51.
9. See, for example, Scottish Education Department: *Relations between Education Authorities and Teachers*, Edinburgh, H.M.S.O., 1962, pp. 19–20.
10. For a fascinating description of school building in the U.S.A., with detailed diagrams, see Ministry of Education. Building Bulletin No. 18: *Schools in the U.S.A.: A Report*, London, H.M.S.O., 1961.
11. The present legal position is laid down in the Education (Scotland) Act, 1962, Sections 8, 9, 10, 21, 67 (2).
12. For an excellent account of the situation which developed in England see CRUICKSHANK, M., *Church and State in English Education*, London, Macmillan, 1963.

CHAPTER 4

Primary Education

"PRIMARY EDUCATION" is generally understood as the designation of the education received by pupils aged 5 to 12 in primary schools and departments. Legally, however, "primary education" includes education in nursery schools and classes.[1] This chapter deals first of all with nursery education, and then with what is generally known as "primary education".

NURSERY EDUCATION

Nursery education in Scotland is provided in separate nursery schools for children between the ages of 2 and 5, and in nursery classes attached to primary schools and departments. The combined nursery/infant school for children aged 2 to 7 is not a feature of Scottish education.

Provision of Nursery Education

The Education (Scotland) Act, 1962 states: "The provision of primary education in nursery schools and classes shall be deemed to be adequate if such provision is made at centres where sufficient children whose parents desire such education for them can be enrolled to form a school or class of a reasonable size."[2] From this it would appear that if parents desire nursery education for their children, and if they desire it in sufficient numbers, nursery education is likely to be provided. This is far from being the case, as priority has been given to meeting the demands of other sectors of the educational system. A new housing area may well have a space reserved for a nursery school, but the education authority is not usually allowed to build one; it may, however, convert old buildings for use as nursery schools.

As a result of this situation, the number of public and grant-aided nursery schools in 1965 was only ninety-three, and the number of nursery classes attached to public and grant-aided primary schools was forty-four. For various reasons accurate statistics are not available with regard to the number of independent nursery schools and classes.[3] Almost all public and independent nursery schools and classes are situated in the four cities and a handful of counties—for example, Fife, Lanarkshire, Renfrewshire, Ayrshire and Dumfriesshire. About two-thirds of all education authorities make no provision for nursery education, and in the country as a whole only about 5% of children receive such education.

Selection for Nursery Education

Since provision is inadequate, there are waiting lists for most nursery schools, and selection becomes an issue. In the case of most public nursery schools, priority is usually given to two main groups of children: those suffering from some defect, perhaps physical or emotional; and those whose physical or social environment is unsatisfactory—for example those whose background is one of a "broken home", of illness in the family, of overcrowding, or of the loss of a parent. One or two education authorities have added a third category: children whose mothers are employed as teachers, or who are undertaking a course of teacher training.[4]

The situation is somewhat different in independent nursery schools, where those who are able to pay the fees are admitted, or placed on the waiting list. However, a more subtle selection, social and economic, takes place, as a result of the siting of these schools in middle class residential areas. Moreover, where selection is practised, the criteria tend to be those of sound health, above average intelligence, and good social adjustment. The authors of a Report on nursery school provision in Scotland, published in 1958,[5] underline the "positive" nature of the criteria employed in the selection of pupils for independent nursery schools, which contrasts with the "negative" criteria used in the selection of children for public nursery schools.

Public and independent nursery schools differ in various other ways. The typical public nursery school has a roll of around forty pupils; the youngest child is usually about $2\frac{1}{2}$ years old; the school is likely to function in both forenoon and afternoon; and the teacher in charge is likely to be well qualified, recognized as a teacher by the Scottish Education Department, and probably the holder of a nursery school endorsement.

The typical independent nursery school has a roll of around twenty-five pupils; the youngest child is usually about $3\frac{1}{2}$ years old; the school is likely to function only in the forenoon; and the teacher in charge is likely to be much less well qualified than the teacher in charge of a public nursery school, probably not being recognized as a teacher by the Scottish Education Department.

The Value of Nursery Education

Educators from Plato to Dewey have stressed the impact on children of the environment and environmental influences. Most nursery schools are pleasant places in which to be, even those in converted premises not originally intended for nursery work. Rooms are arranged to be as spacious as possible, walls are gaily painted, furniture is simple and pleasing, the place is brightened by flowers and plants. In some well-equipped schools the environment is "tailor-made" for small children: chairs are the right shape and light in weight; toy cupboards are easily accessible; wash basins and lavatories are the correct height. The child may thus be allowed to explore his environment, to master it, and to develop personal skills and self-reliance.

Children in nursery schools are cared for physically. For example, they are under regular medical supervision. Apart from the immediate advantage to the child's health, this has important consequences for the start of his schooling at age 5, as it makes possible the early diagnosis of minor defects which are often associated with initial difficulties experienced in school work. The child gets a balanced diet, milk, orange juice and cod liver oil generally being provided in addition to the midday meal. Rest and sleep are catered for by the institution of the afternoon nap.

From the children's point of view the most attractive feature of the nursery school is the variety of activities in which they can take part. They play safely and under supervision, indoors and out, with sand, bricks, pictures, dolls, paints, rocking horse, jungle gym, Wendy house and so on. They plant seeds, lay tables, climb on apparatus and listen to stories. The various activities cater for both personal and social development, and the established routine of the day provides a framework of stability and security.

Nursery education is especially valuable for only children, for children living in flats with no access to a garden, for children from homes in which parent/child relationships are unhappy, or where the mother has to go out to work. What many educationists would like to see is an extension of nursery school provision, so that all children whose parents wish them to have the experience may have the chance to benefit from nursery education.

There is no doubt that an increased provision of nursery schools could react beneficially on the educational system as a whole. For example, for girls following non-certificate courses of secondary education some experience of nursery school work could be a first-hand, useful and attractive introduction to the care of small children, and could provide a means of integrating theoretical and practical work. This approach has been tried in a few areas, where boys also have been involved in making and repairing equipment and toys for the local nursery school.

The nursery school can exert a beneficial influence on the home. As a result of discussions between mothers and nursery school staffs, common standards of health, hygiene and social behaviour may be set up. Moreover, there may well be established a habit of co-operation between home and school which may carry over to later stages of the child's education.

However, at the present time only one child in twenty receives the benefits which it is believed nursery education can provide, and it seems unlikely that there will be any great improvement in this situation in the near future.

PRIMARY EDUCATION

As a result of the position outlined above, most Scottish children have their first contact with the educational system at age 5, when they enter primary school.

The 1962 Act requires the parent of every child aged between 5 and 15 "to provide efficient education for him suitable to his age, ability and aptitude either by causing him to attend a public school regularly or by other means".[6] While some parents are able to exercise this choice and send their children to independent schools, and a very few provide education for their children at home, the vast majority of parents send their children to the public (state) schools. Such parents have generally little choice with regard to which public school their children will attend. Although education authorities are required to have regard to the general principle that pupils are to be educated in accordance with the wishes of their parents, this is only "so far as is compatible with the provision of suitable instruction and the avoidance of unreasonable public expenditure".[7] Thus it is the common practice for children to be allocated to schools on a territorial basis, and in urban areas a system of "zoning" often determines the school to which children living in a particular part of the town must go.

Intake to Scottish primary schools is usually once a year, at the end of August, although the larger two-stream primary schools have a second intake in February. This use of the term "stream" must not be misunderstood; the criterion is usually one of age. The practice of streaming by ability in terms of intelligence and/or attainment which is common in English primary schools is not at all characteristic of the Scottish system. One important reason for this is simply that most primary schools in Scotland do not have an intake large enough to make streaming a viable proposition; as already shown in Chapter 3, just over half of all primary schools have fewer than 100 pupils on the roll. But another reason is that Scottish educators, while accepting the principle of streaming by ability in secondary schools, have regarded such streaming as undesirable in the primary school. The wisdom of this view, although not originally based on any research findings, has been shown by various investigations in England during the 1950's and 1960's.[8]

Once enrolled in the primary school, the child is exposed for 7 years to the influence of teachers, other children, the curriculum of the school, and the methods of teaching employed. This section is concerned mainly with curriculum and methods.

Curriculum

A basic concern of all educational systems is with ensuring literacy, and this has always been the main aim of Scottish elementary education. For example, in Knox's plan for a national system of education in the *First Book of Discipline*, the first stage was to be concerned with reading plus the elements of the catechism; the core curriculum of the parish schools which gradually spread throughout the country in the seventeenth to nineteenth centuries consisted of reading, writing, reckoning and religion; and the 1872 Act made the duty of parents clear—to ensure that their children were taught the three R's between the ages of 5 and 13.

In the twentieth century the development of the primary school curriculum has shown three clear trends: towards an expansion of the content of the curriculum; towards a revaluation of the subjects of which it is composed; and towards an integration of the various subjects taught.

To illustrate the first trend it is only necessary to compare the content of elementary education in the nineteenth century with the content of present-day primary education. In 1946 the Advisory Council listed the subjects of the primary school curriculum as follows:[9] physical education; handwork; arithmetic; art; spoken English; nature study, geography and history; reading and writing; singing; written composition; spelling and dictation; and later in the Report, religion. *The Schools (Scotland) Code, 1956* laid on primary schools the duty of providing instruction in a similar list of subjects, with the exception of religion.[10]

Several factors have been responsible for this expansion of content: the general expansion of knowledge throughout the twentieth century; the demands of secondary education in an era of secondary education for all; the acceptance of basic literacy as a minimum right of all, rather than the precious possession of a few. But perhaps the most important factor has been a change of aim or purpose, the result of asking the question: what is a primary school for? This kind of question has been asked frequently since the Second World War, and answers have usually stressed the insufficiency of providing a purely intellectual training, and the necessity of catering for other aspects of the lives of growing children. Explicit in the half-dozen main reports on Scottish education in the last twenty years, and implicit now in much school practice, is the basic idea that the duty of the school is to ensure for the pupil "the fullest development of which he is capable"[11]—and this refers to various aspects of development and to all stages of education.

This factor behind curriculum change is linked to the second main trend mentioned, the tendency to revalue existing curriculum content. For example, prior to 1946 few would have disagreed with the assertion that the fundamental subjects of the primary school curriculum were reading, writing, and arithmetic. However, in that year the Advisory Council's report on primary education contained this revolutionary pronouncement: "we discard with little regret the narrow and obsolete view that reading, writing and arithmetic are the three fundamentals of education. . . . If it is necessary . . . to talk about any subject at all being more fundamental than another, we would suggest tentatively, and as a basis for clearer thinking on the subject, that the three fundamental subjects are physical education, handwork, and speech."[12]

The Advisory Council had said in an earlier paragraph of the report that "the curriculum and methods of the primary school should be thought out afresh",[13] but few Scottish teachers could have foreseen that the reappraisal would be quite so radical. The traditional type of teacher had his doubts about the sanity of the members of the Advisory Council, and hoped that they were taking an extreme position in order to bring the traditionalists at least part of the way. In the event, little came of the suggestion, and comfort was taken in a report a few years later which stated bluntly: " . . . despite the importance now rightly attached to physical education, music, art, and handwork, the basic skills of reading, writing and arithmetic can never cease to be fundamental in the primary school."[14]

Nevertheless changes have come, and the twin processes of expansion and revaluation continue. French has been introduced to the curriculum of a considerable number of primary schools; in 1965 almost 1000 classes in some 220 schools were taking the Glasgow ETV programme in primary French. In some schools a course in elementary science is replacing or supplementing traditional work in nature study. Primary mathematics, sometimes called "discovery mathematics" because much of the initiative in learning comes from the children, highlights the importance of practical activities in developing mathematical concepts, as opposed to the traditional emphasis on mechanical computation in arithmetic. Some schools are experimenting with "patch" studies in history and with "sample" studies in geography.

With regard to revaluation, primary school teachers have been more willing of recent years to examine the content of existing subjects in a spirit of critical questioning. Is too much time spent on mechanical arithmetic, in which Scottish pupils tend to shine? Is written English stressed at the expense of spoken English? Is adequate attention paid to reading for comprehension? Is there too much dead wood and too great a stress on memorizing in history and geography?

This kind of critical appraisal was further stimulated by the publication in 1965 of the memorandum *Primary Education in Scotland*,[15] produced by a committee of teachers, H.M. Inspectors, and lecturers in colleges of education. This memorandum examined the principles on which primary education should be based, and gave official support to the third trend mentioned above, the trend towards integration of the subjects taught in the primary school. To date, primary schools have generally been organized in terms of subjects, time-tables, and 30–40 minute periods. Although the concept of "child-centring" is familiar to most teachers, it has tended to be "child-centring" in the rather limited sense of concern for children's needs and interests within the framework of an established and accepted subject curriculum.

The new memorandum constitutes an important statement of the inadequacy of this kind of view. For example, " . . . the curriculum is not to be thought of as a number of discrete subjects, each requiring a specific allocation of time each week or each month. Indeed, it is quite impossible to treat the subjects of the curriculum in isolation from one another if education is to be meaningful to the child."[16] And the memorandum recommends the knitting together of formerly discrete subjects into such groupings as "language arts" (for example, reading, oral and written composition, spelling, poetry), and "environmental studies" (for example, arithmetic, history, geography, science). This trend towards integration, although quite widely accepted in England, is relatively new in Scottish primary education, and tends to encounter considerable opposition from teachers accustomed to the traditional subject approach. It also tends to offend the sense of logical and tidy organization which many teachers value, and which is a reflection of the traditional Scottish emphasis on *teachers teaching* rather than on *children learning*.

The memorandum is heavily biased towards the *children learning* approach, and by giving official Departmental support to more progressive and experimental teaching techniques, it has initiated a general reappraisal of teaching methods in the primary school. No greater service could be performed for Scottish primary education.

Methods

The picture of the traditional Scottish classroom is as follows: the children are sitting, quietly and attentively, in rows of desks; the teacher is at the front of the class, talking. Questions are asked by the teacher, and answered by the pupils. Material is written neatly on the blackboard. There is little communication among the pupils, and little activity apart from the raising and lowering of hands. Everything is planned, orderly, under control. The teacher knows what she wants, and generally gets it. She is there to teach, the pupils are there to learn. The emphasis is on the individual, rather than the group; on competition rather than co-operation.

This is the situation on which more progressive approaches have impinged; to what effect? There are still some classrooms of which the above paragraph is not a caricature, but a description. At the opposite extreme there are a few classrooms—a very few— in which the apostle of ultra-progressivism would feel quite at home. Most Scottish teachers disapprove of such classrooms, and mutter about noise and lack of control. In between are the majority of classrooms, characterized by a general adherence to the traditional techniques of teaching, with some infusion of group work, assignments and projects, and a gradual liberalizing of the classroom atmosphere.

Progressive techniques have made their most noticeable impact in infant departments, that is classes P.I and P.II, where playway, activity methods and informal approaches are quite generally found. In many of these classes children move freely about the classroom, and group and regroup for different activities. They play with blocks, plasticine, paints and crayons. They are introduced informally and gradually to reading, writing and counting by means of pictures, stories, toy shops and so on. They are encouraged to talk by such devices as the "news" period, and the discussion of toys, games and favourite activities. This process, while providing useful word experience as a basis for reading, is aimed at countering the relative lack of verbal fluency which characterizes children in Scottish primary schools when they are compared with children in English junior schools or American elementary schools.

Outside the early years of primary education formal class teaching still occupies much of the school day, although the progressive practices of the infant rooms are gradually being extended. Group teaching is on the increase, mainly in the teaching of reading and arithmetic. The practice of grouping enables individual pupils to advance at a pace which suits them, and has generally been found to develop in pupils both self-reliance and co-operation. Various difficulties account for the fact that group work is by no means universal: large classes, unsuitable rooms and furniture, staff changes, and the demands which group work makes with regard to organization, supervision, correction and class control.

For similar reasons the project method, a commonplace of educational theory for most of the twentieth century, has not had a very great impact on Scottish primary education. The essence of the project method is that some topic is taken as a centre of interest, and that the subjects of the curriculum become integrated in their contribution to this particular topic. Full-scale projects which cut across the traditional organization of the curriculum into specific subjects are becoming more common in Scottish primary schools, but most projects are more modest in scope, being confined to one or two particular subjects. Projects which have been successfully completed include local surveys, the production of school plays and school magazines, improving a school playground, and running a school tuck shop, as well as the more usual run of projects on Coal, Shipping, Dress, Railways, Farms, Housing and so on.

The memorandum *Primary Education in Scotland* recommends the use of group work, activity and discovery methods, project and assignment techniques, and experimentation in such areas as programmed learning and team teaching. The authors of the report note: "The teacher's role is changing as teacher-dominated methods and subject-centred curricula give way to methods and curricula based on the needs and interests of the child."[17] Herein lies the challenge to established teachers in Scottish primary schools.

Assessment

Assessment in the primary school is generally by means of oral and written examinations of the traditional type. Standardized attainment tests, group intelligence tests, and diagnostic tests are certainly used, but by and large teachers set their own examinations in order to ascertain the progress pupils are making, and to evaluate the efficiency of the teaching done. The results of these examinations are generally used to inform parents, through the medium of a report card, of their children's progress at school.

While assessment for such purposes is necessary, it is fair to say that in Scottish primary education an undue emphasis has been placed on examining, so that marks are added together, orders of merit drawn up, "places" in class allocated, and prizes awarded at the end of the session. Two of the last three reports on primary education have been strongly critical of this kind of emphasis,[18] which militates against the developments in curricula and methods described above.

As indicated in Chapter 3, *The Schools (Scotland) Code, 1956* lays down that a pupil's progress record shall be kept for every pupil attending a public or grant-aided school.[19] The card is designed to contain such information as date of birth, parent's occupation, schools attended, results of standardized tests, nursery class records, attainments in the various subjects of the curriculum and background information. Opinion tends to be divided on the usefulness of these cards. A revision of the form and content of the pupil's progress record is in hand. It is to be hoped that the new record will prove of value, not merely for purposes of assessment, but also for advising and guiding the pupil throughout his school career.

One form of assessment demanded of the primary school is that required for the purpose of transfer of pupils from primary to secondary education. This process merits separate consideration.

TRANSFER FROM PRIMARY TO SECONDARY EDUCATION

The historical background to present transfer procedures has been mentioned in the outline of the development of secondary education given in Chapter 1. There it was shown that the Merit Certificate was introduced in 1892 to encourage children to stay at school after age 13. The function of the Certificate soon changed, however, and from 1899 it marked the completion of elementary education at age 12, and served as the condition of admission to post-elementary education.

In 1903 the qualifying examination, designed to be taken at age 12, replaced the Merit Certificate. This examination, a "pass" or "fail" barrier, consolidated the tradition that pupils were expected to "qualify" for secondary education, that is to reach a set standard in basic subjects before being allowed to continue with secondary subjects. Many children never did so. Circular 44 of 1921 led to the replacement of the qualifying examination by the control examination conducted by individual education authorities, and also to the gradual acceptance of the principle that all children should proceed to some form of secondary education—the principle known as the "clean cut", the accepted age for the break being 12.

The idea of the "clean cut" was enshrined in the 1946 Act.[20] This served to focus attention on the various techniques employed in what was termed by the Act "promotion" and what is today known as "transfer" from primary to secondary education. It should be noted that different forces operated to produce the break between primary and secondary education at age 12 in Scotland and 11 plus in England.[21]

At the present time each education authority in Scotland is required to prepare and submit for the Secretary of State's approval a transfer scheme showing the methods to be adopted for transferring pupils from primary to secondary education in the authority's area.[22] There are therefore thirty-five separate transfer schemes in existence. However, most schemes have many features in common; what follows outlines the general position.

The type of secondary education to which pupils are transferred is determined by tests and assessments given in the primary school. Most current transfer schemes provide for the following: firstly, verbal reasoning tests of which two are given in most areas, one usually in P.VI and one in P.VII; secondly, objective attainment tests in English and arithmetic; thirdly, teachers' estimates in English and arithmetic, which in most areas are scaled on the objective attainment tests in English and arithmetic respectively, in order to make the estimates comparable from school to school. This particular test battery is based on research findings, and has proved to be an efficient predictor of success in the secondary school.[23]

In most areas these measures are used to allocate pupils to secondary courses of two main types: certificate courses, that is courses leading to the examinations for the award of the Scottish Certificate of Education; or non-certificate courses. An official recommendation in 1961 was that 35% of an age group should proceed to certificate courses.[24] For various reasons this percentage has increased, and by 1965 the figure for the country as a whole was 40%, although considerable variation still existed from one education authority area to another.

Transfer to secondary education takes place once a year in most education authority areas, and twice a year in the remainder. In each area responsibility for transfer procedures rests with a Transfer Board which usually consists of the director of education, members of the education committee, and representatives of primary and secondary headmasters and teachers.

Parents' wishes with regard to their children's secondary education are taken into consideration, but the 1962 Act makes it clear that a parent is not entitled to select for his child a course of secondary education from which, in the opinion of the education authority, the child shows no reasonable promise of profiting.[25] A parent may appeal to the Transfer Board against its decision, and if he is still not satisfied, he may appeal to the Secretary of State, whose decision is final. In 1965 there were ninety-one appeals to the Secretary of State; the Transfer Board's decision was confirmed in sixty-six of these cases.

Although transfer procedures in general function with efficiency and fairness, they are nevertheless open to criticism. For example, since no system of assessment is infallible, some mistakes in allocation are made, and not all are subsequently rectified; allocation to a certificate or non-certificate course is made on the basis of work done in the primary school before the child has had any experience of secondary education; and the stress on attainment in English and arithmetic tends to have a narrowing and restricting effect on the curriculum of the primary school. For these and other reasons the Scottish Education Department's Circular 614 of 1966[26] suggested that allocation to certificate or non-certificate courses on the basis of present transfer procedures should be discontinued wherever possible, and that decisions about the secondary courses which individual pupils should follow should be the responsibility of the secondary school, and should be made on the basis of the pupil's record both in the primary school and in the initial stage of the secondary school. The circular asked education authorities not to set external tests for primary schools, and advised primary schools to base the information sent to secondary schools on normal primary school work, rather than on internal examinations specifically designed to obtain information for the secondary school. The circular further recommended that the initial stage of secondary education should be regarded as a period of orientation during which pupils explore a variety of subjects to find out for themselves where their interests and abilities lie.

It is therefore certain that the future will see considerable changes in the present pattern of transfer procedures. There is likely to be greater flexibility in schemes and increased co-operation at the direct personal level between the staffs of primary and secondary schools. In this connection it should be noted that personal contact between "sending" and "receiving" headmasters has been part of Glasgow's scheme in its system of transfer panels and group transfer committees established in 1958.

The recommendations of Circular 614 have clear implications for the organization of secondary education, and especially for the institution of a system of comprehensive secondary schools. These issues are discussed in the next chapter.

REFERENCES AND NOTES

1. Education (Scotland) Act, 1962, Section 2 (2).
2. *Ibid.*, Section 2 (3).
3. For example, it is only where an independent school has five or more pupils of school age that the issue arises of admission to the register of independent schools. Thus the Scottish Education Department's list of independent schools excludes all schools which cater exclusively for children under school age. Such schools should be registered with the local health authority, and in 1965 there were 111 premises in the care of local authorities or private individuals. It is difficult to decide, however, how many of these should be classified as nursery schools, as distinct from day nurseries or crèches.
4. The Scottish Education Department's Circular No. 610 of 1st June 1966, announced that the Secretary of State was prepared to allow education authorities to provide new nursery classes (but not nursery schools) in which priority of admission would be given to the children of married women returning to service in the schools.
5. Scottish Council for Research in Education: *A Survey of Nursery School Provision in Scotland*, 1958.
6. Education (Scotland) Act, 1962, Section 31.
7. *Ibid.*, Section 29 (1).
8. See, for example
   DANIELS, J. C., The effects of streaming in the primary school, *British Journal of Educational Psychology* 31, parts I and II, Feb. and June 1961.
   JACKSON, B., *Streaming: An Education System in Miniature*, London, Routledge & Kegan Paul, 1964.
   DOUGLAS, J. W. B., *The Home and the School*, London, Macgibbon & Kee, 1964, Chapter XIV.
9. Scottish Education Department: *Primary Education*. A Report of the Advisory Council on Education in Scotland, Cmd. 6973, Edinburgh, H.M.S.O., 1946, Chapter XI.
10. *The Schools (Scotland) Code, 1956*, Section 21 (1).
11. Scottish Education Department: *Junior Secondary Education*, Edinburgh, H.M.S.O., 1955, Para. 3.

12. Scottish Education Department: *Primary Education*. A Report of the Advisory Council on Education in Scotland, Cmd. 6973, Edinburgh, H.M.S.O., 1946, Paras. 112 and 113.

13. *Ibid.*, Para. 80.

14. Scottish Education Department: *The Primary School in Scotland*, Edinburgh, H.M.S.O., 1950, Para. 10.

15. Scottish Education Department: *Primary Education in Scotland*, Edinburgh, H.M.S.O., 1965.

16. *Ibid.*, p. 37.

17. *Ibid.*, p. 60.

18. Scottish Education Department: *Primary Education*. A Report of the Advisory Council on Education in Scotland, Cmd. 6973, Edinburgh, H.M.S.O., 1946, Paras. 423–7.
    Scottish Education Department: *Primary Education in Scotland*, Edinburgh, H.M.S.O., 1965, Chapter 8.

19. *The Schools (Scotland) Code, 1956*, Section 18 (1).

20. Education (Scotland) Act, 1946, Section 30.

21. For an important study of factors affecting the age of transfer see NISBET, J. D. and ENTWISTLE, N. J., *Age of Transfer to Secondary Education*, London, University of London Press, 1966.

22. Education (Scotland) Act, 1962, Section 30.

23. The classic Scottish investigation is that of MCCLELLAND, W., *Selection for Secondary Education*, London, University of London Press, 1942. A shortened account is given in MCINTOSH, D. M., *Promotion from Primary to Secondary Education*, London, University of London Press, 1948. For subsequent research by McIntosh see *Educational Guidance and the Pool of Ability*, London, University of London Press, 1959.

24. Scottish Education Department: *Transfer from Primary to Secondary Education*. A Report of a Special Committee of the Advisory Council on Education in Scotland, Cmnd. 1538, Edinburgh, H.M.S.O., 1961, Para. 86. See also Scottish Education Department: Circular No. 501: *Transfer of Pupils from Primary to Secondary Education*, 20th June 1962.

25. Education (Scotland) Act, 1962, Section 29.

26. Scottish Education Department: Circular No. 614: *Transfer of Pupils from Primary to Secondary Education*, 29th June 1966.

CHAPTER 5

Secondary Education

ANY account of secondary education in Scotland at the present time must begin with the question of organization which, as indicated in Chapter 3, has become increasingly complex of recent years.

ORGANIZATION OF SECONDARY EDUCATION

The two main factors responsible for this increasing complexity are the move towards a system of comprehensive secondary education, and changes in the examination structure of the secondary school. As a result, an account in accordance with the familiar terminology of "junior secondary" and "senior secondary" schools is no longer adequate. Perhaps the most satisfactory classification of secondary schools at the present time is in terms of courses and combinations of courses provided. A classification used by the Scottish Education Department is shown in Table 4.[1]

A few comments on Table 4 may be helpful.

The schools in category A1, which provide non-certificate courses only, are still commonly called "junior secondary" schools. Such schools are found in all but seven education authority areas, although their number has been decreasing each year—from 503 in 1960 to 306 in 1965. This is due partly to the centralization of educational provision in various areas, and partly to the general tendency for such schools wherever possible to "grow" a fourth year and present their most able pupils for the Ordinary grade of the Scottish Certificate of Education, a process which transfers the schools concerned from category A1

TABLE 4. CLASSIFICATION OF SECONDARY SCHOOLS

Classification	No. of schools	Approx. no. of pupils
A. SELECTIVE SCHOOLS		
1. Offering non-certificate courses only	306	53,000
2. Offering certificate courses only	70	62,000
B. COMPREHENSIVE SCHOOLS		
Offering non-certificate courses, and complete Ordinary and Higher grade certificate courses	134	95,000
C. PART-SELECTIVE, PART-COMPREHENSIVE		
1. Offering non-certificate courses, and years I and II of both Ordinary and Higher grade certificate courses	33	4,500
2. Offering non-certificate courses, years I and II of Higher grade and years I to IV of Ordinary grade certificate courses	66	30,000
3. Offering non-certificate courses, and years I to IV of Ordinary grade certificate courses (no Higher grade)	59	31,000

to category C3. These two factors, coupled with the future development of comprehensive secondary education, will operate to reduce still further the number of "pure" junior secondary schools.

The schools in category A2, which offer certificate courses only, are the "senior secondary" schools, selective and intellectual in orientation, which have for many years given the academic type of secondary education for which Scotland is well known. Some of the most famous secondary schools in the country, many of them with a long and distinguished history, fall into this category. The seventy schools are spread over eighteen education authority areas.

The schools in category B, "all-through" comprehensive schools, are found in all but three education authority areas. This category includes the traditional "omnibus" type of secondary school common in various parts of Scotland for very many years, and also the new comprehensive schools established by such authorities as Glasgow and Edinburgh. This distinction is explained below in the context of the comprehensive issue in general.

The schools in category C1, small schools in areas of scattered population, provide non-certificate courses, and also the first 2 years of certificate courses for pupils who then transfer to a larger secondary school, often a considerable distance from home.

The schools in category C2 are fully comprehensive for their first 2 years, after which the brightest pupils proceed to secondary schools providing courses up to fifth and sixth years, while the other pupils remain to complete non-certificate courses or certificate courses to Ordinary grade standard only. In some counties—for example Fife and Renfrewshire—schools in this category have been established as part of a two-tier comprehensive system of junior and senior high schools.

The schools in category C3 are almost all former junior secondary schools (category A1) which have developed a fourth year and present some of their pupils for the Ordinary grade of the Scottish Certificate of Education, as well as providing non-certificate courses for the majority of their pupils. Pupils who are successful in Ordinary grade examinations may transfer from schools in this category—and from schools in category C2 above —to larger secondary schools for fifth and sixth year studies.

The pattern of organization of secondary education varies from one education authority area to another, and varies also within individual areas. For example, in 1965 one area had schools in all six of the above categories, seven areas had schools in five categories, and six areas had schools in four categories. The present trend, however, is towards a reorganization of secondary education on comprehensive lines. The intention is to have all secondary pupils in schools which provide both certificate and non-certificate courses; in 1965 almost 60% of secondary pupils were in such schools. Thus the future is likely to see a quite rapid decline in the number of category A schools (selective schools) and an increase in the numbers of category B and C schools—but especially in category B, the "all-through" comprehensive schools. Some general issues with regard to comprehensive schools merit separate consideration.

THE COMPREHENSIVE SCHOOL

Since most of the public debate on comprehensive schools has been conducted in the context of English education, it may be useful to take the situation in England as a point of departure. In the period after the Second World War English secondary education was characterized by a tripartite organization in terms of secondary grammar, secondary technical, and secondary modern schools, and children were allocated to these different schools according to their performance in the "11 plus" examination. The aim of many parents was to secure for their children entry to the grammar school—roughly the equivalent of the Scottish senior secondary school—but in the 1950's grammar schools were taking only 20% of an age group, and this figure varied widely from area to area, in some areas being as low as 10%. Moreover, the "11 plus" came increasingly under fire: it caused stress and anxiety to children and parents; final decisions about a child's future were being made at the tender age of 11; and grammar school "failures" and secondary modern "successes" threw doubt on the predictive validity of the "11 plus" procedures. In this kind of situation support grew for the idea of the comprehensive school which would take all the children of a particular area for their secondary education, and would not be divided into clearly defined "sides". Consequently, in various parts of England today comprehensive schools coexist with selective grammar schools, and the trend, as in Scotland, is towards comprehensive schools.

The situation in Scotland has differed from that in England in two main ways. In the first place a higher percentage of each age group has been admitted to senior secondary schools; when the national figure for entry to English grammar schools was 20%, the comparable figure for entry to Scottish senior secondary schools was 35%. Hence there have been fewer parents in Scotland who have felt their children deprived of an academic education. In the second place, because of the distribution of the population in Scotland, certain areas have for many years had schools which have taken all the pupils of the area for their secondary education —"omnibus" schools—and to this extent have been comprehensive. It must be noted, however, that such schools have tended to be bi-lateral rather than comprehensive, in that pupils have usually been firmly allocated, before entry to the secondary school, to certificate or non-certificate courses, and once in the secondary school have usually been separated by fairly rigid streaming into two distinct "sides". In fact the majority of the 134 schools entered in Table 4 as "comprehensive" fall into this bi-lateral category. However, this segregation under one roof has not been so obvious and hence has evoked less public complaint.

Thus the comprehensive debate has been less fierce in Scotland than in England, although similar arguments have been advanced in favour of the comprehensive principle. For example, since the comprehensive school takes all the children of an area for their secondary education, it promotes social unity, and as long ago as 1947 the Advisory Council had stated: "this is the natural way for a democracy to order the post-primary schooling of a given area."[2] Selection problems are minimized, allocation to courses taking place within the one school, decisions frequently being based on the performance of pupils in secondary rather than in primary education. Subsequent transfers are more easily effected, as no change of school is involved; all that may be required is a change of sets. As a comprehensive school is usually large, a wide range of school subjects and extra-curricular activities can be provided; this, coupled with the principle of "setting" by ability in individual subjects, means that there is a good chance of finding subjects and levels of difficulty to suit individual pupils.[3]

On the other hand, critics of the comprehensive principle have tended to doubt the extent and sometimes even the desirability of the social mixing which takes place. They are concerned about the large size of comprehensive schools, with their attendant dangers of impersonality. They fear that academic pupils may make less progress than they would under a selective system, and also on the other hand that non-academic pupils will be denied experiences of responsibility and leadership which they would have had as the senior pupils in a junior secondary school.

While the debate continued in Scotland, official action was taken. The government's intention to further the reorganization of secondary education on comprehensive lines was announced in Circular No. 600,[4] in which a clear preference was expressed for the "all-through" type of comprehensive school, although it was recognized that local conditions and resources might make such variations as a two-tier system necessary. Education authorities were asked to review their existing arrangements and to inform the Scottish Education Department by 31st March 1966 of their general intentions for reorganization.

Clearly such reorganization has created problems for many areas: external problems such as choice of system, the economic use of existing accommodation, the place of grant-aided schools; and internal problems such as class organization, the adoption of setting by ability in individual subjects, provision for mixed ability grouping in certain subjects and in extra-curricular activities, the establishing of a genuine house system, and so on. And over all has hung the knowledge that the action which education authorities take in the late 1960's is likely to determine the organization of secondary education in their areas for many years to come.

CERTIFICATE COURSES

Although the pattern of organization of secondary education has been shown to be complex, the courses provided in secondary schools may be classed in two broad groups: certificate courses which lead to the examinations for the Scottish Certificate of Education on Ordinary and/or Higher grades; and non-certificate courses which lead to no national external examination or certificate.

The percentage of the age group in certificate courses has risen steadily; it was 30% in 1950, 35% in 1960, and just over 40% in 1965. The sections which follow explain the main reasons for this increase.

Traditional Courses. The Scottish Leaving Certificate

It has already been pointed out in Chapter 3 that Scotland has been noted for producing able academic pupils from its secondary schools, where the main emphasis has tended to be placed on individual intellectual excellence. Consequently the curriculum has, throughout the present century, included the traditional secondary subjects: English, modern languages, ancient languages, science, mathematics, history, geography. It is true that schools have also taught homecraft, technical subjects, art, music, commerce and physical education; but the really "important" subjects for most secondary schools have been the academic ones. The Leaving Certificate examinations, introduced as long ago as 1888, have provided standards for the schools and a goal for the pupils.

It is only since the Second World War that successful attempts have been made to broaden the rather narrow academic basis of secondary education, and to loosen rather rigid examination requirements. The first step was taken in 1947 by the publication of the Advisory Council's classic report, *Secondary Education*.[5] In this report wise words were written about aims in secondary education and about curriculum content; current methods of teaching were criticized and various experimental approaches recommended; the organization of secondary education was examined and a comprehensive-type system advocated; the pattern of examinations was analysed and a new structure suggested.

Although this report influenced both the direction and the quality of thinking about secondary education in Scotland, there were no immediate dramatic changes. Full secondary education continued to be a 5-year course in a fairly stereotyped range of subjects, and continued to be dominated by the Leaving Certificate examination. Certificate courses had to be approved by the Scottish Education Department, and had to provide for the study, by each pupil following a certificate course, of specific subjects at certain stages of the course. In connection with most subjects there were two grades of the Certificate, Higher and Lower, both planned to be taken generally in the fifth year of secondary education. Up till 1950 candidates had to pass in a group of subjects in order to gain the Certificate—for example, two Highers and three Lowers in the 1940's—but from 1950 the position was eased a little in that the Certificate was awarded on the basis of passes in individual subjects. In the 1950's, of those who started a certificate course—30–35% of an age group—only one-third obtained the Scottish Leaving Certificate; the majority left school during the third and fourth years.

The situation outlined above was the background to the publication in 1959 of the *Report of the Working Party on the Curriculum of the Senior Secondary School*,[6] which suggested changes in both curriculum and examination structure. Almost all the proposals of the Working Party were accepted, the majority having been implemented in 1962. What follows outlines the present position.[7]

New Courses. The Scottish Certificate of Education

With regard to the examination structure, the Scottish Leaving Certificate has been renamed the Scottish Certificate of Education, and is now open to external candidates as well as to school pupils.[8] The Higher grade in each subject remains unchanged, but the Lower grade has been replaced by a less exacting Ordinary grade taken one year earlier, in fourth year. The intentions behind the introduction of the Ordinary grade were: to cut down wastage by encouraging pupils to stay at school and complete a fourth year; to effect a closer integration of secondary education with further education; to provide a certificate of use to a wider range of employers; and if possible to encourage successful Ordinary grade candidates to remain in school for fifth and even sixth years.

In all these aspects the Ordinary grade has proved a distinct success. For example, greatly increased numbers of pupils now sit the Certificate examinations: in 1961, 18,562 candidates were presented for the Scottish Leaving Certificate; in 1962, the first year of the Scottish Certificate of Education, 42,276 candidates were presented; in 1965 the figure had risen to 68,937, including 39,131 candidates presented on subjects on the Ordinary grade only.[9] Between 1961 and 1964 there was a 17% increase in the number of pupils remaining at school after age 15. One of the most striking statistics in present-day Scottish education relates to the number of pupils aged 17 and over still in attendance at public and grant-aided schools: between 1955 and 1965 the increase was of the order of 129%.

One result of the introduction of Ordinary grade was unexpected: the original intention was that able pupils would by-pass Ordinary grade, and make straight for Higher grade in fifth year. In practice many able pupils take Ordinary grade in passing as a kind of insurance policy.

With regard to curriculum, certificate courses need no longer be submitted to the Scottish Education Department for approval, and no subject is made compulsory at any stage of certificate courses, responsibility for the content of the courses followed by individual pupils having been passed to headmasters. New subjects have been introduced to the curriculum—for example biology, modern studies, applied mathematics, horticulture, navigation. Former composite subjects such as science, homecraft, technical subjects and commercial subjects have been subdivided into appropriate branches, and separate passes may be obtained in each branch; for example, in science five subjects are offered on Ordinary grade, and four on Higher grade.

As a result of these developments outlined above, certificate courses are now more varied and flexible than ever before. The first 2 years of such courses are fairly general, and many schools now try to avoid overburdening pupils at the start of their secondary courses. With the switch to a more specialized course at the beginning of third year, an increased number of subjects is offered and pupils have a greater freedom of choice, so that there is now the possibility of tailoring a course to suit the individual, whereas previously individuals were forced into the mould of an established and rather rigid curriculum.

In this connection the fear has been expressed that the abolition of compulsory subjects, taken in conjunction with the earlier differentiation of courses in preparation for Ordinary grade examinations, may lead to an abandoning of the broad-based general education traditional in Scotland. Evidence suggests that in general this is being avoided.[10] Up to fourth year or beyond, English remains basic to all courses, and more than two-thirds of all certificate pupils study at least one foreign language; history and geography are normally taken in the first 2 years, and one or other is usually continued till at least the fourth year, or replaced by modern studies; arithmetic is retained until the fourth year by almost all pupils, and over 75% study mathematics to the end of their certificate course; the majority of certificate pupils study one or more sciences throughout the course; practically every pupil takes physical education. The one weakness would appear to be on the aesthetic side—the inadequate provision of courses in music and more particularly in art.

As already mentioned certificates are now within the reach of an increased number of pupils, so that wastage has been cut down. Secondary education is more closely linked with further education —for example the normal requirements for entry to National Certificate courses are expressed in terms of relevant Ordinary grade passes. Finally, secondary education is now seen by both pupils and parents as more relevant to life outside the school; future vocational requirements are taken into account in planning pupils' courses; and Ordinary grade passes secure entry to a variety of occupations.

In comparing secondary education in Scotland with that in England, differences in the pattern of secondary school examinations must be borne in mind. The Ordinary grade of the Scottish Certificate of Education is taken after 4 years of secondary education, and the Higher grade after 5 or sometimes 6 years. In England the Ordinary level of the General Certificate of Education is taken after 5 years of secondary education and the Advanced level after 2 years—sometimes 3—of specialized work in sixth form. While the Scottish Ordinary grade is of a similar standard to English Ordinary level, the Scottish Higher grade is lower in standard than English Advanced level. The introduction in Scotland of a post-Higher grade examination, an issue which has been under consideration for some time, is referred to below.

The Scottish Certificate of Education Examination Board

One result of the large increase in the number of candidates for the Scottish Certificate of Education was that responsibility for the Certificate examinations, which had been conducted by the Scottish Education Department since 1888, passed in 1965 to the new Scottish Certificate of Education Examination Board.[11]

The Board consists of thirty-eight members—thirty-three appointed from persons nominated by bodies representing educational interests, and five, including the chairman, appointed directly by the Secretary of State. The main functions of the Board are to advise the Secretary of State on matters relating to examinations for pupils receiving secondary education, to conduct the annual examinations for the Scottish Certificate of Education, and to award the Certificate in accordance with such conditions as the Board, with the approval of the Secretary of State, from time to time prescribes.

The Board has set up three Standing Committees—a Finance Committee of nine members, a General Purposes Committee of twelve members, and an Examinations Committee of twenty-four members. For each subject or group of subjects the Examinations Committee has appointed Subject Panels, on which are represented such interests as teachers, the universities, the colleges of education, further education, and the Inspectorate. These panels work in close collaboration with the Examiners, Setters, and Assistant Examiners responsible for each examination.

As the first Report of the Board shows,[12] the conduct of the Certificate examinations each year is something of a major operation.

The Sixth Year

Whereas pupils in English sixth forms are usually specializing in depth on a relatively narrow front, pupils in Scottish sixth years are pursuing a variety of ends. Some are taking additional subjects on the Higher grade; some are resitting examinations in subjects in which they failed in fifth year; some are converting Ordinary grade passes into Higher grade passes; some are resitting examinations in subjects in which they already have Higher grade passes in order to raise the level of their passes and increase their chance of university entry; some are taking short courses in additional subjects to add breadth; some are preparing for one or other of the University Bursary Competitions; some are just there to mature and perhaps to acquire the techniques of independent study.

It is against this background that proposals for the introduction of a post-Higher grade examination have been discussed. The suggestion for an Advanced grade examination, first made in 1947,[13] was revived in 1960 when a Special Committee of the Advisory Council proposed the introduction of an Advanced grade examination to be taken in sixth year, and also recommended that the Higher grade of the Certificate be retained.[14] The idea was to provide papers of a more advanced character in order to develop the talents of the ablest pupils; to give "direction and focus" to sixth-year work, in which it was claimed the pattern of studies was "ragged and diffuse"; and to lead pupils into "habits of positive and rewarding private study". Critics tended to doubt whether the introduction of an Advanced grade was the most desirable way of ensuring these desirable ends, and fears were expressed on a number of counts. For example there was the possibility of introducing to Scottish schools the rather narrow specialization which characterizes English Advanced level work, and the danger that the "Highers" might disappear as the ablest pupils by-passed them for Advanced grade passes to which, in the end, university entry might become tied.[15]

In spite of these and similar objections work on a possible Advanced grade continued. Syllabuses and specimen question papers produced in 1963 and 1964 were adversely criticized, however, and plans to introduce Advanced grade examinations in 1964 were dropped. In September 1964 the Scottish Certificate of Education Examination Board was asked to advise the Secretary of State on the form, standard and content of a post-Higher grade examination, and the Board's *Circular 2 (1966)* announced the establishing of a "Certificate of Sixth Year Studies". Syllabuses and specimen question ,papers have been prepared in respect of six subjects—Art, Commerce, English, French, Geography, Physics—and papers will be available in these subjects for the first awards of the Certificate in 1968. Papers in other subjects are expected to be available in 1969 and succeeding years.

The Certificate of Sixth Year Studies is meant to supplement and not to replace the existing certificates, and it is not intended that it should come to be regarded by the universities or the professions as a formal requirement for entrance. It is thus already a disappointment to those who hoped for a Scottish equivalent of English Advanced levels. At the moment its precise status is uncertain and its probable impact on the work of the secondary schools is a matter of conjecture.

Individual Subjects and Methods

So far, attention has been focused on courses in general and the examinations to which these courses lead. Changes have also been taking place in the content of individual subjects and in methods of presentation. It is not possible in a general survey to deal with such developments in detail, but mention must be made of important developments in the teaching of mathematics, modern languages, and science.

In 1965 more than 75% of all pupils in the first year of certificate courses were following a new syllabus produced by the Mathematics Syllabus Committee set up by the Scottish Education Department in 1963. This syllabus entails a new approach to traditional work, and contains a number of topics not previously taught in schools. Pupils' textbooks and teachers' notes have been produced, and the series is planned to cover 5 years' work. Examination papers in "the new mathematics" are likely to be set at Ordinary grade in 1968, and at Higher grade in 1969. It has been claimed that these developments put Scotland in the forefront of mathematics teaching in Britain, and probably in Europe.

Modern language teaching has been revitalized by a new emphasis on the aural-oral approach, enabling the spoken word to have the place in language learning that it has lacked in Scotland, where the formal textbook with its emphasis on the grammatical and literary aspects of a language has tended to be at the centre of teaching. While experiments have been conducted using a variety of audio-visual aids, the most important development has been that of language laboratories in which each pupil sits in an individual booth with tape-recorder and headphones, listens to expert pronunciation, and can record and play back his own efforts. The teacher sits at a console which enables him to contact any child individually. The first language laboratory was installed in a Scottish school in Fife in 1962 and now various authorities make a point of providing language laboratories in all their new secondary schools.

In science, the introduction of alternative syllabuses in physics and chemistry has transformed the work done in schools. For example in physics the old syllabus omitted most of the new discoveries in modern physics, and led to teaching which was characterized by a didactic approach, an emphasis on learning definitions and laws, and a lack of provision for discovery by the pupils themselves. The new syllabus in physics, introduced in

1962,[16] entailed changes in both content and method. The content is no longer based on the traditional division into branches—mechanics, heat, light, sound, electricity and magnetism—but on the fact that certain fundamental concepts run through the whole of physics, and that by studying certain fundamental phenomena —energetics, flow, field phenomena, waves and atomic physics— the most important aspects of physics can be covered. With regard to method, the aim now is not to inculcate a body of factual knowledge but to arrange for the study of ideas and concepts in an exploratory way, to teach pupils to exercise judgement, and to establish theories which are of wide significance. In 1965 over 90% of secondary schools with certificate courses were following the new physics syllabus.

Although certain new approaches are generally accepted, it is a fair generalization to say that methods in certificate course teaching in Scotland remain fairly traditional. Project and assignment techniques are certainly employed here and there; there are experiments with programmed learning and teaching machines; there are genuine attempts to provide for independent study in many sixth-year classes; and Glasgow's closed-circuit ETV Service, inaugurated in August 1965, has transmitted a first-year mathematics course to fifty secondary schools in the city. In general, however, in spite of the criticisms of the Advisory Council many years ago,[17] class teaching is still the rule, although a more favourable teacher/pupil ratio means that classes in the later years of certificate courses tend to be smaller, so that what amounts to group work is possible. Most experiments which entail any radical departure from traditional class-teaching methods have been conducted in connection with non-certificate courses.

NON-CERTIFICATE COURSES

Approximately 60% of all children transferred from primary to secondary education follow non-certificate courses in secondary schools. It is only comparatively recently that real efforts have been made to devise courses and employ methods suited to the needs of these pupils.

Curriculum and Methods

The development of junior secondary education has been outlined in Chapter 1. The tendency for many years was to give non-academic pupils a "watered-down" academic secondary education. The inadequacy of this approach was finally brought home after 1947, when the raising of the school-leaving age kept all pupils, non-academic as well as academic, at school until age 15, and made possible the provision of a minimum of 3 years of secondary education for all. It should be noted that by no means all pupils have been completing three years of secondary education. Since Scottish pupils are transferred to secondary schools about age 12—some a little older—many attain the age of 15 and leave school during their third year, thus only receiving 2 years and several months of secondary education. In 1961 only 56% of pupils leaving 3-year non-certificate courses had completed the course;[18] this figure had risen only to 67% by 1965.[19]

Immediate problems of accommodation and staffing following the raising of the school-leaving age were acute, but by about 1950 some teachers and headmasters were having success with new courses devised for non-certificate pupils. The way ahead was charted by the publication in 1955 of *Junior Secondary Education*, one of the most important memoranda produced by the Scottish Education Department. The tone was set on the first page: "If junior secondary education is to achieve success, it must develop its own philosophy, devise its own approach to its own problems, and build up its own traditions . . . it must resist the tendency to imitate blindly the senior secondary school."[20]

The memorandum favoured the retention of a traditional subject curriculum, but advocated integration of subjects whenever possible. Recommended subjects for all pupils were: English, mathematics, geography, history, science, art, music, physical education; thereafter there might be a choice from technical, rural, nautical, homecraft, and commercial subjects. For determining the content of individual subjects the criteria suggested were utility and interest, and to further the process of integration it was suggested that one teacher might be responsible for teaching more than one subject to each class.

With regard to method, the report emphasized the importance of a sense of purpose, the idea being that the pupil must see some point in what is done in school, and must see the relevance of school work to life outside. The interest motive was stressed, the assignment method received favourable mention, group methods were advocated, and projects and hobbies periods were recommended. Almost every point in method represented a move away from the traditional chalk-and-talk class lesson, and was therefore wholly in keeping with the stated aim for the junior secondary school of devising "its own approach to its own problems".

The writers of the report were concerned with two further problems: the need to cater for the social education of pupils, and the need to combat the isolation of the school from the local community. As a consequence, great importance was attached to promoting the corporate life of the school by means of clubs and societies, social functions, house organization, even school meals and the morning assembly; and to effecting co-operation between school and community agencies such as the home, the church, local industries, the youth employment service, and further education.

The above points from the report have been detailed because to a large extent the history of the development of non-certificate courses in the years since 1955 has been one of gradual implementation of the recommendations then made. In this, some schools have been more successful than others, and an interim progress report in 1962[21] dispensed both praise and criticism of developments to that date.

At present various schools are developing their own individual approaches. In some schools an approach is made on a "how things work" principle: a wireless set, motor-cycle, or fourth-hand car is the starting-point, and from the actual object, and perhaps its failure to work in practice, the teacher proceeds to the theory behind the object's functioning. Happily more and more teachers in Scotland are proving the theory that for the non-academic pupil the approach is from the practical to the theoretical, the concrete to the abstract, and not the other way round. "How things work" may be the approach adopted by a science department or a technical department.

A similar practical approach may express itself in terms of courses in handyman jobs, gardening, household management, the last not being a restricted course in cookery and laundrywork, but a complete preparation for running a home, frequently involving knowledge of materials and design, value for money, budgeting, sex education and the care of children.

Some schools have experimented with courses on a particular topic which will integrate various curriculum subjects, although not all have claimed that they were running projects. For example, "Life in Our Community" involved for one school lessons on health, local government, local public services, the history of the development of the community, its geographic features, population trends, knowledge of local employment, visits to local industries, and the investigation of opportunities for service in the community. Occasionally a school will specialize in one particular line, the line usually being determined by staff resources. The approach may be through nautical studies, car-driving and motor mechanics, outward-bound activities of various kinds, retail distribution courses, making and sailing dinghies, running an imaginary business, voluntary social service. A few schools have gone further, and have departed quite radically from traditional concepts of curriculum and method.[22]

The "Vocational Impulse"

The schools which originally adopted the various approaches indicated above usually emphasized that the particular lines were developed as vehicles for the general education of their pupils. However, in the early 1960's a vocational bias became increasingly apparent in much of the work being done. The 1955 Report had approached the issue of vocational education very tentatively: "In the interests both of the individual pupil and of the community it is one of the duties of the school to equip its pupils to enter the employment of their choice with a reasonable chance of success." The next sentence quickly adds: "This duty will be discharged primarily by giving each boy and girl a sound general education."[23] In 1955 opinion was not yet ready for the idea that a fairly pronounced vocational bias should be given to school work; it was then still held clearly in mind that the raising of the school-leaving age to 15 in 1947 was intended to give boys and girls a further year of general education before the working world claimed them.

Thus it was 8 years later before the report *From School to Further Education* articulated clearly, and gave official backing to, the concept of the "vocational impulse" in secondary education. This Working Party report, usually referred to by the name of its chairman as the Brunton Report, is the Scottish equivalent of the English Newsom Report.[24] There is no equivocation about this statement: "We believe, and we are supported in this by very many of those whom we have consulted, that the case is unanswerable for the use in schools of the vocational impulse as the core round which the curriculum should be organized."[25] This is the basic idea inherent in project work—that curriculum subjects become integrated in a meaningful way round some centre of interest; but here the centre of interest is to be the vocational aspirations of the pupils.

The recommendations of this report, plus the prospect of a school-leaving age of 16 from 1970, have provoked secondary schools in Scotland to a rethinking and replanning of their non-certificate courses. There has been widespread acceptance of the concept of the vocational impulse—perhaps a too uncritical acceptance.[26] To say this is not to imply rejection of the validity of the concept, but rather to express a fear that excessive concentration on vocational aspects may warp the curriculum, so that aspects other than the vocational may be under-emphasized and under-valued—for example, general education, social education, education for leisure.[27]

If secondary education to age 16 is to be meaningful for pupils following non-certificate courses, there are three main requirements: firstly, the acceptance and implementation of the Brunton Report's recommendations with regard to the "vocational impulse"; secondly, a re-examination of the concept of "general education" for such pupils, involving, among other things, a more flexible approach by teachers to literature, films, music and art; and thirdly, a concern for social education, conceived not merely in terms of "good citizenship" in the future, but in terms of the nature and quality of the social interaction for which the school provides. All this constitutes a formidable task for the schools, and entails a considerable reorientation of thinking on the part of many teachers.

Assessment

The procedure with regard to assessment in non-certificate courses varies from one school to another, but in most schools such assessment is by means of internal written examinations of the traditional type. As implied by the label "non-certificate", pupils in these courses are not aiming for the Scottish Certificate of Education or any certificate awarded at a national level, although in some areas local certificates are provided. Official opinion has been strongly opposed to the introduction of any national certificate to be awarded on the basis of an external examination set at the end of a 3-year course of secondary education, on the grounds that it would impose uniformity on the schools, lead to a concentration on the bookish and the verbal, and cut down on experimental approaches.[28]

Moreover, there has not as yet been any demand in Scotland for a national external examination below Ordinary grade, on the lines, for example, of the English Certificate of Secondary Education. This situation is a result of the dissimilar organization of the educational systems of the two countries: with only about

20% of an age group securing entry to English grammar schools, the secondary modern schools have had fairly able and hence more examinable "tops" than have the Scottish junior secondary schools. In such a situation secondary modern schools have presented candidates for Ordinary level of the General Certificate of Education, and more recently for the sub-Ordinary level Certificate of Secondary Education. Whether or not there will be a demand for a certificate below the standard of Ordinary grade of the Scottish Certificate of Education, when all pupils have to remain at school till age 16, remains to be seen.

TRENDS AND DEVELOPMENTS

It is probably true to say that change in Scottish secondary education has never been so extensive or so rapid as it has been in the 1960's. For example, developments are in progress or pending with regard to the following widely differing aspects of secondary education: an investigation into the part which the school teaching of classics has to play in a modern, industrial society; the extension of social education through school clubs and societies; a consideration of how the certificate subject of modern studies may be adapted for use with non-certificate pupils; further development of the house system in large secondary schools; the provision of real work experiences for pupils in non-certificate courses; the possible institution of Scottish Certificate of Education examinations in religious education; the use of teaching machines and various audio-visual approaches.

Such is the scope and complexity of curriculum development alone that in 1965 the Secretary of State set up a Consultative Committee on the Curriculum, consisting of twenty-three members including serving teachers, H.M. Inspectors, educational administrators, college principals and university professors. The Committee has a threefold remit: to maintain a general oversight of the whole school curriculum, primary as well as secondary; to draw the Secretary of State's attention to any aspect of the curriculum which seems to call for consideration by specialist bodies;

and to give the Secretary of State its comments on the recommendations made by any working party which the Secretary of State
appoints on its advice.

It may be helpful to pull threads together by looking at the
pattern and direction of the main developments in contemporary
Scottish secondary education. These are: the raising of the school-
leaving age to 16 in 1970; the establishing of a complete system
of comprehensive schools; the provision of an increased number
of subjects in certificate courses; the modernization of the content
of individual subjects; the adoption of various new teaching
methods; the provision of certificates at Ordinary and Higher
grades of the Scottish Certificate of Education and the introduction of the Certificate of Sixth Year Studies; the acceptance of the
"vocational impulse" in non-certificate courses; the development
of meaningful courses of "general" education for non-academic
pupils. It should be borne in mind, moreover, that the institution
of a system of comprehensive schools will mean that all these
developments may affect every secondary school.

In education as elsewhere, one development tends to entail a
further development. For example, if the curriculum is characterized by variety and flexibility, the need for guidance of pupils
arises, and it is almost certain that the immediate future will see
important developments in the sphere of guidance and counselling
in secondary schools. Moreover, if these varied courses are being
provided in large comprehensive schools, the development of a
system of housemasters and housemistresses would seem im-
perative; such a system has been introduced, for example in a
number of Glasgow schools, where housemasters are expected to
know every pupil in their house—his or her abilities, weaknesses,
interests, family circumstances, proposed career, and so on.

Thus, although the concept of "secondary education for all"
has for long been accepted in Scotland, it is fair to say that it is
only in comparatively recent years that the implications of the
concept have been fully realized. Action consequent on this
realization will be put to the test from 1970 on.

REFERENCES AND NOTES

1. Scottish Education Department: *Education in Scotland in 1965*, Cmnd. 2914, Edinburgh, H.M.S.O., 1966, Table A, p. 33. The figures in Table 4 are as at October 1965, and thus differ slightly from those given in Table 3, which are as at January 1965.
2. Scottish Education Department: *Secondary Education*. A Report of the Advisory Council on Education in Scotland, Cmd. 7005, Edinburgh, H.M.S.O., 1947, Para. 164.
3. For a concise and useful statement of the case for the comprehensive school see PEDLEY, R., *The Comprehensive School*, Penguin Books, 1963.
4. Scottish Education Department: Circular No. 600. *The Reorganisation of Secondary Education on Comprehensive Lines*, 27th Oct. 1965.
5. Scottish Education Department: *Secondary Education*. A Report of the Advisory Council on Education in Scotland, Cmd. 7005, Edinburgh, H.M.S.O., 1947.
6. Scottish Education Department: *Report of the Working Party on the Curriculum of the Senior Secondary School*, Edinburgh, H.M.S.O., 1959.
7. For a more detailed account see HUNTER, S. L., Scottish Education: changes in the examination structure in secondary schools, *International Review of Education*, Vol. IX/1963–4/No. 3.
8. Details with regard to S.C.E. examinations are published annually; for example, Scottish Certificate of Education Examination Board: *Scottish Certificate of Education Examination. Conditions and Arrangements 1967*, Edinburgh, 1966.
9. Scottish Education Department: *Education in Scotland in 1965*, Cmnd. 2914, Edinburgh, H.M.S.O., 1966, p. 31.
10. Scottish Education Department: *Education in Scotland in 1964*, Cmnd. 2600, Edinburgh, H.M.S.O., 1965, pp. 40–1.
11. The Board was appointed by the Secretary of State in the spring of 1964 under Section 1 of the Education (Scotland) Act, 1963, and in terms of the *Scottish Certificate of Education Examination Board Regulations, 1963*.
12. Scottish Education Department: *Scottish Certificate of Education Examination Board. Report for 1965*, Edinburgh, H.M.S.O., 1966.
13. Scottish Education Department: *Secondary Education*. A Report of the Advisory Council on Education in Scotland, Cmd. 7005, Edinburgh, H.M.S.O., 1947, Chapter VIII.
14. Scottish Education Department: *The Post-Fourth Year Examination Structure in Scotland*. A Report of a Special Committee of the Advisory Council on Education in Scotland, Cmnd. 1068, Edinburgh, H.M.S.O., 1960.
15. For a viable alternative to an examination structure involving an Advanced or post-Higher grade, see NISBET, S., A pattern for examinations, *Times Educational Supplement Scotland*, 19th Nov. 1965.
16. Scottish Education Department: Circular No. 490. *Alternative Physics*, 24th Apr. 1962.
17. Scottish Education Department: *Secondary Education*. A Report of the Advisory Council on Education in Scotland, Cmd. 7005, Edinburgh, H.M.S.O., 1947, Chapter VI.

18. Scottish Education Department: *Transfer from Primary to Secondary Education.* A Report of a Special Committee of the Advisory Council on Education in Scotland, Cmnd. 1538, Edinburgh, H.M.S.O., 1961, Para. 38.

19. Scottish Education Department: *Education in Scotland in 1965*, Cmnd. 2914, Edinburgh, H.M.S.O., 1966, p. 15.

20. Scottish Education Department: *Junior Secondary Education*, Edinburgh, H.M.S.O., 1955, Para. 2.

21. Scottish Education Department: *New Ways in Junior Secondary Education*, Edinburgh, H.M.S.O., 1962.

22. See, for example, MACKENZIE, R. F., *A Question of Living*, London, Collins, 1963.

23. Scottish Education Department: *Junior Secondary Education*, Edinburgh, H.M.S.O., 1955, Para. 20.

24. Ministry of Education: *Half Our Future.* A Report of the Central Advisory Council for Education (England), London, H.M.S.O., 1963.

25. Scottish Education Department: *From School to Further Education*, Edinburgh, H.M.S.O., 1963, Para. 55.

26. It should be emphasized that there is no warrant in the Brunton Report for the adoption of narrow vocational courses. See, for example, para. 58 of the Report.

27. See STENHOUSE, L., Reservation on Brunton, *Times Educational Supplement Scotland*, 29th Apr. 1966.

28. Scottish Education Department: *Secondary Education.* A Report of the Advisory Council on Education in Scotland, Cmd. 7005, Edinburgh, H.M.S.O., 1947, Paras. 233 and 234.
Scottish Education Department: *Junior Secondary Education*, Edinburgh, H.M.S.O., 1955, Paras. 162–4.
Scottish Education Department: *From School to Further Education*, Edinburgh, H.M.S.O., 1963, Paras. 133–41.

CHAPTER 6

Special Education

THE LEGAL POSITION

In the 1962 Act "special educational treatment" is defined as "education by special methods appropriate to the special requirements of pupils who suffer from disability of mind or body";[1] such education must be given in special schools approved by the Secretary of State for the purpose, or by other approved means.

It is the duty of each education authority to ascertain which children in its area who have attained the age of 5 years require special educational treatment, or are suffering from such a disability of mind as to make them unsuitable for education or training in a special school. If necessary for the purpose of this duty the authority may require a parent to submit his child for medical examination by a medical officer of the authority who, if required, must issue a certificate showing the nature and extent of any disability of mind or body from which the child is suffering. Important phrases in the previous sentence are "if necessary" and "if required". It has unfortunately become rather a common practice to issue such certificates; yet the Act states clearly that a certificate should only be issued if in the opinion of the authority it is necessary in order to ensure that a child requiring special educational treatment receives it. A parent may appeal to the Secretary of State against the issue of such a certificate; such certificates may be withdrawn by the Secretary of State or by a medical officer of the education authority.

If the education authority decides that the child is suffering from such a disability of mind as to make him unsuitable for education or training in a special school, the authority must issue to the local health authority a report of its decision, plus a copy of any document which was taken into account in making the decision. Before issuing such a report the authority must inform the parent, who may refer to the Secretary of State the question of whether such a report should be issued. It is the responsibility of the local health authority to provide the special care required for pupils unsuitable for education or training in a special school —for example, care centres on a daily basis, or hospitalization. Section 65 of the 1962 Act provides for the periodic review by the education authority of its decision.

Since in many cases handicap is obvious before a child attains the age of 5, a parent may request the education authority to have his child medically examined at any time after the child's second birthday. In spite of this provision the majority of handicapped children are not found to be so until they come to school, where teachers have close and continuous opportunities for detecting various disabilities.

Thus the responsibility for ascertainment of handicap rests with education authorities. In the case of most handicaps the process of ascertainment involves the co-operation of educational psychologists, medical officers, and teachers. It should be noted that from its use in Section 54 of the 1946 Act, the term "ascertainment" has come to be used in a technical sense to mean "assessed by the education authority as suffering from the particular handicap to such an extent as to require special educational treatment".

The term "special school" has been used above in the legal sense. For statutory purposes "special school" includes child guidance clinics and occupational centres, as well as special classes which form part of primary and secondary schools. In the rest of this chapter, unless otherwise stated, the term "special school" will be used in the narrower sense which excludes child guidance clinics and occupational centres.

CATEGORIES OF HANDICAP

In January 1947 the Advisory Council on Education in Scotland was asked by the Secretary of State to review the provision made in Scotland for the primary and secondary education of pupils who suffer from disability of mind or body or from maladjustment due to social handicaps, and to make recommendations. The Council submitted seven Reports.[2] In 1954 the Secretary of State issued Regulations[3] defining the categories of pupils requiring special educational treatment, and in 1955 a circular[4] commenting on the various recommendations made in the Advisory Council's Reports. This circular, the seven Reports, and the 1954 Regulations form the basis for the present organization of special educational treatment in Scotland.

The categories as defined in the 1954 Regulations are noted below.

1. *Deaf pupils:* pupils who, because of defective hearing, are without naturally acquired speech or language.
2. *Partially deaf pupils:* pupils whose sense of hearing is defective but who possess naturally acquired speech or language.
3. *Blind pupils:* pupils who have no sense of sight or whose sense of sight is, or is likely to become, so defective as to be of no practical value for reading or writing.
4. *Partially sighted pupils:* pupils whose sense of sight is, or is likely to become, defective but is, and is likely to remain, of practical value for reading or writing.
5. *Mentally handicapped pupils:* pupils who have little natural ability.
6. *Epileptic pupils:* pupils who suffer from severe or frequent epileptic seizures or who, by reason of epilepsy, behave in such a way as to make it inexpedient that they should be associated with other children.
7. *Pupils suffering from speech defect:* pupils who suffer from defect or lack of speech not due to deafness or mental handicap.

	Deaf	Partially deaf	Deaf and partially deaf	Blind	Partially sighted	Blind and partially sighted	Mentally handicapped	Physically handicapped	Mentally and physically handicapped	Epileptic	Spastic	Maladjusted	Totals
Day Special Schools	2	2	4		2		24[1]	2	23	1	1[2]	1	60
Residential Special Schools		1	2[5]	1				6			1[3]	5	13[4]
Residential cum Day Special Schools	2					1	3		1		2		11
Special Classes attached to Ordinary Schools		1					53	1	1			1	57
Totals	2	3	6	1	2	1	80	9	25	1	4	7	141[6]

Notes [1] Includes one which also caters for deaf, partially deaf, partially sighted, and spastic children; one which also caters for partially sighted, partially deaf, and epileptic children; and six which also cater for partially sighted children.

[2] Also takes aphasic children.

[3] For mentally handicapped spastics.

[4] There are, in addition, two schools run on Rudolf Steiner principles, which cater for various categories of handicap.

[5] One takes a few blind children.

[6] This total differs from the total given in Table 2, as it relates to a later date in 1965.

TABLE 6. PUPILS IN PUBLIC AND GRANT-AIDED SPECIAL SCHOOLS
AND CLASSES: ANALYSIS BY TYPE OF HANDICAP

	Day pupils	Resident	Total
Deaf	202	210	412
Partially deaf	274	50	324
Blind	9	157	166
Partially sighted	212	3	215
Mentally handicapped	6626	166	6792
Epileptic	51	—	51
Speech defect	23	—	23
Maladjusted	73	139	212
Physically handicapped	911	278	1189
Totals	8381	1003	9384

8. *Maladjusted pupils:* pupils who suffer from emotional instability or psychological disturbance.
9. *Physically handicapped pupils:* pupils who suffer from a physical disabiiity which is, or is likely to be, permanent or protracted and which does not bring them within any of the foregoing categories.

SCHOOLS AND PUPILS

In November, 1965 there were 141 public and grant-aided special schools and classes attended by over 9000 pupils; in addition some 1500 severely mentally handicapped pupils were attending fifty-four occupational centres. Table 5 gives an analysis of schools and classes by type of handicap catered for, and Table 6 an analysis of pupils by type of handicap.

The Code[5] lays down the maximum class size for the various categories of handicap as follows: ten in a class for deaf or partially deaf pupils; fifteen in a class for blind or partially sighted pupils; twenty-five in a class for physically handicapped pupils; and twenty in a class for each of the other categories of handicap.

DEAF AND PARTIALLY DEAF CHILDREN

Early ascertainment in the case of the deaf is of crucial importance; delay entails not only a lost opportunity of receiving appropriate educational treatment, but also the possibility of the acquisition of ineffective methods of communication. A deaf child may even be suspected of being mentally handicapped. Audiometric and other tests have been devised to assist in the early ascertainment of defects in hearing, and children from about age 2 can be trained in lip-reading and can make a beginning in the use of speech. There are conflicting views on the virtues of finger spelling, and a National Working Party has been concerned with the question of communication for the deaf.

The official terms are "deaf" and "partially deaf". Partially deaf children are those who have defects of hearing sufficient to prove a handicap in ordinary classroom conditions, but whose disability is not grave enough to have caused their failure to learn to speak as children and to acquire language through the ear as hearing children do. The more detailed classification currently employed is as follows:[6]

GRADE I. Children with defective hearing who can, nevertheless, without special arrangements of any kind, benefit from the education provided in an ordinary school.

GRADE II. Children whose hearing is defective to such a degree that they require for their education special arrangements or facilities, but not the educational methods used for deaf children without naturally acquired speech or language.

Grade II has two subdivisions:

GRADE IIA. Those children within Grade II who can make satisfactory progress in ordinary classes in ordinary schools provided they are given some help, whether by means of favourable position in class, individual hearing aids, or tuition in lip-reading.

GRADE IIB. Those children within Grade II who, even with the help of favourable position in class, individual hearing aids or tuition in lip-reading, fail to make satisfactory progress in ordinary classes in ordinary schools.

GRADE III. Children whose hearing is so defective and whose speech and language are so little developed that they require education by methods used for deaf children without naturally acquired speech or language. This grade includes the totally deaf.

In grading a deaf child, various factors must be taken into consideration—medical history, intelligence, language development, educational progress—but the crucial factor, naturally, is hearing. For purposes of grading, the Advisory Council recommended a team consisting of medical officer, educational psychologist, and teacher of the deaf.[7]

The determination of the incidence of deafness in school children according to the above grades is a matter of some difficulty. The Advisory Council estimated[8] that the total incidence of all degrees of deafness among children on school rolls was probably not less than 5%; and that future planning should be on the basis of a suggested figure for special schools and classes of $1 \cdot 2$–$1 \cdot 7$ per thousand of the school population. In 1965 the proportion of deaf and partially deaf children actually enrolled in special schools and classes was $0 \cdot 8$ per thousand.

Pupils in Grades I and IIA remain in schools for normal children, though Grade IIA pupils, if they are to make progress, require such help as can be given by means of position of seating in the class, the use of a hearing aid, or instruction in lip-reading.

In order to make satisfactory progress, Grade IIB children must be educated in special schools, apart from normal children. Since they have a certain amount of naturally acquired speech and language, it is desirable that they should not be in the same school as Grade III deaf. This, however, is not always possible to arrange. Since the chief handicap of the children is lack of facility in speech and language, it is important that the curriculum should aim at the development of language and verbal skills, with the help of individual and group hearing aids. On the other hand, since many will be concerned with forms of work and leisure which depend on craftsmanship and manual skills rather than on linguistic skills, provision must be made for drawing and painting, modelling in various materials, working in wood and metal, and for various practical activities. The aim is to provide a varied curriculum which will approximate as far as possible to that for normal children.

Children in Grade III have failed to acquire speech, and the attempt has to be made to enable them to do so, even though they may hear no sound or virtually no sound from the words spoken by the teacher. The attempt is most likely to succeed if the children are in small groups, and if the educational environment is so planned as to stimulate the desire to communicate. Where numbers make it possible, organization is in the form of a nursery and infant stage for the 3–7 year olds, and a senior stage for the 8–16 year olds.

At the nursery and infant stages the curriculum resembles that for hearing children, but lays special emphasis on stimulating the desire to communicate and teaching the techniques of speech and language. The child has to learn to speak and lip-read the names of everyday objects; to follow instructions by lip-reading; to articulate consonants and vowels; to string words together into statements and questions; to associate the word lip-read with the word printed. Everything has to be mastered by a direct act of learning. All this constitutes a formidable task; that a considerable degree of success is achieved borders on the miraculous.

Because of the complexities and difficulties in connection with communication, a considerable amount of time must continue to be devoted by senior pupils, the 8–16 year olds, to the development of speech and language; but the aim must also be to give a varied experience of the subjects which form the primary school curriculum for hearing children. Since average Grade III children are retarded by 4 or 5 years in linguistic ability, such children cannot attempt studies appropriate to the normal secondary school. Those few who can may attend a school in England, though a secondary unit for Grade III deaf children will eventually evolve at Donaldson's School for the Deaf, Edinburgh.

The Advisory Council pronounced quite strongly in favour of vocationally slanted work for under 16's, and for those who elect to remain in school after age 16, and schools for the deaf are involved in the general reassessment of the "vocational impulse" in secondary education.

For teachers of the deaf, there is a 1-year course—for certificated teachers—at Manchester and Dublin.

BLIND CHILDREN

It is on a visit to a special school for the blind or partially sighted that the observer is made forcibly aware of the dependence of educational experiences on vision, whether the experience is of reading, arithmetic, geography, art, physical education or nature study. Moreover, recent developments in teaching methods tend to highlight the importance of sight—for example film strips, projects, assignment cards, television, activity methods, teaching machines. There is thus the constant danger that "the handicap of nature is magnified by educational inequality".[9]

As for the deaf, the value for the blind of early ascertainment cannot be overemphasized. While the condition of a pupil's sight is normally the most important factor determining selection for a special school for the blind, other factors may be involved—for instance general health, intelligence, educational attainment. It is this fact which led the Advisory Council to suggest[10] the use of an ascertainment team consisting of an ophthalmologist, medical officer, psychologist, and specialist teacher acquainted with the educational opportunities available for children with defective sight.

The anticipated incidence of blind children is $0 \cdot 25$ per thousand of the school population; in 1965 the proportion of blind children actually enrolled in schools for the blind was $0 \cdot 18$ per thousand of the school population.

For the blind child, the acquisition of the skills of reading, writing, and counting becomes a difficult task; there is the danger that concepts remain words, or in Whitehead's phrase "inert ideas" devoid of meaning and unrelated to experience. The simple activities involved in physical education become hazardous ventures. Problems of social adjustment are in some cases acute.

Because of the various difficulties involved, it is generally accepted that the most satisfactory method of organizing education for the blind in Scotland is to gather all blind children together in one residential school, the Royal Blind School, Edinburgh. Here there are facilities for the intellectual, physical, social and emotional education of blind children which cannot be provided in small day or residential schools, and still less in a class within a school for the physically handicapped. Outwith the Royal Blind School there is provision for the blind at St. Vincent (Tollcross) School, Glasgow, and for a handful at Duncarse, Dundee.

At the Royal Blind School the curriculum consists of the subjects usually studied in schools for normal children. Oral teaching naturally predominates; good speech is encouraged; handwork is used as a means to promote acquaintance with things through touch; physical education creates self-confidence in movement; pleasant social relationships are encouraged and furthered through informal club activities. For children aged 5 and over there are nursery and infant units, and provision is made for primary, secondary, and further education.

With regard to vocational training, the Advisory Council recommended[11] that training directed to a specific vocation should not be given until the pupil reached the age of 16, and that after age 16 general education should continue to be given along with vocational training. The range of occupations open to the blind has increased; to the traditional activities such as piano-tuning, music, basket-making, shoe-repairing, have been added shorthand and typing, machine-knitting, switchboard-operating, physiotherapy, and recently there has been a new venture into light engineering.

About a fifth of blind children of school age have an additional physical or mental handicap. Some of the mentally handicapped blind children are ineducable, but those who are capable of receiving education in a special school are catered for at the Royal Blind School. Children who are totally deaf as well as totally blind, and who show promise of profiting from instruction, attend Condover Hall, a boarding school in England opened by the Royal National Institute for the Blind in 1948. Children who are totally blind and partially deaf are educated in schools for the blind, provided they have acquired normal speech. Children who are totally blind and physically defective are educated in the residential school for the blind provided adequate care can be given to their physical disability.

Teachers of the blind are normally certificated teachers; they may attend lectures at Moray House College of Education, Edinburgh, and sit examinations for a diploma awarded by the College of Teachers of the Blind. There is also a 1-year course at Birmingham.

PARTIALLY SIGHTED CHILDREN

Defects in vision are usually discovered by means of sight-testing with the Snellen test card, which is a normal part of school medical examinations. Sight-testing remains the responsibility of the medical officer, although the Advisory Council, in an attempt to secure the earliest possible ascertainment, suggested that preliminary testing might be done by class teachers.[12]

The incidence of partially sighted children in Scotland is estimated at 0·75 per thousand of the school roll; in 1965 the proportion of such children actually enrolled in special schools and classes was 0·23 per thousand.

It is generally accepted, for a variety of reasons, that partially sighted children should not attend a school for the blind. At the present time they are educated in two day special schools and one residential cum day special school; the latter also has a few blind pupils. Some eight special schools for pupils who are physically handicapped and/or mentally handicapped also cater for partially sighted children, who either form a class of about fifteen, or are scattered throughout classes for the physically handicapped. The Advisory Council recommended[13] the establishment in Edinburgh of a residential special school for partially sighted children, but this recommendation has not been implemented.

Present policy is to make the education of partially sighted children as like the education of normal children as their visual handicap will permit. Their handicap naturally affects methods of teaching in such areas as reading, writing, and spelling; there must be more emphasis on speaking and listening; and in the case of most other school subjects, content and method have to be adapted for partially sighted children. They use large-print books —the first in the new trend of such books was produced by Glasgow education authority—and are helped by the use of Keeler, Leeds, and London lenses. In general the aim is to get such children to use, as far as possible, the ordinary tools of learning.

It should be noted that there is a greater number of partially sighted children in ordinary schools than in special schools and classes, and the tendency has grown to allow these children, especially those of fairly high intelligence, to remain in ordinary schools if possible; the advice of ophthalmic surgeons that harm does not generally come from the use of eyes with impaired vision has done probably as much as the use of lenses to allow partially sighted children to enjoy a much wider range of educational activities. The present situation is thus a far cry from the old "sight-saving" days, when partially sighted children were encouraged to use the eyes as little as possible.

Teachers of the partially sighted take the course for teachers of mentally and physically handicapped children, which is provided at Jordanhill and Moray House Colleges of Education.

MENTALLY HANDICAPPED CHILDREN

The incidence of mental handicap in the school population is in the region of 1.5%, and is slightly higher among boys than among girls. Mental handicap accounts for the presence of 73% of the children in special schools.

In the field of mental handicap there are three groups of handicapped children:

1. Children who receive education in a special school or class; such children are usually termed "educable"; the usual IQ range is from 55 to 70.
2. Children who receive training in an occupational centre; such children are usually termed "trainable"; the usual IQ range is from 40 to 55.
3. Children who are cared for by the local health authority; such children are usually termed "untrainable"; the IQ range is from 40 downwards.

Although in theory such a classification appears crisp and clean-cut, in practice this is not so; these groups shade gently into each other. It is this which makes the problem of ascertainment acute; this plus the difficulties created by a public attitude which is not as yet wholly enlightened. In Scotland many people still regard mental handicap as a stigma on the child so handicapped, and even on his parents; and the term "daft school" has not completely disappeared. This situation has created the need for various euphemisms, whose ambiguity may create comfort at the expense of clarity. Some psychologists and educationists deplore the process of formal ascertainment, and classification into categories, for a variety of reasons—for example, the fact that the development of borderline cases is hard to predict, or that once deprived of a rich educational environment the child may well conform to the category in which he has been placed. However, present organization is in accordance with the categories listed above.

"Educable" Children

The really crucial borderline is that which separates children who are capable of being educated in an ordinary school from those who, though educable, require special educational treatment. The unsatisfactory practice of regarding IQ 70 as a watershed is gradually dying out. The Working Party on Standards of Ascertainment for Scottish Schoolchildren recommended[14] that in all cases of suspected mental handicap there should be a complete medical and psychological examination of the child, including individual intelligence and attainment tests, a study of the home and school situations, close observation of the child under favourable conditions of teaching—for example in adjustment or tutorial classes for backward and retarded children, manned by teachers working in close co-operation with the child guidance service of the area. The Working Party also recommended that for the purpose of screening, a non-verbal group test of intelligence should be applied to all 7 year olds, and that all those scoring below a fixed point should receive individual tests of intelligence and educational attainment. A limited number of education authorities employ screening tests, and in areas where there are sole psychologists, this work is burdensome.

In Scotland there are various arrangements to meet the needs of mentally handicapped children: in some cases a class is attached to an ordinary school; there are a few residential schools—for example Drummond School, Inverness, and Raddery House in Ross-shire; but the most usual method is to establish special day schools, preferably for mentally handicapped pupils only, although in practice mentally handicapped and physically handicapped children are to be found attending the same special school, often in separate wings. A large authority like Glasgow can have separate schools for primary and secondary stages, the usual age ranges being 5–13 and 13–16.

Compared with pupils in ordinary schools, children in special schools for the mentally handicapped are taught in smaller classes, by individual and group methods, and at a pace suited to their intellectual level. They take longer to learn the processes involved in reading, and much effort must be expended in the attempt to establish a level of skill which will endure after school-leaving age. Work in arithmetic must be designed to meet the simple practical needs of everyday life. History and geography, to be successful, have generally to be presented in colourful story form. Some mentally handicapped children show a surprising ability in art or music, physical education or handwork; but "surprising" is a relative term; the work will usually be below the standard achieved by normal children; the theory of "compensation" is in general a false one.[15] Older girls receive training in homecraft, boys in woodwork and metalwork.

In a special school mentally handicapped pupils can experience success at their own level. The importance of this cannot be overemphasized, particularly for the child who has for years tagged along well below the bottom of his class in the ordinary school. The special school has more limited aims; the curriculum content is more obviously practical; there is not the same necessity to cover the ground or prepare for an examination. All this highlights the twofold need: for early ascertainment, since delay extends the period of failure and shortens the time available for special educational treatment; and for encouragement to parents not to oppose their child's being sent to a special school. Enlightened and interested class teachers in ordinary schools can play a part in meeting both of these needs.

As already noted, the incidence of mental handicap in the school population is in the region of $1 \cdot 5\%$. This would lead one to expect about 13,700 mentally handicapped children to be receiving special educational treatment in 1965; in fact there were 8351 mentally handicapped children in special schools, special classes, and occupational centres in that year. Many more children could be receiving special education if there were more buildings, improved facilities, more teachers, and perhaps most important, a stronger belief among the public in the value of such special educational treatment.

For certificated teachers wishing to work in this field there is a 4-month course at Jordanhill College of Education, Glasgow, followed by 6 months' continuous teaching in a special school, under the supervision of the college's department of Remedial Education. This course leads to an endorsement for teaching mentally handicapped and physically handicapped children. A similar type of course is provided by Moray House College of Education, Edinburgh.

"*Trainable*" *Children*

The second group of mentally handicapped children consists of those who are not capable of receiving education in a special school, but are able to benefit from training in an occupational centre. As stated above, the normally accepted IQ range of such pupils is 40–55, sometimes 35–55, although the Working Party on Standards of Ascertainment preferred IQ 50 rather than 55 as the lower limit of the special school range.[16] The Working Party was of the opinion that intelligence tests should not play such an important part in deciding between a special school and an occupational centre as they should in deciding between an ordinary school and a special school, and suggested certain practical criteria which a child should be able to satisfy if he is to benefit from education in a special school as distinct from an occupational centre.[17] Some children are placed in a preparatory class in a special school for observation before being assigned to special school or occupational centre.

A child in an occupational centre receives a training which aims at promoting the highest degree of independence, adjustment, and personal competence of which he is capable. He learns acceptable habits of dress, cleanliness, feeding, social behaviour; indulges in activities to facilitate speech and muscular co-ordination; learns to follow simple directions; takes part in music, simple games, and craftwork. Formal education in reading and arithmetic is rarely possible, but elementary work is attempted along such lines as recognizing signs and notices, and learning the value of coins. In some cases the patience and perseverance of instructors in occupational centres have shown that children of very low intelligence, given proper care and guidance, may attain a standard of personal and social competence which has hitherto been thought to be beyond them. In general, however, these children will not be capable of earning their own living, and many will require to be cared for throughout life.

Occupational centres are manned by instructors for whom an 8-week course of training, plus 8 months' supervised work in centres, is provided by Jordanhill College of Education. Those in service before 1st April 1958 have from the Scottish Education Department a letter of recognition based on an Inspector's report.

"*Untrainable*" *Children*

The third group of mentally handicapped children consists of those who are "untrainable", and thus unable to profit from the training provided by occupational centres. Such children are often identifiable early in life, before the age of compulsory schooling. They become the responsibility of the local health authority, which may provide junior care centres on a daily basis, although there is not a large number of such centres in Scotland. In some cases junior care centres and junior occupational centres, with an age range of $6\frac{1}{2}$–16, are under the same roof.

There may be doubt as to whether a child is more suited to an occupational centre or a care centre; in such cases problems of testing are considerable, and the figure of IQ 40 as the lower limit for children regarded as "trainable" is a very approximate one. The Working Party on Standards of Ascertainment stated certain general criteria for deciding whether a child at the age of 5 or later should be given a trial in an occupational centre,[18] but was of the opinion that if a child over age 7, after such a trial period and any necessary treatment, failed with regard to any one of these criteria, the occupational centre should not be expected to cope with him.

Since there is no widespread provision of care centres on a daily basis, children in this category are often hospitalized, or remain in their own homes.

EPILEPTIC CHILDREN

Epileptic children are to be found in their own homes, in institutions, in ordinary schools (if they have mild and infrequent seizures), in schools for physically handicapped children, or in a special school with residential provision nearby but under separate auspices. In the Regulations the category "epileptic" is confined to children with severe or frequent epileptic seizures; the estimated incidence is $0 \cdot 3$ per thousand of the school population.

The national centre for Scotland is the Colony for Epileptics at Bridge of Weir, Renfrewshire, which caters for between thirty and forty children aged 5–16. The aim of the school is to give as normal an education as possible. Basic primary school subjects are taught, individual and group methods are employed, and emphasis is placed on arts and crafts and practical work. It is important that epileptic children should be occupied in interesting pursuits, but unfortunately the nature of their handicap sets limits on their activities. The main ameliorative development of recent years has been the use of electro-encephalography and new drugs to cut down the frequency of seizures.

The range of occupations, as of activities, is limited for epileptics. They may be employed in certain forms of factory work, clerical work, dressmaking, agriculture and labouring.

CHILDREN WITH SPEECH DEFECTS

Although speech defects are not uncommon among school children, it is seldom that the defect is so severe as to necessitate education in a special school or class; in 1965 only twenty-three children fell into this category. Treatment is provided for most children with speech defects without removing them from ordinary schools.

The most common forms of speech disorder are defects of articulation (dyslalia) and stuttering; other defects include mutism, complete loss of voice (aphonia), defective voice (dysphonia), and perceptual disorders of speech (aphasia and dysphasia). The first day aphasic unit in Britain has been established in Glasgow at Kelbourne School for spastics.

There is fairly general agreement with regard to the incidence of stuttering—about 1% of the school population—but variations exist in estimates of the frequency of other defects. A total figure of 4–5% is probably a reasonable guide, but such is the shortage of speech therapists that there has been no recent comprehensive survey to establish a thoroughly reliable figure.[19] The incidence of defect is much higher among boys than among girls.

As in the case of all defects, early ascertainment is important, not only for the child's personal development, but also for his educational progress, as speech defect is associated with educational backwardness. It is desirable that class teachers refer all cases of speech defect to the speech therapist or the school medical officer, and that all defects should be entered on the pupil's medical record card.

Most authorities in Scotland have appointed speech therapists, who work in collaboration with the medical officer in most areas, although in some counties, for example Ayrshire and Lanarkshire, they work in collaboration with the child guidance service.

Speech therapists have a 3-year course of training at the School of Speech Therapy, which is now part of Jordanhill College of Education.

MALADJUSTED CHILDREN

Maladjusted children are officially defined as those "who suffer from emotional instability or psychological disturbance".[20] This is a very general statement. A more specific definition was suggested by the Underwood Committee in England: "a child may be regarded as maladjusted who is developing in ways that have a bad effect on himself or his fellows and cannot without help be remedied by his parents, teachers and the other adults in ordinary contact with him."[21]

The Scottish Working Party on the Ascertainment of Maladjusted Children was of the opinion that the nature and scope of maladjustment could most helpfully be indicated by describing the groups of children among whom the maladjusted are mainly to be found, and the characteristics of maladaptive behaviour.[22] Eleven such groups are listed: for example, children who have been deprived of normal early life experiences such as individual mothering, association with other children, normal play opportunities; children living with parents who are handicapped in the parental role by their own childhood experiences; children whose parents are known invalids or mentally ill; children who have been over-protected and indulged in early childhood and have inadequate resources for meeting stress. Characteristics frequently associated with maladaptive behaviour—twenty are listed—include high level distractibility; tendency to marked swings of mood; persistent demanding of attention; regression to infantile behaviour patterns; unusual degrees of self-assertiveness or self-effacement. Although there are dangers attached to using a check-list of symptoms of maladjustment, it is particularly important that teachers should learn to recognize symptoms, and have some knowledge of the major underlying causes.

In the case of maladjustment, early ascertainment does not necessarily mean early in terms of years lived; since maladjustment can manifest itself at any stage of a child's development, the aim should be to detect as soon as possible those children of all ages who need help because of maladjustment.

The Working Party on the Ascertainment of Maladjusted Children strongly endorsed the Advisory Council's repeated recommendation that ascertainment should be based on team work, and suggested that the ascertainment team should consist of an educational psychologist, a school medical officer, and a social caseworker. There should also be consultation with the child's headmaster and family doctor. In all cases close co-operation between medical services and child guidance services is essential.

The Advisory Council estimated the incidence of maladjustment at about 5% of children of school age,[23] but the figure may well be considerably higher than this. Though the precise figure may be in doubt, there is no doubt that the facilities at present available in Scotland are grossly inadequate, especially for maladjusted adolescents.[24] In the whole of the industrial belt there is virtually no provision for maladjusted children, though at the time of writing Glasgow is to reopen its residential school at

Nerston, East Kilbride.[25] As a consequence of this situation, most maladjusted children remain in ordinary day schools, from which they may or may not be sent to child guidance clinics for treatment; some are in residential special schools; and a smaller number in day special schools.

As well as being concerned, as is any school, with educational progress, the special school for maladjusted children has three overriding aims: to help the children to feel secure; to allow them to experience success; to assist them to overcome difficulties of behaviour. The day is usually clearly structured, with certain established routines and set times; whenever possible individual or small group work is planned. The atmosphere may be more permissive—this depends on the philosophy and/or psychology of the teachers in the school; play and creative activities may be consciously used for therapeutic purposes; physical education may aim at improving physique and posture, and relaxing the tensions which may militate against skilled performance in games.

Teaching maladjusted children makes particular demands on the teacher. He needs patience, sensitivity, tolerance, psychological insight, and a more than ordinary degree of emotional maturity. The children he teaches may be aggressive, withdrawn, suspicious, destructive, uninterested. The methods of the ordinary day school may be inappropriate, and may have to be discarded in favour of the experimental and untried. Moreover, the teacher's success or failure is clearly seen. The teacher of the blind or the deaf educates children who nevertheless remain handicapped; the teacher of the maladjusted is expected to reduce their handicap, and if possible return them to ordinary schools.[26]

There are, however, few of such special schools and few of such teachers in Scotland. The Working Party on the Ascertainment of Maladjusted Children included the following in a list of urgently needed facilities: both primary and secondary day and residential schools for maladjusted children of average intelligence; residential schools for maladjusted children who are also mentally handicapped; day child guidance clinics and residential child guidance clinics for short-term treatment of 6 to 12 months.

We are probably many years and one or two official reports distant from the adequate provision of such facilities.

PHYSICALLY HANDICAPPED CHILDREN

The category of "physically handicapped" includes children who are so physically disabled as to be unable to attend ordinary classes in ordinary schools—for example, children with heart disease, cerebral palsy, muscular dystrophy, tuberculosis of bones and joints, poliomyelitis, and, increasingly, spina bifida. Such children require an education specially planned to meet their needs, not only because of their physical handicap, but also because such handicap frequently brings in its train problems of social and psychological adjustment. These needs are further varied by the fact that some of the ailments are progressive, some cause severe crippling, some require constant therapeutic measures. The estimate of incidence of physical handicap made by the Advisory Council[27] was $5 \cdot 0$–$9 \cdot 0$ per thousand of the school population, but for various reasons this figure is probably too high for the present day.

It may be useful to take as an example the case of children suffering from cerebral palsy, which afflicts almost two in every thousand school children. Children with cerebral palsy are usually known as "spastics", although not all who are generally included in the term are spastic in behaviour. The majority of such children are disabled from birth; a mild case may have only slight disability, whereas the more severely affected child may be completely paralysed, unable to speak, walk, or use his hands. All grades of severity between these two extremes are found. For many of the children the simple operation of putting out a hand to grasp an object may require special training; walking may have to be taught with great deliberation; speech may be incomprehensible unless careful tuition is given. Early treatment is essential if certain elementary habitual actions are to be mastered effectively.

There are consequently many problems with regard to the education of children with cerebral palsy, treatment and education requiring co-operation between medical and educational services. Before the child can make progress in reading he must often have help from the speech therapist; while learning to write he may need help from the physiotherapist; he is frequently absent from the classroom because of the extended treatment he requires. Success may be measured in simple terms: tying his own shoes; writing the figure "3"; feeding himself without spilling his food.

Not all forms of physical handicap are so dramatically obvious as that of cerebral palsy. The average school for physically handicapped children may appear at first glance like an ordinary day school, but closer inspection will reveal the presence of the occasional wheel-chair, crutch, and calipers; the special medical rooms; the arrival of the special bus to transport the children to and from school.

Whenever possible the education of physically handicapped children proceeds along normal lines. The same variety of curriculum as in ordinary day schools is provided, though lessons are usually shorter, as many of the children tire easily; wherever possible individual and small group methods of instruction are employed. Throughout, constant attention is paid to the main concern of the school, the promotion and maintenance of health; or, if this is not possible, to a gradual advance towards improved physical and mental adjustment.

PRESENT NEEDS AND FUTURE DEVELOPMENTS

There are many current needs in Scottish special education, and any list of these must of necessity be selective. What are probably the most important needs are noted below.

1. A need for a more knowledgeable and enlightened attitude on the part of the general public to special educational treatment; it would be a real advance in attitude if special education came to be regarded simply as education that is specially adapted to meet a child's needs.[28]

2. A need for up-to-date statistics of incidence of the various forms of handicap; it is disappointing to record that in many cases the figures given by the Advisory Council over 15 years ago are the latest figures. We need to forecast trends in incidence, and this can best be done on a basis of research and epidemiological studies.

3. A need for uniformity in ascertainment procedures; at present these procedures vary from county to county, and in some cases the determining factor is one of accommodation.

4. A need for an increase in the number of qualified staff: at present some 50% of teachers in special schools and classes for physically and mentally handicapped children are over age 50, and 75% over age 40.[29] There is a twofold need: to encourage young teachers to undertake this work, and to expand provision of initial and refresher courses for serving teachers.

5. A need to devise new tests of social adjustment and "real life ability" as alternative criteria to traditional intelligence tests for ascertaining mental handicap.

6. A need to provide after-care and further education services for mentally handicapped children who leave special schools at age 16. For those leaving occupational centres there is a need for senior training centres and sheltered workshops.

7. A need to reassess the vocational content of education in special schools in the light of the "vocational impulse" generated by the Brunton Report. This is particularly necessary as a boost to the morale of physically handicapped children. Although what is possible is limited by the type of handicap, there is nothing in this country like the work done, for example, in Sweden, where industrial contracts are taken, and pupils may be engaged in making boxes for Camembert cheese.

8. A need for increased attention to the problem of maladjusted children. This would involve studies of social and emotional development, the improved provision of residential schools, in-service training of teachers as school counsellors, and the attaching of trained social workers to schools on the lines established by Glasgow's School Welfare Service.

It is to be hoped that future developments, say in the next 10 years, will succeed in meeting these needs. To do so will involve the expenditure of time, effort, and money. To the hard-headed who question the wisdom of such expenditure a hard-headed answer can be given:

> The vast majority of the handicapped, however, can *with appropriate education* become self-supporting. The uneducated and untrained blind or deaf person is practically unemployable; the educated one can support himself and a family. The uneducated mentally retarded child grows up into an unemployable or unstable casual worker; the educated one into a more dependable and useful citizen. The uneducated cripple is a burden to his family; the educated one may become a useful worker. This applies to every category of the handicapped. It is a matter of common prudence as well as humanity to do everything possible to equip these children to take their place as self-reliant and responsible members of the community.[30]

REFERENCES AND NOTES

1. Education (Scotland) Act, 1962, Section 5 (1).
2. Scottish Education Department: Reports of the Advisory Council on Education in Scotland, Edinburgh, H.M.S.O.:
   Pupils who are Defective in Hearing, Cmd. 7866, 1950.
   Pupils who are Defective in Vision, Cmd. 7885, 1950.
   Pupils with Physical Disabilities, Cmd. 8211, 1951.
   Pupils with Mental or Educational Disabilities, Cmd. 8401, 1951.
   Pupils Handicapped by Speech Disorders, Cmd. 8426, 1951.
   Pupils who are Maladjusted because of Social Handicaps, Cmd. 8428, 1952.
   The Administration of Education for Handicapped Pupils, Cmd. 8432, 1952.
3. *The Special Educational Treatment (Scotland) Regulations, 1954.*
4. Scottish Education Department: *Circular No. 300*, 21st Mar. 1955.
5. *The Schools (Scotland) Code, 1956*, Section 15 (3).
6. Scottish Education Department: *Pupils who are Defective in Hearing*, Cmd. 7866, Edinburgh, H.M.S.O., 1950, Para. 46.
7. *Ibid.*, Para. 223.
8. *Ibid.*, Paras. 73–9.
9. Scottish Education Department: *Pupils who are Defective in Vision*, Cmd. 7885, Edinburgh, H.M.S.O., 1950, Para. 7.
10. *Ibid.*, Paras. 26–7.
11. *Ibid.*, Para. 71.
12. *Ibid.*, Para. 90.
13. *Ibid.*, Paras. 131–5.
14. Scottish Education Department: *Degrees of Mental Handicap*, Edinburgh, H.M.S.O., 1961, Paras. 21–4.
15. Scottish Education Department: *Pupils with Mental or Educational Disabilities*, Cmd. 8401, Edinburgh, H.M.S.O., 1951, Para. 38.

16. Scottish Education Department: *Degrees of Mental Handicap*, Edinburgh, H.M.S.O., 1961, Para. 34.
17. *Ibid.*, Para. 35.
18. *Ibid.*, Para. 46.
19. Some figures are given in Scottish Education Department: *Pupils Handicapped by Speech Disorders*, Cmd. 8426, Edinburgh, H.M.S.O., 1951, Chapter 3.
20. *The Special Educational Treatment (Scotland) Regulations, 1954*, Section 2 (8).
21. Ministry of Education: *Report of the Committee on Maladjusted Children*, London, H.M.S.O., 1955, Para. 89.
22. Scottish Education Department: *Ascertainment of Maladjusted Children*, Edinburgh, H.M.S.O., 1964, Appendix B.
23. Scottish Education Department: *Pupils who are Maladjusted because of Social Handicaps*, Cmd. 8428, Edinburgh, H.M.S.O., 1952, Para. 38. See also Para. 115.
24. For the relevance of this situation to the wider problem of juvenile delinquency see Scottish Home and Health Department; Scottish Education Department: *Children and Young Persons Scotland*, Cmnd. 2306, Edinburgh, H.M.S.O., 1964, Paras. 175–8, and 181.
25. For some interesting proposals with regard to maladjusted children see Scottish Council for Educational Advance: *The Emotionally Handicapped (Maladjusted) Child*, Memorandum, 1965.
26. For an outline of the work of residential schools for maladjusted children in England see Department of Education and Science, Education Pamphlet No. 47: *The Education of Maladjusted Children*, London, H.M.S.O., 1965.
27. Scottish Education Department: *Pupils with Physical Disabilities*, Cmd. 8211, Edinburgh, H.M.S.O., 1951, Para. 25.
28. For evidence of an official trend in this direction in special education and allied fields see the general tenor and specific recommendations of the Kilbrandon Report: *Children and Young Persons Scotland*, Cmnd. 2306, Edinburgh, H.M.S.O., 1964.
29. Association for Special Education, Scottish Committee: *Survey of Staffing Position in Special Schools and Classes in Scotland*, 1965.
30. Ministry of Education, Pamphlet No. 5: *Special Educational Treatment*, London, H.M.S.O., 1946, Para. 108.

CHAPTER 7

Approved School Education

INTRODUCTORY

Approved schools are the modern descendants of the industrial schools and reformatories of the nineteenth century.

Industrial schools, established by voluntary bodies, were not penal institutions; they were intended to cater for the needs of children aged 7–14 whose surroundings made delinquency seem inevitable—for example, children who were orphans, vagrants, beggars, the associates of criminals. The first industrial school in Scotland, a "ragged school", was established by Sheriff Watson in Aberdeen in 1841. The school provided food, industrial training, and elementary education. The movement spread and schools were set up in Glasgow, Edinburgh (three by 1847) and in other parts of the country.

Reformatories, on the other hand, were for young offenders under age 16. They were thus intended to correct the erring, whereas industrial schools aimed at turning destitute children into useful citizens. The first Scottish reformatory was the Glasgow House of Refuge for Boys, 1837.

The terms "industrial school" and "reformatory school" were used until the distinction between the two was abolished by the Children and Young Persons (Scotland) Act, 1932. This Act renamed such schools "approved schools", that is, schools for the education and training of juveniles[1] sent there in pursuance of the Act, and approved and certified for the purpose by the Secretary of State; "approved" also implies eligibility for government grant. The term "approved" does not appear in the public titles of such schools.

136

Much of current practice is based on the Act of 1932, which came into operation on 1st November, 1933. The sanctions for such practice, however, are always quoted in terms of the Children and Young Persons (Scotland) Act, 1937, which consolidated previous legislation, plus relevant sections of the Education (Scotland) Act, 1962 and the Criminal Justice (Scotland) Act, 1963.

In England and Wales the central Department responsible for approved schools' administration is the Home Office; in Scotland it is the Scottish Education Department. Approved schools thus form a recognized part of the Scottish educational system.

COMMITTAL AND DETENTION

Almost all the pupils in approved schools have been sent there on the authority of a committal order from a court of law. The four main categories of children who may be committed to approved schools are noted below.

1. *Offenders.* Children over the age of 8, at present the age of criminal responsibility in Scotland, who have been found guilty of an offence punishable, in the case of an adult, with imprisonment.

2. *Children in need of care or protection.* Children who, through lack of proper care and guardianship, are falling into bad associations, are exposed to moral danger, or are beyond control; children who have been the victims of certain offences; children who are vagrants and are thus not receiving normal education.

3. *Truants.* Children who have failed to attend school regularly and in the opinion of the court require to be sent to an approved school in order to ensure that they receive adequate education.

4. *Refractory children.* Children shown by their parents or guardians to the satisfaction of a court to be beyond control.

About 75% of children committed to approved schools are offenders, and about 65% of such offenders have had more than two court appearances. Thus many children in approved schools are extremely difficult children who have not responded to other methods of treatment.

The layman occasionally expresses concern that children in need of care or protection mix in approved schools with children who are offenders, fearing that the delinquent may mislead the unfortunate. In fact, children of both categories are usually the victims of similar circumstances and come from similar environments; often it is a matter of chance that one appears in court as an offender, and another as in need of care or protection. Moreover, many experienced approved school teachers maintain that children in need of care or protection are often more of a problem than the delinquent.

The allocation of a child to a school rests with the court, the most suitable school being indicated by the Scottish Education Department on the basis of relevant reports on the child, and information about vacancies in appropriate schools. The court also sends to the headmaster of the receiving approved school information about the child being committed. The record consists of three forms: Form A is concerned with general information, including home circumstances; Form B consists of educational information; Form C of medical information.[2] In most cases there is also a Social Inquiry Report prepared by the probation officer. No one over the age of 17 may be committed by a court to an approved school.

For children aged under 16 when committed the period of detention—that is, the maximum period for which a person may legally be detained in an approved school by virtue of an approved school order—is 3 years, or until the age of 15 years 4 months, whichever is the longer. In the case of children aged 16 or over when committed, the period ends at 19. In certain circumstances the period may be extended by a period not exceeding 6 months.

At any time during a person's period of detention, the managers of the school may release him, though no person may be released during the first 6 months of the period of detention without the consent of the Secretary of State.[3] At present the usual time spent in an approved school is from 15 to 21 months.

A person released from an approved school remains for 2 years under the supervision of the managers of the school, who concern themselves with his welfare, employment, place of residence, and so on. Details of after-care arrangements are given later in the chapter.

CLASSIFICATION OF SCHOOLS

In 1965 there were twenty-six approved schools in Scotland, and 1305 boys and 205 girls were on the registers of these schools on 15th January, 1965. Thus approximately $1 \cdot 7$ per thousand of the school population are in approved schools.

Approved schools are classified according to the age, sex, and religious persuasion of the pupils committed to them. The present position is shown in Table 7.

Typical age ranges are noted below, though placing may be varied according to particular circumstances.

Junior schools—8–15: committal normally under age 13.

Intermediate schools—13–17: committal normally between 13 and 15.

Senior schools—$14\frac{1}{2}$–19: committal normally between 15 and 17.

An important development in England is that of the classifying school, a school in which newly committed pupils have a short stay during which they are carefully observed before a decision is made as to which approved school will best meet their needs. Though strongly recommended by the Scottish Advisory Council on the Treatment and Rehabilitation of Offenders,[4] and supported by the Advisory Council on Education in Scotland,[5] a classifying school has not as yet been set up in Scotland. There are various reasons for this: for example, there are fewer Scottish approved schools from which a choice may be made; these schools are in general not characterized by specialization in type

TABLE 7

CLASSIFICATION OF SCHOOLS

| | Junior | | Jun./Inter. | | Intermediate | | Inter./Sen. | | Senior | | Total | | Total all schools |
	Prot.	R.C.	Prot.	R.C.	Prot.	R.C.	Prot.	R.C.	Prot.	R.C.	Prot.	R.C.	
Boys	4	1		2	3	1	1		4	2	12*	6	18
Girls	2	1			1				3	1	6	2	8
Total	6	2		2	4	1	1		7	3	18	8	26

* Two schools for Protestant boys also accept R.C. boys if desired.

of pupil, activity, or approach; there are problems created by the geography of Scotland. As a consequence the present tendency, within the limits imposed by a classification of schools according to age, sex, and religion, is to place the child in the school nearest to his own home.[6]

WORK OF THE SCHOOLS

Approved schools are not juvenile prisons; their aims are not punitive or repressive. The intention is to assist the children committed to them to become normally adjusted citizens. To this end the schools provide general education, social training, occupational preparation, and an introduction to a variety of leisure-time pursuits.

In four junior schools all pupils of school age attend local day schools, and in four schools selected pupils do so. In all the other schools children of school age receive education in the usual school subjects within the approved school itself, where they are taught by teachers with qualifications approved by the Scottish Education Department. As approved school pupils are characterized by low intelligence—average IQ is about 85—and educational backwardness, much of the time is spent on the three R's in an attempt to establish basic literacy and numeracy. In the larger junior schools it is possible to group pupils according to ability rather than chronological age, and wherever possible group and individual methods of teaching are employed.

For older pupils practical work of various kinds is provided—for example farm-work, carpentry, metalwork, building, painting and decorating, tailoring, for boys; cookery, laundrywork, housewifery, commercial subjects, for girls. Although as already noted schools in general do not develop any main specialization which would determine placement, some schools develop sidelines of their own. For example, farming has been successfully developed at Rossie Farm, near Montrose; Kibble, Paisley, has helped to equip other approved schools by making furniture; Mossbank, Glasgow, has painting, decorating, and building, and intends to develop catering when the school is moved to Stevenston, Ayrshire.

As an approved school is a boarding school, various activities outwith school work have to be provided—for example football, swimming, life-saving, boxing, mountaineering, athletics, drama, country dancing. There are also domestic activities—cleaning shoes, making beds, working with vegetables and fruit. Pupils over school age in some schools undertake seasonal employment; a few years ago the boys at Rossie Farm school earned over £2000 at potato harvesting; half of this was divided among the boys concerned, and the other half went towards the expenses of the school; thus "proceeds of industry" can still figure in the income of approved schools.

The physical and mental health of pupils is of prime importance. Medical examinations are held on admission, quarterly, and before leaving. Dental inspections are arranged on admission and at least every six months. There are three psychologists specifically concerned with approved school work, and most schools have at least one social welfare officer who takes a personal interest in each new pupil, visits the home, gets to know parents, covers court appearances, and so on. Some schools are experimenting with group counselling techniques.

The daily life of the approved school may exert its own beneficial influence—a stable environment, an ordered routine, relationships with staff and other pupils.[7] Pupils receive letters and parcels from home, have a weekly allowance of pocket money, and from time to time get home leave for a night, a week-end, or longer. In appropriate cases additional home leave is given towards the end of a pupil's period of detention in order to facilitate his return to ordinary life. Most pupils spend a period at a camp each summer.

Not unnaturally, discipline in an approved school presents its own problems. Individual schools have their own individual approaches, but the most frequently used sanction is the withdrawal of privileges. The whole issue of punishment is closely controlled by the Rules[8] which place limits on the forms of punishment permitted. Corporal punishment, for example, may be inflicted only under certain conditions, and the headmaster must keep a punishment book in which relevant details are entered. Although these statements about discipline rather emphasize the negative aspect, in the actual day-to-day life of the approved school much that is of positive value in leading to self-discipline, rather than submission to external control, is achieved, largely as a result of the relationships fostered between staff and pupils.

STAFF

Teachers of school subjects in approved schools must be certificated teachers. Although the Advisory Council[9] as long ago as 1946 recommended a 3-month full-time additional course for such teachers, there is as yet little special training for approved school work. This situation may change when facilities for the in-service training of teachers in general are expanded. At present in-service training is in the form of release for short week-end or week courses, or if the teacher is nearing the status of third-in-charge, a year's course at Durham or Newcastle.

The standard salary scales are increased by £170 per annum for working in an approved school, and by up to around £280 per annum for extraneous duties, payment for the latter being on an hourly basis.

Instructors in the work departments of approved schools are qualified tradesmen, graded according to qualification. Grade I qualification is the standard of a Final City and Guilds Certificate; Grade II is about the standard of the Intermediate City and Guilds Certificate.

In appointing staff for approved school work attention must be paid not only to academic and technical qualifications. The work is demanding, and personal qualities are at a premium.

AFTER-CARE

It is the duty of managers to release each pupil as soon as he has made sufficient progress; consequently they must review his progress and all the circumstances of his case at least quarterly.

On release from an approved school the pupil is under the supervision of the school managers for 2 years from the date of release, or until he attains the age of 21, whichever is earlier. The managers' obligations are: "to cause him to be visited, advised and befriended and to give him assistance (including, if they think fit, financial assistance) in maintaining himself and finding suitable employment".[10]

In this after-care work managers are assisted, in thinly populated areas, by probation officers and other local agencies, and in the more populous areas by over twenty welfare officers. After-care is now carried out to a considerable extent on a school basis rather than, as formerly, on a purely geographical basis. The arrangement is for each welfare officer to be responsible for the after-care of all the pupils who are released from one or more particular schools and who live in a prescribed part of the country. Welfare officers work in close co-operation with the headmasters of the schools with which they are concerned. They try to establish personal relations with the pupils and their families, report on homes to headmasters and managers, assist in finding accommodation, if necessary, and suitable employment.

Throughout the period of supervision welfare officers maintain contact with pupils by means of visits and correspondence, and report to the managers. If progress reports are unsatisfactory, managers may recall a person under supervision; he is then liable to be detained in the school until the expiration of his period of detention or the expiration of 6 months from the date on which he is brought back to the school, whichever is the later. A person may not be thus recalled to, or retained in, an approved school after age 19. If recalled and again released, the person's period of supervision continues to run from the date of original release.

If the managers are requested by a person under their supervision, they may continue his after-care until the expiration of 3 years from the end of his period of detention, or until he attains the age of 21, whichever is earlier.[11]

ADMINISTRATION AND FINANCE

Since 1920 approved schools have come under the jurisdiction of the Scottish Education Department, which supervises the various arrangements for the health, welfare, education, release, and after-care of pupils. The schools are inspected by various members of the Inspectorate, including two with special knowledge and experience of the needs of delinquent and maladjusted children.

Apart from two schools run by Glasgow education authority, approved schools are managed by boards of managers, individual managers generally being appointed by the voluntary bodies to whom the schools belong. Boards of managers consist of responsible citizens, and frequently include representatives of local authorities. Names of managers must be notified to the Secretary of State, who has power to appoint additional managers. The Secretary of State also has power to make an order regulating the constitution and proceedings of the managers of any voluntary approved school.[12]

Once a child is admitted to an approved school the managers have assumed all the legal rights and responsibilities which were formerly vested in the child's parents. Managers are responsible for the general control and running of the school, and must arrange for the school to be visited by one or more of their number at least once a month. Managers are responsible for the appointment and dismissal of staff, though for the post of headmaster, deputy headmaster, or third-in-charge, the prior approval of the Secretary of State is necessary.[13]

Total expenditure on approved schools is currently running at over £1 million per annum. About 47% of the expenditure is met by exchequer grants, and 47% by payments from the education authorities from whose areas the children in approved schools have come. The remaining 6% is met from donations, pupils' earnings, sale of produce, parental contributions, and payment by staff for accommodation and services. The amount of education authority contributions is fixed from time to time by the Secretary of State; from 1st April 1966 the weekly contribution payable by education authorities in respect of each pupil sent to an approved school from that authority's area was £10 4s. 9d.[14]

COMMENT

Many problems face those who work in approved schools. Although there has of late been an improvement in the building of new schools—for example Loaningdale School, Biggar, 1963; Geilsland School, Beith, 1964; St. Andrew's School, Shandon, 1964—many approved schools are housed in buildings which date from the late nineteenth and early twentieth centuries. Mossbank School, Glasgow, was built in 1869. Thus much of the work has to be done in unpromising and sometimes depressing surroundings.

The work itself makes great demands. As already indicated, the great majority of pupils in approved schools are offenders, and many of them are recurrent delinquents. Well over 80% of the pupils are emotionally disturbed, as compared with about 12% in the non-delinquent population. Many feel rejected, insecure, or inadequate. The staff of the schools require patience, understanding, sympathy, and the ability to withstand disappointment. Yet for a number of teachers the work brings its own rewards. For many of the pupils the approved school becomes the best home they have known, and many "old boys" return to visit headmaster and staff.

Experimental work is not neglected. At Rossie Farm, a senior boys' school near Montrose, a special section for the care and training of seriously disturbed boys and persistent absconders was opened in March 1962. This section, which draws its pupils from other approved schools, is virtually a "closed block" cut off from the rest of the school, with its own workshops, playrooms, etc. The ratio of staff to pupils can be as high as 1 to 2·5. Even then success is by no means assured, but the justification of the experiment is that without some such system the approved schools could not keep such boys long enough to have even a chance of influencing them for good.

As far back as 1947 an official suggestion for the establishment of a short-term approved school was made.[15] In January 1963 Loaningdale School, Biggar, was opened, for eighteen boys originally, with the prospect of ultimately catering for forty. The initial experiment was to provide for selected Protestant boys aged 13 and over a shorter and more specialized period of training, perhaps of 6 to 9 months' duration. Although problems of selecting the type of boy suited to this course have proved considerable, the experiment is continuing, and will no doubt be subject to further development in the light of experience.

The question is often asked: how successful are approved schools? The most commonly used criteria of success are those of regular employment and absence from court appearances on the part of former pupils. Inquiries made in 1965 about pupils released from approved schools in the year ended 31st March, 1962 showed that:

64% of the girls and 44% of the boys were in regular employment;

83% of the girls and 43% of the boys had not come before the courts in the 3-year period;

6% of the girls and 37% of the boys had been recommitted to approved schools, or sentenced to Borstal, detention centre or prison.[16]

Even taken at face value, these statistics demand interpretation, which involves a value judgement. For example, is it success when over two-fifths of these boys do not appear before the courts in the 3-year period? Is it failure when almost three-fifths of them do? Moreover, the criteria can be challenged: are these adequate criteria, or are they employed because the relevant statistics are obtainable? Sense of security, degree of adjustment, happiness, feeling of personal adequacy—these are difficult to measure; yet by these criteria someone who has a further court appearance may be a success, and someone who steers clear of the courts may be a conspicuous failure.

Those in close touch with approved school work are fairly confident on two points. Firstly, bearing in mind the type of pupil with whom the school has to deal, it is gratifying to find the success rate, in terms of the figures quoted above, as high as it is; secondly, there are areas of human behaviour in which there is achieved success of a subjective, qualitative kind, which is not amenable to statistical tabulation.

THE FUTURE OF APPROVED SCHOOLS

The publication in 1964 of the Report of the Kilbrandon Committee[17] raised questions about the precise future of approved schools. The two main recommendations of the Committee concerned the establishing of "juvenile panels" and "social education departments".

The Committee suggested that existing juvenile courts should be abolished and their place taken by juvenile panels with power to assume jurisdiction over juveniles under age 16 and to order special measures of education and training according to the needs of the juvenile concerned. Such panels would consist of lay men and women, and would only deal with cases where the facts were agreed and admitted; disputed cases would go for trial to the sheriff. Cases would be presented to the panel by an independent public official to be called "the reporter", who would refer cases on the basis of reports from the police, the agencies of local government, and other sources.

The Committee further proposed that as part of each education authority there should be established a department of social education under the charge of a director with the status of a deputy director of education. This department would be responsible for the child care service, the child guidance service, the school medical services, and the school welfare service. It would take charge of children's homes and education authority special schools. Its officers would take over the duties of the probation officers in connection with children under age 16.

With regard to approved schools in particular, the Committee suggested that they should come under the wing of the new social education departments; that they should be called simply "residential schools"; that in them an increased emphasis should be placed on social education; that short-term residential "adjustment" courses should be provided for cases of truancy; and that "after-care" as such should disappear, and be replaced by supervision by a social worker of the social education department. The whole trend of the Report was thus towards regarding approved schools, not as separate, "different" establishments, but as part of a flexible system of residential schools for children whose needs could not be met within the normal educational provision.

The Report of the Kilbrandon Committee aroused widespread interest, discussion and, in some cases, concern. The concept of children's panels met with general approval, and the principle of establishing such panels was accepted by the government in 1965. There were reservations, however, about the setting up of a social education department as part of each education authority, and a government White Paper of 1966[18] has proposed instead the establishing in each county and county of a city of a separate social work department under a director of social work, to undertake the functions of various existing services including the child care service, the school welfare service, and the probation service. It is *not* proposed that the new department should be responsible for the work of the child guidance service or the school health service.

The White Paper follows the Kilbrandon Committee's recommendations closely in proposing to abolish existing statutory distinctions between certain types of residential establishments for children. The range of establishments to which panels will have the power to send children will include the existing approved schools, which will no longer be known by this generic name, and "will no longer be a separate category of establishment but will become an integral part of a range of establishments providing a variety of regimes and special treatments".[19]

What will be the precise impact of the Kilbrandon Report and the 1966 White Paper on the work of the present approved schools remains to be seen.

REFERENCES AND NOTES

1. Although legally a "child" is a juvenile under age 14, and a "young person" is a juvenile over age 14 but under age 17, the word "child" is used in this chapter to cover both categories.
2. *The Approved Schools (Form of Court Record) (Scotland) Regulations, 1949.*
3. Criminal Justice (Scotland) Act, 1963, Section 18 (1).
4. Scottish Education Department: *Approved Schools.* Report by the Scottish Advisory Council on the Treatment and Rehabilitation of Offenders, Edinburgh, H.M.S.O., 1947, Paras. 23–5.
5. Scottish Education Department: *Pupils Who are Maladjusted because of Social Handicaps.* A Report of the Advisory Council on Education in Scotland, Cmd. 8428, Edinburgh, H.M.S.O., 1952, Para. 212.
6. For official comments on classification see Scottish Education Department: *Circular No. 317,* 13th Oct. 1955, Paras. 9–13.
7. For an interesting approach to social education in an approved school see WILSON, J. T., *The Treatment of Juvenile Delinquency—An Appraisal of the Scottish Approved School System,* Glasgow University Library, B.Litt. Thesis—2153—1963, Vol. 2.
8. *The Approved Schools (Scotland) Rules, 1961,* Rules 28–32.
9. Scottish Education Department: *Training of Teachers.* A Report of the Advisory Council on Education in Scotland, Cmd. 6723, Edinburgh, H.M.S.O., 1946, Appendix III, para. 24.
10. Children and Young Persons (Scotland) Act, 1937, Second Schedule, para. 12 (2).
11. For full details in connection with release and supervision see Criminal Justice (Scotland) Act, 1963, Section 18 and Schedule 2.
12. *Ibid.,* Section 22.
13. Managers' duties are defined in detail in *The Approved Schools (Scotland) Rules, 1961.*
14. *The Approved Schools (Contributions by Education Authorities) (Scotland) Regulations, 1966.*
15. Scottish Education Department: *Approved Schools.* Report by the Scottish Advisory Council on the Treatment and Rehabilitation of Offenders, Edinburgh, H.M.S.O., 1947, Paras. 26–30.
16. Scottish Education Department: *Education in Scotland in 1965,* Cmnd. 2914, Edinburgh, H.M.S.O., 1966, p. 80.
17. Scottish Home and Health Department; Scottish Education Department: *Children and Young Persons Scotland,* Cmnd. 2306, Edinburgh, H.M.S.O., 1964.
18. Scottish Education Department; Scottish Home and Health Department: *Social Work and the Community,* Cmnd. 3065, Edinburgh, H.M.S.O., 1966.
19. *Ibid.,* Para. 71.

CHAPTER 8

Welfare and Guidance Services

As INDICATED in the first chapter, one of the most noticeable trends in Scottish education in the twentieth century has been towards an extension of the concept of "education" to cover the development of the individual in directions other than the purely intellectual. Complementary to this trend has been the development of services designed to enable pupils to take full advantage of the educational facilities provided. Both of these trends are reflected in the growth of the various welfare and guidance services described in this chapter.

SCHOOL MEALS SERVICE

School meals first found a place in Scottish educational legislation in the Education (Scotland) Act, 1908, which empowered school boards to supply school meals exclusive of the cost of the food. Nowadays it is the duty of education authorities to provide a midday meal for pupils attending schools under their management.[1] The duties of authorities with regard to the provision of premises and equipment for the School Meals Service, the ensuring of cleanliness, the employment of staff, and so on, are laid down in official Regulations.[2] Midday meals must be of good quality, adequate as the main meal of the day, well prepared and cooked, attractively served under hygienic conditions; they must be planned to secure a varied and balanced diet. Practically every authority has now appointed an Organizer of School Meals, and there is ample evidence to show that the various requirements are being met, in spite of the unpromising implications of the official definition of food: " 'Food' means any article used or intended to be used as food or drink for the meals service."[3]

The two-course meal may be cooked on the premises in a specially designed kitchen, or brought to the school from a central kitchen serving a number of schools. There are still, however, over fifty schools in Scotland without meals facilities; these schools are mainly small schools where either there is no demand for midday meals, or it is impossible to meet a demand because of their remoteness.

Education authorities are required to ensure that suitable arrangements are made for the supervision and social training of pupils during meals,[4] and many schools make considerable efforts to turn the midday meal into an integral part of the pupil's day-to-day education. For example, the method of serving school meals known as "family service" aims at reproducing in the school dining room the conditions of a good home. Small groups, usually of eight pupils, dine together as "families" and the meal is served at the table. This arrangement reduces movement to a minimum and creates conditions in which good table manners and civilized conversation may be encouraged. In some schools various departments have made contributions to the amenities of the dining room in the form of murals, place-mats, flower holders and menu cards.

Teachers are active in the voluntary supervision of school meals; only in a few areas has anything come of a suggestion[5] that persons recruited perhaps from existing school meals staff might assist teachers in such supervision. Moreover, in some areas teachers still undertake a variety of clerical and accounting duties in connection with school meals, although of recent years such duties have increasingly been undertaken by clerical staff.

The Secretary of State is empowered to prescribe the charges to be made for school meals, and each education authority must submit for approval a scheme of charges and reduced charges for midday meals. For example, the present basic charge is one shilling per meal, but reduced charges are made when two or more pupils belonging to the same household are provided with midday meals, and there is further provision for the remission in whole or in part of the charge or reduced charge in cases of financial hardship. In 1965, 42% of pupils in attendance at public and grant-aided schools took school meals, and 19% of those who took meals received them free of charge. Excluding capital costs, the estimated average cost per meal in 1965–6 was $11\frac{1}{2}d.$ for food and $1s. 6\frac{1}{4}d.$ for overheads. Estimated average income per meal was $8\frac{1}{4}d.$, so that the net cost per meal was estimated at $1s. 9\frac{1}{2}d.$[6]

The Milk in Schools Scheme was launched in the 1930's, and all children whose parents so desired were able to obtain one-third of a pint of milk per day for one halfpenny. After the war school milk was provided free, and the present position is that all school pupils are entitled to one-third of a pint of milk per day free of charge, as are students below age 18 in colleges of further education; pupils in special schools are entitled to two-thirds of a pint per day free of charge. About 90% of all children in public and grant-aided schools take school milk; the cost of provision per child for the school year 1965–6 was estimated to be £2 9s. 2d.[7]

SCHOOL HEALTH SERVICE

An impetus was given to the medical inspection of school children by the Boer War, as medical examinations for the army revealed the poor physical condition of many British youths. A few of the school boards in Scotland experimented with schemes of medical inspection in the first few years of this century, and as a result of the Education (Scotland) Act, 1908, school boards were empowered, and some of the larger boards were compelled, to provide for the medical examination and supervision of pupils attending schools in their districts.

At the present day it is one of the duties of education authorities to provide for the medical inspection, at appropriate intervals, and for the medical supervision of all pupils in attendance at schools under their management. For this purpose they may require parents to submit pupils for medical inspection, and a parent may be fined for non-compliance with this requirement.

They also have the duty of ensuring that comprehensive facilities are available to pupils for free medical and dental treatment.[8]

Each authority must appoint a Chief Administrative School Medical Officer to be responsible to the authority for the administration of the School Health Service, a Chief Executive School Medical Officer, a Chief Dental Officer, and such other medical and dental officers, nurses, and other officers as are necessary for securing the efficiency of the Service. Unless the Secretary of State has agreed otherwise, the medical officer for the education authority area is the Chief Administrative School Medical Officer.[9]

Medical inspections take place on such occasions as the Secretary of State may direct, and on such other occasions as the education authority, with the approval of the Secretary of State, may determine. At present, routine medical examinations are carried out when children are aged 5, 9, 13, and 16. The typical procedure is as follows: the school medical officer advises the headmaster that a particular age group is to be examined on a specified date. The headmaster sends to the parent or guardian of each child to be examined a form requesting information about the child's past illnesses, and inviting the parent to be present at the examination; about 80% of parents whose children are involved attend the examination of 5 year olds, but thereafter attendance of parents drops steeply. Next, the school nurse visits the school, weighs and measures the children, tests vision, observes posture and general cleanliness. Finally the school medical officer makes his inspection. The parent is notified of any defect discovered, and may have the child treated by the family doctor, or take advantage of such facilities for treatment as are provided by the School Health Service in the area.

As well as routine medical examinations, there are special examinations of any children suspected, for example by a teacher, parent, or nurse, to be suffering from some disability. Moreover, in many areas school medical officers are managing to visit schools once a term, and in some areas once a month.[10] Most areas now also have some form of audiometric service available to them, so that children have their hearing tested at age 5, and some have a second test before leaving the primary school.

All relevant information is entered on school medical records, which must be kept by each authority for all pupils who are medically inspected. Continuity of information is an important factor. In many areas the duties of the maternity and child welfare service and of the School Health Service are carried out by the same medical officers, and in every area there is a procedure whereby information in the hands of the child welfare service may be passed to the School Health Service when the child enters the school. The form of the school medical record has been under review by the Scottish Home and Health Department, and it will be an advantage if the new form provides for a single comprehensive medical record of the child's development from birth to school-leaving age.

The role of the school with regard to the physical welfare of pupils has become increasingly recognized. Teachers are encouraged to be on the lookout for minor physical defects in pupils, for example defects of sight, hearing, speech, and nose and throat infections, all of which are frequently correlated with poor performance at school. The basic aim is to enable pupils to attain and to maintain good physical health. The gradual realization of this aim will eventually allow the School Health Service to concentrate less exclusively on physical health, and concern itself more closely with mental health and, in co-operation with the child guidance service, with the ascertainment and treatment of maladjusted children.

CLEANLINESS AND CLOTHING

A further safeguard of the health of school children lies in the power which an education authority has to enforce cleanliness.[11] The authority may authorize one of its medical officers to cause examinations to be made of the bodies and clothing of any of the pupils in attendance at the authority's schools, and if necessary a notice may be served on the parent requiring him "to cause the body and clothing of the pupil to be cleansed". If this is not done within 24 hours, the cleansing may be carried out under arrangements made by the authority. If there is a recurrence of the condition, and this recurrence is due to parental neglect, the parent may be prosecuted.

The necessity to enforce cleanliness does not arise often at the present, although in some schools infestation of the hair remains a persistent problem.

Education authorities have also the duty of providing clothing for any pupils attending schools under their management if such pupils are unable, by reason of the inadequacy or unsuitability of their clothing, to take full advantage of the education provided. The cost, or part of it, is recoverable from the parent, unless the authority is satisfied that the parent is unable to pay without financial hardship.[12] Although the number of cases where such provision is necessary has declined over the years, there were still 4285 pupils being supplied with clothing free of charge in 1965.[13]

GRANTS

In the history of Scottish education there are various references to the provision of bursaries by beneficent lairds and merchants, and in this century the Acts of 1908 and 1918 empowered school boards and education authorities respectively to award bursaries. However bursaries, especially for pupils still at school, were not plentiful until after the 1945 Act.

The present position is that education authorities are responsible for awarding certain school and further education bursaries. Official Regulations[14] prescribe how education authorities are to calculate the value of higher school bursaries—that is, those awarded to pupils who are over age 15, and in the fourth or subsequent years of secondary schooling—and bursaries awarded to students who are following full-time courses of further education which are not of university or comparable standard.

Three important points must be emphasized. First of all, the decision whether or not to grant a bursary or other allowance to any applicant rests with the authority; the Regulations merely require the authority to conform to prescribed conditions when a decision has been made to grant a bursary of a type covered by the Regulations. Secondly, part-time further education bursaries, correspondence-course bursaries, and bursaries for school fees and school clothing are not covered by the Regulations, but are granted and assessed entirely at the discretion of education authorities, a situation which leads to considerable variation in the practice of different authorities. Thirdly, the Regulations do not apply to awards for full-time courses at universities or colleges of education, or for advanced full-time or sandwich courses at other further education establishments; such awards are granted by the Secretary of State for Scotland.

Bursaries awarded by education authorities are normally tenable for the duration of the course, but the amount payable is calculated annually. Authorities are required to estimate each year the expenditure which will be incurred by the student in following his course, and to deduct from it the amount, if any, of the contribution towards that expenditure which can be made by him and his parents. The amount actually payable is the excess of the estimated expenditure over the contribution. Details with regard to the various items which are to be taken into account in assessing estimated expenditure, and with regard to the parental contribution which is required to be deducted from the estimated expenditure in assessing the bursary, are given in Schedules 1 and 2 respectively of the 1963 Regulations. At present the maximum higher school bursary for a pupil in the fourth year of a secondary course is £70 per annum, and £100 per annum for a pupil in a fifth or subsequent year.

In session 1964–5, 28,500 education authority bursaries were being paid, at a total cost to these authorities of over £1,300,000.

Allowances to students attending full-time courses at universities and colleges of education, and advanced full-time or sandwich courses at other further education establishments, are awarded by the Secretary of State for Scotland. Arrangements and conditions for the award of such allowances are prescribed in *The*

Students' Allowances (Scotland) Regulations, 1962. The maximum student's allowance consists of the fees payable for the course plus a standard maintenance allowance, and in some cases additional allowances for dependants, vacation courses, etc. The award paid to any student is this maximum allowance reduced by the amount of the parental contribution, which is calculated on a prescribed income scale, and also by the amount by which the student's personal income, including income from other awards, exceeds £100. A minimum allowance of £50 per annum is paid to all eligible students, regardless of their own or their parents' financial circumstances.[15] From the beginning of session 1965–6 the amount of the standard maintenance allowance was £340 per annum for students living in halls of residence, hostels, and lodgings, and £275 per annum for students living at home.

In the academic year 1964–5, 27,345 students were receiving allowances, at a cost to public funds of almost £8 million.

CHILD GUIDANCE SERVICE

The origin of the Child Guidance Service in Scotland was in 1926–7, when an "educational clinic" was opened by Dr. William Boyd of the Education Department at Glasgow University, and a "psychological clinic" was established by Professor James Drever of the Psychology Department at Edinburgh University. The term "child guidance clinic" was first used in 1931, when Notre Dame Child Guidance Clinic was opened in Glasgow, and Glasgow was the first education authority to set up a child guidance clinic on a full-time basis in 1937.[16] In all, seven education authorities had established Child Guidance Services prior to the 1945 Act, which empowered education authorities to provide a Child Guidance Service as part of their educational provision. By 1965 a Child Guidance Service had been established in the areas of twenty-four education authorities, and five authorities had made specific arrangements with other areas; the remaining six authorities made no provision for a Child Guidance Service. A residential child guidance clinic has been in operation at

Kirkmichael, Ayrshire, since 1957, and Glasgow is to reopen its residential school and clinic at Nerston, probably in 1967.

The function of the Child Guidance Service is stated in the 1962 Act to be "to study handicapped, backward and difficult children, to give advice to parents and teachers as to appropriate methods of education and training and in suitable cases to provide special educational treatment for such children in child guidance clinics".[17] Thus the main functions are educational and psychological.

Children may be sent to child guidance clinics for a variety of reasons—for example, a general failure to learn by ordinary methods of teaching; a specific disability in some school subject; a behaviour problem such as temper-tantrums, restlessness, lying, or aggressiveness; delinquent behaviour in such forms as theft, destructiveness, truancy, fire-raising; physical/nervous disorders such as enuresis, asthma, tics, stammering. Thus many of the children who attend child guidance clinics come into the category of maladjusted children considered in Chapter 6.

Children are referred to child guidance clinics from various sources—for example teachers, school medical officers, family doctors, parents, children's departments, courts. The most common source of referral is the schools, and it must be stressed that the Child Guidance Service in Scotland is essentially an educational service—a child guidance clinic is included in the statutory definition of the term "special school".[18] Thus, as well as being involved with the attempt to understand and treat sometimes quite dramatic forms of maladjustment, educational psychologists visit schools, administer intelligence, attainment and diagnostic tests, discuss cases with teachers and headmasters, interview and advise parents, and give remedial educational work to individual pupils or small groups at school or clinic. Psychologists have also played an important part in the development and use of the various forms of assessment involved in the transfer of pupils from primary to secondary education.

An ideal has generally been that the staff of a child guidance clinic should consist of three elements: psychiatrist, psychologist, and psychiatric social worker. Although Notre Dame was the first clinic to have such a staff, this particular team approach has not developed to any extent elsewhere in Scotland. Psychiatrists are not available in the numbers required for education authority child guidance clinics, and although in a few areas psychiatrists attend such clinics on a sessional basis, in most areas children in need of psychiatric treatment are referred to the psychiatrist at a hospital clinic. There is likewise an acute shortage of psychiatric social workers, and the demand for their services in many branches of the mental health service is so great that there is no likelihood of their making a large contribution to the work of education authority clinics in the foreseeable future. Consequently education authority child guidance clinics are staffed largely by educational psychologists, with a smaller number of social workers, and, in one or two cases, health visitors. All educational psychologists are graduate, certificated teachers with experience of class teaching, and the majority hold the degree of Ed.B. (now M.Ed.), a Scottish higher degree in Education and Psychology.

The situation in Scotland thus differs from that in England. The distinction which is made in England between the school psychological service, which is under the direction of an educational psychologist, and the child guidance clinic, which has a medical director, has never been present in Scotland. The authors of the report *Ascertainment of Maladjusted Children* saw no reason to depart from the arrangements operating in Scotland, since, they claimed, good relationships exist in general between the Child Guidance Service and the School Health Service; moreover, the fact that the Child Guidance Service is part of the educational provision affords it contact with the whole child population and with a large variety of professional workers.[19] On the other hand, the authors of the report *Medical Services for Child Guidance* were less happy about the existing situation, stressed the lack of liaison between child guidance clinics and hospital child psychiatric clinics, and recommended that a more prominent role be played by medical services.[20]

In view of this recommendation, it must be borne in mind that not all children referred to the Child Guidance Service present medical problems, and that a comprehensive Child Guidance Service has varied functions. These functions are stated by the Glasgow Child Guidance Service to include:[21] individual case-work—for example, participation in the ascertainment of children requiring special education, and the detection, diagnosis and treatment of children showing problems of behaviour and/or educational retardation; the organization of forms of special educational treatment—advising the education authority on the general provision and planning of special schools, organizing formal provision for disturbed and retarded children, carrying a direct responsibility for the day-to-day functioning of schools and classes for maladjusted children; consultation with other casework agencies—the probation service, school welfare officers, youth employment officers, the juvenile court, and so on; advisory work in schools, including the preventive aspects of child guidance, the positive furtherance of the educational guidance of normal children, the study of problems of discipline and the behaviour of groups; advisory work on procedures of transfer to secondary education; certain forms of community service; research.

Very few Child Guidance Services in Scotland could carry the burden of all these functions. Only about a third of all education authorities have really well-developed Services, and some have no Service at all. A desirable development would be legislation to make the provision of a Child Guidance Service mandatory on all education authorities, and not optional as it is at present. This move was suggested by the Advisory Council as long ago as 1952,[22] but the Secretary of State was not at that time prepared to accept the recommendation. However, recent evidence[23] shows that this development may not be long delayed. It would certainly be a considerable advance if the excellent work done by the best child guidance clinics could become a feature of all education authority areas.

YOUTH EMPLOYMENT SERVICE

The Youth Employment Service, known as the Juvenile Employment Service until 1948, was established in its present form as a result of the recommendations of the Ince Report of 1945.[24] Under the Employment and Training Act, 1948, the Minister of Labour is responsible to Parliament for the Service, which operates throughout Great Britain. Responsibility for the central administration, organization and operation of the Service is placed upon the Central Youth Employment Executive, which consists of senior officers of the Ministry of Labour, the Department of Education and Science, and the Scottish Education Department. The CYEE gives guidance on policy and methods, and seeks to ensure that the service provided is broadly the same throughout the country.

The Minister of Labour appoints and is advised by a National Youth Employment Council; an Advisory Committee on Youth Employment for Scotland and one for Wales report to the National Council.[25] At the local level Youth Employment Committees, generally composed of representatives of the education authority, teachers, both sides of industry, and independent members, advise on all matters relating to the effective operation of the Service in their areas.

The Youth Employment Service is operated locally either by the Ministry of Labour through its local offices, or by the education authority in accordance with arrangements approved by the Minister of Labour. In Scotland, twelve of the thirty-five education authorities have responsibility for the Service in their areas[26] and these areas include about 64% of the total school population.

The Service is officially concerned with "persons under the age of 18 years and persons over that age who are for the time being attending school".[27] The functions of the Youth Employment Service with regard to such young people are: to give them vocational guidance; to assist them to find suitable employment (and also to assist employers to find suitable workers); to follow up their progress in employment and to give them any further help and advice they may need.

In order to carry out these functions, youth employment officers are appointed. There were 136 in Scotland in 1966, eighty-three employed by education authorities and fifty-three by the Ministry of Labour. These officers visit the schools in their areas. The usual plan has been to give a general talk to pupils intending to leave school at 15, in their penultimate term at school, in order to stimulate interest and direct thought about future careers. This has been followed by parents' interviews and individual school leaving interviews in the final term. This general plan is being altered in many areas. For example, under the impact of the Brunton Report[28] the initial group talk and discussion is tending to take place in the second year; and in an increasing number of areas arrangements are made for visits to places of employment, and for the use of invited speakers and/or television programmes on various occupations.

To assist the youth employment officer in his work with pupils who leave at the statutory age, many schools fill in a Confidential School Report, Form Y15, which provides for information with regard to health and physique, educational attainments, general ability, and aptitudes. This form has been found to be rather inadequate in the areas in which it is used, and a more comprehensive form is likely to be produced. The Brunton Report suggested a new school-leaving report which would serve the needs both of the Youth Employment Service and of colleges of further education.[29]

Although attendance of young people for individual interviews with youth employment officers is entirely voluntary, the majority of pupils who leave school at the statutory leaving age are interviewed, and about 40% of them are placed in employment by the Service. Their progress is reviewed after 4–6 months in employment, and further reviews are undertaken where necessary. The response to "open evenings" varies from about 30% to 50% of young people invited, and some areas are experimenting with alternative methods of reviewing progress.

For older pupils leaving school with various passes in the Scottish Certificate of Education examinations, or proceeding from school to higher education, talks and interviews may be given by specialist officers. In areas where the Service is operated by the Ministry of Labour these officers are known as careers advisory officers, of which there are at present nine in Scotland. In most of the areas in which education authorities operate the

Service, the careers advisory work is an integral part of the youth employment officer's normal duties.

One important development, though much less common in Scotland than in England, is the appointment in secondary schools of a member of staff to serve as careers master or mistress.[30] As yet few of such teachers have received specific training in this work, and often the time and facilities provided for their special duties are inadequate. Where a school has made such an appointment, co-operation with the youth employment officer has generally been facilitated, the careers master contributing a detailed knowledge of individual pupils, the youth employment officer a detailed knowledge of a variety of occupations.

In order to be fully effective in his work, the youth employment officer must be acquainted with occupational requirements in general throughout the country; but he must also have a thorough knowledge of the local job situation, a knowledge best acquired by close and frequent contact with local employers. By means of such contacts the youth employment officer can also keep employers informed about trends and developments in the schools, thus serving as a two-way channel of communication between school and employment.

There is a variety of "aids" at the disposal of the youth employment officer. For example, the CYEE produces the "Choice of Careers" series of booklets, and other publications; various professional bodies and industrial organizations produce their own material; and there are films, film strips and television programmes dealing with particular careers or groups of occupations.

Future development of the Youth Employment Service depends upon an adequate supply of youth employment officers. Officers employed by education authorities are drawn from a variety of sources including teaching, industry, commerce, social service work, and branches of local government. Ministry of Labour youth employment officers are recruited from officers already serving in the Department, who usually spend only 5 years or so in youth employment work, before moving on to other work in the Ministry, either by promotion or transfer.

At present it is not necessary to have had a course of specific training in order to be appointed as a youth employment officer, but a variety of training facilities exists.[31] In 1966 all youth employment officers employed by the Ministry of Labour in Scotland, and two-thirds of those employed by education authorities, had had full-time courses of training. The majority of the remaining education authority youth employment officers were long-service, experienced officers, who had been trained "on the job" by their senior officers.

The work of the Youth Employment Service is inspected by Inspectors of the CYEE, who work in association with H.M. Inspectors of Schools in the areas concerned. Although full-scale formal inspections still take place, the tendency is to move towards shorter, more informal contacts with officers in the field; in the Youth Employment Service, as in the schools, the concept of the Inspector as a consultant is gaining ground.[32]

The opinion of teachers and pupils as to the value of the Youth Employment Service varies from area to area, doubtless being dependent on the efficiency and interest shown by individual youth employment officers.[33] Certainly the need for the Service exists, and is likely to grow as the result of various educational, social, and occupational developments—for example, the adoption of vocationally-based courses for non-academic pupils in secondary schools; the development of further education courses of various types; the trend towards voluntary staying on at school, often to improve career prospects; the increasing speed of technological change, with the consequent demand for new skills, and the creation of completely new jobs. These and other factors are likely to affect the extent and direction of development of the Youth Employment Service in the 1970's.

REFERENCES AND NOTES

1. Education (Scotland) Act, 1962, Section 53.
2. *The Meals Service (Scotland) Regulations, 1953.*
3. *Ibid.*, Regulation 1 (1) (e).
4. *Ibid.*, Regulation 5 (9).

5. Scottish Education Department: Circular No. 431: *The School Meals Service and the Schools*, 25th Apr. 1960, Para. 6.
6. Scottish Education Department: *Education in Scotland in 1965*, Cmd. 2914, Edinburgh, H.M.S.O., 1966, pp. 22–3.
7. *Ibid.*, p. 24.
8. Education (Scotland) Act, 1962, Sections 57–60.
9. *School Health Service (Scotland) Regulations, 1947*, Regulations 2 and 3.
10. A recommendation to move towards a system of more continuous supervision was made in Scottish Home and Health Department: Circular 58/1962, 31st Aug. 1962.
11. Education (Scotland) Act, 1962, Section 61.
12. *Ibid.*, Sections 54–6.
13. Scottish Education Department: *Education in Scotland in 1965*, Cmnd. 2914, Edinburgh, H.M.S.O., 1966, p. 24.
14. *The Education Authority Bursaries (Scotland) Regulations 1963. The Education Authority Bursaries (Scotland) (Amendment No. 1) Regulations 1965*.
15. Full details are given in a *Guide to Students' Allowances*, available from the Scottish Education Department.
16. McCALLUM, C., Symposium on Psychologists and Psychiatrists in the Child Guidance Service. IV. Child Guidance in Scotland, *British Journal of Educational Psychology*, Vol. 22, Part 2, June 1952.
17. Education (Scotland) Act, 1962, Section 1 (6).
18. *Ibid.*, Section 145 (46).
19. Scottish Education Department: *Ascertainment of Maladjusted Children*, Edinburgh, H.M.S.O., 1964, Paras. 41 and 42.
20. Scottish Home and Health Department; Scottish Health Services Council: *Medical Services for Child Guidance*, Edinburgh, H.M.S.O., 1962, Paras. 52–69.
21. The Corporation of Glasgow, Education Department: *Report on Child Guidance Service*, Session 1964–5, Part IV.
22. Scottish Education Department: *Pupils who are Maladjusted because of Social Handicaps*. A Report of the Advisory Council on Education in Scotland, Cmd. 8428, Edinburgh, H.M.S.O., 1952, Para. 58.
23. Scottish Education Department: Circular No. 602/1965. Health and Welfare Services Circular No. 23/1965. 14th Dec. 1965, Appendix "A", 8.
24. Ministry of Labour and National Service: *Report of the Committee on the Juvenile Employment Service*, London, H.M.S.O., 1945.
25. The constitution of these bodies is given in: Employment and Training Act, 1948, First Schedule.
26. Aberdeen, Edinburgh, Glasgow, Banffshire, Clackmannanshire, Dunbartonshire, East Lothian, Fife, Lanarkshire, Perth and Kinross, Stirlingshire, Zetland.
27. Employment and Training Act, 1948, Section 7 (2).
28. Scottish Education Department: *From School to Further Education*, Edinburgh, H.M.S.O., 1963, Chapter VII.
29. *Ibid.*, Paras. 121–5, and Appendix 2.

30. A useful account of current developments in careers work is given in Department of Education and Science, Education Pamphlet No. 48: *Careers Guidance in Schools*, London, H.M.S.O., 1965.

31. For details see Ministry of Labour; Central Youth Employment Executive: *The Future Development of the Youth Employment Service*. Report of a Working Party of the National Youth Employment Council. London, H.M.S.O., 1965, Chapter IX, and Appendixes VIII and IX.

32. General information about the activities of the Service is given in Ministry of Labour; Central Youth Employment Executive: *The Work of the Youth Employment Service, 1962–1965*. A Report by the National Youth Employment Council, London, H.M.S.O., 1965.

33. For an illuminating account of the impact of the Youth Employment Service on a sample of pupils in Lanarkshire, see JAHODA, G. and CHALMERS, A. D., The Youth Employment Service: a consumer perspective, *Occupational Psychology*, Vol. 37, No. 1, Jan. 1963.

CHAPTER 9

Independent School Education

THERE is very little published material on independent schools in Scotland, apart from a few histories of individual schools. This chapter sets out some of the basic facts about the independent schools, explains the process of registration, and then deals more generally with the place and role of independent schools in the state system.

BASIC FACTS

The statutory definition of an independent school is: "a school at which full-time education is provided for five or more pupils of school age (whether or not such education is also provided for pupils under or above that age), not being a public school or a grant-aided school."[1]

There are at present 140 independent schools in Scotland, with just over 18,000 pupils on the rolls. The schools are unevenly distributed throughout the country—for example there are thirteen education authority areas in which there are no independent schools, and one area in which there are as many as twenty-four. The distribution of independent schools by education authority area is shown in Table 8.[2]

The type of education provided is shown in Table 9. In interpreting this Table it should be noted that, when giving information about independent schools, the Scottish Education Department uses the terminology of the state system. This can be misleading, as the age ranges in the two systems do not always correspond. Confusion is most likely to occur in the case of the

TABLE 8. INDEPENDENT SCHOOLS: DISTRIBUTION BY
EDUCATION AUTHORITY AREA

Area	No. of schools	Area	No. of schools
Counties		*Counties*	
Aberdeen	4	Peebles	1
Ayr	8	Perth and Kinross	13
Dumfries	7	Renfrew	11
Dunbarton	8	Roxburgh	4
East Lothian	6	Stirling	5
Fife	8	Sutherland	1
Inverness	1	West Lothian	1
Kincardine	3		
Kirkcudbright	2	*Burghs*	
Lanark	6	Dundee	2
Midlothian	6	Edinburgh	24
Moray and Nairn	5	Glasgow	14
		Total	140

two categories called in Table 9 "Nursery + Primary", and
"Primary + Secondary". It might be expected that "Nursery +
Primary" would cover the age range 3 or 4 to 11 or 12. This is so
in the case of only about a third of the schools in this category. In
the case of almost half of the schools the upper age limit is 8 or 9.
Thus in the terminology of the independent sector, many of the
schools in this category are "pre-preparatory".

Again, it might be expected that "Primary + Secondary"
would cover the age ranges 5–15 or 5–18. In fact most schools in
this category take children from the age of about 8 till the age of
13 or 14, being in the terminology of the independent sector
"preparatory" schools, preparing pupils for entry to "public"
schools.

Of the total of 140 schools, 48 are for boys only, 17 are for girls
only, and 75 cater for both boys and girls; 15 of these 75 have a
different age range for each sex, being primarily girls' schools, and
taking boys in the younger age groups only.

TABLE 9. INDEPENDENT SCHOOLS: TYPE OF EDUCATION PROVIDED

Type of education	No. of schools
Nursery or Kindergarten	2
Primary	17
Secondary	19
Nursery + Primary	40
Primary + Secondary	41
Nursery + Primary + Secondary	15
Special (Handicapped)	4
Others	2
Total	140

The general public tends to associate independent school education with boarding school education. This is by no means the case. Of the 140 independent schools, thirty-nine are residential, thirty-six are partly residential, and sixty-five are day schools.

There is a further tendency to associate the idea of an independent school with that of the large English "public" school. Again, this is not the case in Scotland. At the present time only eight Scottish independent schools are members of the Headmasters' Conference, membership of which is limited to the headmasters of some 200 boys' secondary schools, and is dependent on such factors as the degree of independence enjoyed by the headmaster and his school, the academic standards of the school as shown by the proportion of boys pursuing advanced studies, and the number of Old Boys at universities.[3] The eight Scottish schools are: Loretto, Gordonstoun, Strathallan, Trinity College Glenalmond, Edinburgh Academy, Fettes College, Merchiston Castle School, and Glasgow Academy.

Moreover, the majority of independent schools in Scotland are not large; sizes are indicated by the number of pupils on the rolls, as shown in Table 10.

TABLE 10. INDEPENDENT SCHOOLS: SIZE AS INDICATED
BY NUMBER OF PUPILS ON ROLLS

Number of pupils	Number of schools
1–25	20
26–50	19
51–100	48
101–200	25
201–300	13
301–400	10
401–500	2
501–600	1
901–1000	1
1001–1100	1
Total	140

Thus over a quarter of Scottish independent schools have rolls of fewer than fifty pupils; three-fifths have rolls of fewer than 100 pupils; and only five schools have rolls of over 400 pupils. The two largest are Glasgow Academy, with around 900 pupils, and Edinburgh Academy, with just over 1000 pupils.

With regard to status, equipment, amenities, curriculum, methods, qualifications of staff, and quality of education provided, there are very wide variations among the independent schools. At one extreme is the small independent school run in an ordinary house, where one or two people provide elementary education for a handful of pupils in a narrow age range. At the other extreme stands the large independent "public" school, in ample buildings and spacious grounds, with a well-qualified staff providing a balanced education for several hundred pupils, and sending the brightest to some well-known universities.

REGISTRATION OF INDEPENDENT SCHOOLS

All independent schools must be registered; it is an offence to conduct an unregistered school. One of the officers of the Scottish Education Department has been appointed by the Secretary of State to be Registrar of Independent Schools in Scotland, and it is his duty to keep a register of independent schools, which is open to public inspection "at all reasonable times".[4]

The procedure for registration is laid down in regulations[5] which prescribe the particulars to be furnished to the Registrar of Independent Schools by the proprietor of any independent school applying for registration, and also the circumstances in which a school may be deleted from the register if the proprietor fails to inform the Registrar of changes in the particulars. Changes in the name of the school, in the address to which communications are to be sent, in the premises used by the school, or in the ownership of the school must be notified within one month by letter to the Registrar. Changes in staff and in the roll of the school must be notified in January of each year.[6]

The usual procedure is for a school to be provisionally registered, and after it has been inspected by one or more of H.M. Inspectors, the Secretary of State decides, in the light of the Inspector's report, whether or not the registration is to be confirmed. While strict demands are made with regard to such matters as safety precautions, somewhat lenient demands are made with regard to the standard of education provided. There is not in Scotland the system which obtains in England, where there are two categories of independent schools, those which are registered, and those which, in addition to being registered, are "recognized as efficient".

There are certain specific grounds on which the Secretary of State may decide that a registered or provisionally registered school is "objectionable". These grounds are: that efficient and suitable instruction is not being provided; that the school premises or parts of the premises are unsuitable for a school; that the accommodation provided is inadequate or unsuitable; that the proprietor or any teacher employed in the school is not a proper person to be the proprietor of an independent school or to be a teacher in any school, as the case may be.[7] In such cases the Secretary of State may serve upon the proprietor a notice of complaint, giving particulars of the matters complained of, stating the remedial measures deemed necessary, and specifying the time within which the measures are required to be taken. If it is alleged in the notice that a person employed as a teacher at the school is not a proper person to be a teacher in any school, that person is sent a copy of the notice.

Any person who receives such a notice of complaint has the right of appeal to an Independent Schools Tribunal, consisting of the sheriff of the county in which the school is situated, and two members drawn from an educational panel of persons appointed by the Secretary of State to act, when required, as members of such a tribunal.[8] Rules have been made with regard to the manner of making appeals to the Independent Schools Tribunal, the proceedings before such tribunals, and matters incidental to or consequential on such proceedings.[9]

Although the procedure outlined above is laid down in detail, the Independent Schools Tribunal, at the time of writing, has not yet had to meet. The procedure for registration of independent schools has in general worked smoothly, almost all schools provisionally registered eventually being finally registered.

THE PLACE AND ROLE OF INDEPENDENT SCHOOLS

The place of independent schools in the Scottish educational system is, from a quantitative point of view, a small one: 140 schools catering for just under 2% of the school population. This contrasts with the situation in England, where some 3500 independent schools cater for about 6% of the school population. As a consequence, the issue of the existence of independent schools and their relationship with the state system has occasioned less controversy in Scotland than in England. However, the arguments for and against independent schools are much the same on both sides of the border.

The case for independent schools tends to be argued on such grounds as these: that freedom of choice is in itself a good thing; that in a democracy an individual has the right to spend his money (within certain broad limits) as he pleases, and that he should not be prevented from buying for his children a type of education which he believes to be worth having; that it would be undesirable for the state system to have a monopoly; that independent schools set standards for the state system to aim at; that they provide the necessary freedom to experiment,[10] a situation which may well react beneficially on the state system itself.

Those who are opposed to independent schools tend to argue along lines such as these: that the freedom of choice is not really meaningful, since it is limited by the ability to pay school fees; that in a democracy it is not right that educational privilege should be bought; that independent education is socially divisive, perpetuating undesirable class distinctions; that a small number of children gets a disproportionate share of teaching resources; that the state system is actually weakened by the existence of independent schools, since the fact that important and powerful elements of society opt for the independent sector leads to a lessening of pressure to improve the state schools; that the "old school tie" still leads to unfair social and occupational advantages in later life.

An examination of the complexities of the controversy is not within the scope of this book, but it will be observed that the above constitutes an interesting mixture of reasons and rationalizations. Moreover, a number of the arguments appear to be based on ideas about English public schools, rather than on knowledge of the factual situation in Scotland. It has already been shown that comparatively few of the independent schools in Scotland are in this category. Eight schools are members of the Headmasters' Conference—and also of the Association of Governing Bodies of Public Schools. In addition, three schools are members of the Association of Governing Bodies of Girls' Public Schools: St. Leonards and St. Katharines at St. Andrews; St. George's School for Girls, Edinburgh; and Esdaile School, Edinburgh. These eleven schools account for only 28% of all pupils enrolled in independent schools in Scotland.

Thus the fairly common idea of the average "independent" pupil as attending a large "public"-type school, paying fees of £500 or £600 per annum, proceeding to Oxford or Cambridge, and acquiring a particular social cachet for life, is a false one. The average "independent" pupil is more likely to be attending quite a small school—the average roll of all independent schools is only 130; to be paying quite modest fees; and to be there not necessarily for the snob value of social exclusiveness, but because his parents can point to quite clear, practical, educational advantages such as smaller classes, more individual attention, greater flexibility of curriculum and sometimes methods, a larger number of extra-classroom activities, and less frequent changes of staff.

Nevertheless, for those who do attend the best-known Scottish independent schools, the advantages are considerable. The average product of the state system who may visit some of these schools is immediately conscious of the gulf between his own educational experiences and those of the pupils attending such schools. The privileges which money can buy are very real. The environment makes its own impact, with impressive, long-established buildings, and spacious, well-kept playing fields. The chapel frequently plays a prominent role in the life of the school, conveying a sense of security, tradition, "roots". The academic standards of the school are generally high, the aim for many being Advanced level passes in the English General Certificate of Education, and preparation for the universities. The curriculum is usually well balanced, with due regard paid to aspects of development other than the intellectual, and a particular emphasis on physical activities and skills. The internal organization of the school—houses, housemasters, prefects, clubs and societies, even dining arrangements—all contribute to the sense of the school as a community; school rules and traditions give a sense of continuity, and of belonging to a group with its own particular standards and ideals. These features, plus the relationships formed between staff and pupils, and among the pupils, contribute to the training in responsibility, leadership, and self-confidence for which these schools are known.[11]

Whatever anyone may think of this kind of education, no one doubts that it has an impact, and often a profound impact, on those exposed to it.[12] At the present time that amounts to approximately $0 \cdot 6\%$ of the school population in Scotland.

Faced with such a situation, various lines of action may be suggested. The schools could be abolished; some scheme could be devised to increase the numbers attending such schools, and/or to diversify their social class composition; the function of the schools could be altered—they could be converted to sixth-form colleges, or colleges of further education; they could be integrated with the state system of schools; they could be left alone. It may be because almost every proposed "solution" to the "problem" posed by the existence of independent schools creates further problems, that the independent schools have been left alone for so long.

However, the present trend towards comprehensive secondary education has served to highlight anew the place and role of such schools, and a first tentative move in the direction of "integration" has been made. In December 1965 a Public Schools Commission was set up under the chairmanship of Sir John Newsom, its terms of reference being to advise the government on the best way of integrating the public schools with the state system of education. The statement made at the time by the Secretary of State for Education and Science indicated the lines of possible future development:

> The Government are determined that the public schools should make the maximum contribution to meeting the educational needs of the country, and that this should be done in such a way as to reduce the socially divisive influence which they now exert. This implies that the schools should like other parts of the educational system, become progressively open to boys and girls irrespective of the income of their parents; that the schools should move towards a wider range of academic attainment, so that the public schools sector may increasingly play its own part in the national movement towards comprehensive education; and in particular that the schools should seek to meet any unsatisfied need for boarding education among wider sections of the population.[13]

For the purpose of the commission "public schools" were defined as those independent schools in membership of the Headmasters' Conference, Governing Bodies Association, or Governing Bodies of Girls' Schools Association. The commission is to recommend in due course whether any action is needed in respect of other independent schools. As the commission's work extends to Scotland as well as England and Wales, this means that the eleven Scottish independent schools mentioned above come within the scope of the commission; the other 129 independent schools do not—as yet.

The future of the independent schools thus appears to be uncertain, and the controversy which their existence provokes is likely to continue. As indicated by Table 8, there is no problem for thirteen education authorities in Scotland, for the simple reason that they have no independent schools in their areas. At the opposite extreme is Edinburgh, with twenty-four independent schools. There are also eight grant-aided schools in Edinburgh, and in addition some 6000 children attend education authority schools which charge fees. The net result is that some 25% of all pupils in Edinburgh are fee-paying pupils. This situation creates various problems, not the least of which is the effect on the standards and morale of the non-fee-paying education authority schools which are "creamed" in this way.

What the Public Schools Commission will report about independent schools will no doubt make interesting reading. The Fleming Report[14] certainly did, but it achieved little. In this connection one characteristic of independent schools has not so far been mentioned: their resource and resilience under attack.

REFERENCES AND NOTES

1. Education (Scotland) Act, 1962, Section 145 (23).
2. The statistics in this section were kindly supplied by the Scottish Education Department, March 1966.
3. For information with regard to schools in this category see *The Public and Preparatory Schools Year Book*, London, A. & C. Black. Published annually.
4. Education (Scotland) Act, 1962, Section 111.
5. *The Registration of Independent Schools (Scotland) Regulations, 1957.*
6. *Ibid.*, Regulation 2 and Schedule.
7. Education (Scotland) Act, 1962, Section 112.
8. *Ibid.*, Section 113 and Seventh Schedule.
9. *The Independent Schools Tribunal (Scotland) Rules, 1961.*
10. It is certain that the experimental, progressive work of people such as A. S. Neill would have been impossible within the bounds of the state

system. See NEILL, A. S., *Summerhill. A Radical Approach to Education*, London, Gollancz, 1964. An account of the work of fourteen progressive independent schools (including Kilquhanity House, Castle Douglas) is given by the respective heads in: CHILD, H. A. T., *The Independent Progressive School*, London, Hutchinson, 1962.

11. For an interesting and perceptive account of the public school system, and one which frequently contrasts appearance with reality, see WILSON, J., *Public Schools and Private Practice*, London, Allen & Unwin, 1962. Of interest also is DANCY, J., *The Public Schools and the Future*, London, Faber & Faber, 1963.

12. An account of the impact of one rather specialized independent school is given in Arnold-Brown, A., *Unfolding Character. The Impact of Gordonstoun*, London, Routledge & Kegan Paul, 1962.

13. Mr. Anthony Crosland, quoted in *The Times Educational Supplement Scotland*, 24th Dec. 1965.

14. Board of Education: *The Public Schools and the General Educational System*, London, H.M.S.O., 1944.

CHAPTER 10

Further Education

FOR the student of Scottish education the field of further education is extensive, and complex to the point of confusion. As Burgess notes of the sphere of further education in England: "It is like the vegetation of South America: it contains anything you can think of. Much of it is jungle; there are weird and exotic growths and there are some very large areas of desert."[1] Moreover, there has developed a bewildering descriptive terminology. For example, the types of education may be labelled technical education, vocational education, cultural education, informal education, social and recreational education, adult education. Courses may be day release, block release, sandwich, pre-apprentice, pre-vocational; they may be for technologists, technicians, craftsmen, operatives; they may lead to university degrees, college associate-ships, college diplomas, Ordinary or Higher National Diplomas, Ordinary or Higher National Certificates, City and Guilds of London Institute Basic Craft, Advanced Craft, or Full Techno-logical Certificates, certificates of the Scottish Council for Commercial, Administrative and Professional Education—or to no certificate at all.

The reader in this field will find that the material is scattered, and that there are gaps in the published information. All that can be attempted in this chapter is a general outline of the system of further education, its institutions, courses, and awards. The definitive study of further education in Scotland remains to be written.

DEFINITION AND SCOPE OF FURTHER EDUCATION

The term "further education" was defined in the Education (Scotland) Act, 1946, as including:

> (a) compulsory part-time and in exceptional cases full-time courses of instruction approved in terms of the code given in colleges (hereinafter referred to as "junior colleges") to young persons not exempt from attendance . . . and designed to enable them to develop their various aptitudes and capacities and to prepare them for the responsibilities of citizenship;
> . (b) voluntary part-time and full-time courses of instruction for persons over school age; and
> (c) voluntary leisure-time occupation, in such organised cultural training and recreative activities as are suited to their requirements, for persons over school age.[2]

With this legal definition in mind, it is possible to give a working definition of further education as it has developed in Scotland: "education intended primarily for persons who have left school, through provision secured either by the Secretary of State for Scotland, or by education authorities in accordance with appropriate schemes or plans approved by the Secretary of State." This definition excludes educational provision in secondary schools, colleges of education, universities, private establishments unaided by an education authority or the Secretary of State, and establishments conducted under the aegis of ministers other than the Secretary of State. It should be noted that as yet nothing has come of the plan to have "junior colleges" ("county colleges" in the 1944 English Act) to provide compulsory part-time education for all young persons under age 18 who are not undertaking other recognized forms of full-time or part-time education.

The field of further education, although limited by the above definition, remains an extensive one. The Advisory Council suggested an analysis into three broad areas: technical education; cultural education; social and recreational education.[3] A defect here lies in the use of terms which tend to be emotionally loaded, and call to mind Whitehead's strictures about the false antithesis between the "technical" and the "liberal".[4] Perhaps the simplest classification is in terms of "Vocational" and "Non-vocational" courses, the former being closely tied to present or future occupations, the latter being given as general education, adult education, and/or for recreative purposes. The "Non-vocational" sector may be further subdivided into "Formal" and "Informal" branches, "Formal" being primarily intellectual in its appeal, and "Informal" being primarily recreational. Thus:

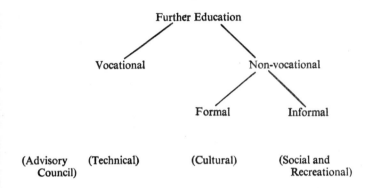

The above classification is open to criticism: for example, the dividing line between Vocational and Non-vocational may be difficult to draw in some instances; much of the Formal Non-vocational further education is given quite informally; a term such as Informal Non-vocational further education is clumsy. Nevertheless, this classification provides a useful framework for describing the system of further education in Scotland; the term "technical" will also be used, as technical education is the largest single element in the vocational sphere.

INSTITUTIONS PROVIDING FURTHER EDUCATION

Further education is provided in Scotland in establishments of two main types—Central Institutions and Colleges of Further Education (formerly Further Education Centres).[5]

Central Institutions

Central Institutions, so called since 1901, have formed "the keystone of the system of technical education"[6] in Scotland. They have been responsible for developing a wide range of courses in the higher branches of technical education, and have also exerted a powerful influence on the provision made by education authorities at the more elementary levels.

At the present time there are thirteen central institutions; three of them are agricultural colleges, for which the Department of Agriculture is responsible; the ten others fall within the administrative sphere of the Scottish Education Department. The complete list is noted below.

Aberdeen	North of Scotland College of Agriculture.
	Robert Gordon's Institute of Technology.
Dundee	Dundee College of Technology.
Edinburgh	Edinburgh and East of Scotland College of Agriculture.
	Edinburgh College of Art.
	Edinburgh College of Domestic Science.
	Leith Nautical College.
Glasgow	West of Scotland Agricultural College.
	Glasgow School of Art.
	Royal Scottish Academy of Music.
	Glasgow and West of Scotland College of Domestic Science.
Paisley	Paisley College of Technology.
Galashiels	Scottish Woollen Technical College.

Three of Scotland's best-known central institutions have attained university status. In Glasgow the Royal College of Science and Technology and the Scottish College of Commerce became the University of Strathclyde in 1964; in Edinburgh the Heriot-Watt College became the Heriot-Watt University in 1966.

The central institutions are not under the control of education authorities, but are managed by governing bodies which consist of representatives of education authorities, of other educational interests, of commerce, industry and art in the area served by the central institution. The institutions function largely on a regional basis, though some, like the Royal Scottish Academy of Music and the Scottish Woollen Technical College, provide for the country as a whole.

The tendency originally was to regard the specifically technical institutions as responsible for all types and levels of technical education, but now these institutions are regarded as responsible for higher technical education, elementary work wherever possible being transferred to colleges of further education. Thus central institutions generally provide courses leading to external degrees, internal diplomas and associateships, and Higher National Diplomas.

In 1965 over 13,000 students were enrolled in vocational courses in central institutions, and of that number almost 6000 were following full-time courses.

Colleges of Further Education (formerly Further Education Centres)

In the first three decades of this century almost all the day-time instruction in technical education was given in the central institutions, elementary technical education being provided in the evenings in day school buildings. When the demand for day and evening courses in technical education grew in the 1940's and 1950's, the great lack of facilities at the local level in the form of further education centres became apparent. The situation in Scotland contrasts with that in England: Scotland did not begin— as England did—with a large number of local colleges as a base on which higher institutions could later be built, but rather with a small number of central institutions round which the local further education centres were later to grow. This growth has, until recently, been a slow one, having been hindered to some extent by the very success of the central institutions in providing all types of courses. Indeed it is only in the 1950's and 1960's that there has been noticeable progress in the building, equipping and staffing of further education centres.

As a result of this historical development, the older term "further education centre" denotes a wide range of establishments. It may signify, at one extreme, simply a day school which is used for evening classes; at the other, a specially built institution with facilities for a wide variety of full-time and part-time day and evening courses. It is the development of such institutions which has led to the use of the new term "college of further education".

In 1965 some 150,000 students were enrolled in vocational courses in colleges of further education/further education centres; of that number almost 10,000 were following full-time courses.[7]

VOCATIONAL FURTHER EDUCATION

In this section attention will be focused on the largest area of vocational further education, namely, specific technical education for industry and commerce.

Levels of Qualification, and Courses

Although lines of demarcation are not always sharply defined, there are four main levels of qualification in industry.

Technologist. The technologist is usually a fully qualified engineer or applied scientist, competent, by virtue of his education and practical training, to apply scientific method to the analysis and solution of technological problems. He may have responsibility for design, research, development, and construction, as well as the supervision of the technical work of others; he may be expected to push forward the frontiers of knowledge in his chosen field.

For technologists, full-time degree or degree level courses are provided in central institutions. There are also full-time courses of

4 years' duration leading to Associateships of the central institution concerned; these are provided in various sciences, many branches of engineering, and in building technology. An important development has been the acceptance of courses leading to certain associateships as courses leading to degrees of the Council for National Academic Awards, a body set up in 1964 with powers to award degrees to students following certain approved courses in non-university institutions.

Central institutions also provide courses of 3 years' duration leading to Higher National Diplomas and College Diplomas in various branches of science and technology. Some of these are "sandwich" courses, consisting of alternate periods of full-time study at college and of supervised experience in industry.

Technician. It is only in recent years, and not yet in all industries, that technicians have come to be recognized as a separate category. The technician is qualified by specialist technical education and practical training to work under the general direction of a technologist. His work usually involves the supervision of skilled craftsmen, and his education and training must be such that he can understand the reasons for the operations for which he is responsible. To this end he needs a good knowledge of mathematics and science related to his own speciality.

For technicians there are courses leading to National Certificates in fifteen subjects including building and various branches of engineering. Ordinary and Higher National Certificate courses, each normally lasting 2 years, are provided on a part-time basis only. The normal requirement for entry to ONC courses is the possession of three appropriate Ordinary grade passes in the Scottish Certificate of Education examinations;[8] and for entry to HNC courses, possession of the appropriate ONC.

Courses for Ordinary and Higher National Diplomas are full-time, often "sandwich" courses, normally extending over 2 and 3 years respectively. The normal requirement for entry to OND courses is possession of four appropriate SCE Ordinary grade passes; for HND courses, possession of certain SCE Higher and Ordinary grade passes, or the appropriate ONC or OND.[9]

Schemes for National Certificates and Diplomas are administered by Joint Committees representative of the Scottish Education Department and relevant professional institutions in collaboration with the Scottish Association for National Certificates and Diplomas, a national co-ordinating body which was set up in 1962 to perform functions with regard to syllabuses, examination papers, schemes of work, and so on.

In 1965 some sixty centres offered National Certificate courses to over 15,000 students. Under certain circumstances students with National Certificates may transfer to higher courses given in central institutions; over 200 did so in 1964–5. Holders of Certificates or Diplomas may secure exemption from certain examinations of relevant professional institutions.

It seems likely that two factors, the raising of the school-leaving age to 16 (thus increasing the pool of potential SCE Ordinary grade candidates) and the national need for an increased number of technicians, will combine to ensure that National Certificate schemes play an even more prominent role in the further education of the 1970's.

Craftsman. The craftsman has the skill necessary to follow established techniques under the general direction of a technician or technologist. He must be able to understand technical descriptions, work from blueprints, make components under supervision, follow established practices in erecting, maintaining or servicing engineering machinery. Craftsmen represent the skilled labour force of manufacturing industry, and account for more than a third of its manpower.

For craftsmen, there is a wide range of courses, many of them leading to certificates of the City and Guilds of London Institute. The aim of the Institute has been, since its founding in 1878, to set nationally recognized standards of attainment and to provide machinery whereby industries can develop, on a national basis, schemes of further education which are integral components of apprenticeships and training schemes. For each subject or group of subjects there is an expert advisory committee representative of the industry, relevant professional institutions, educational and other interests. Each committee ensures that each scheme for courses and examinations is geared to meet the needs of the particular category of industrial employee. Thus there are courses in many subjects and at various levels; not only at craftsman level—"junior", "average", and "higher grade"—but also at operative, technician, and technologist levels. City and Guilds courses are available at institutions of further education throughout the country; many are on a day release or block release basis, and an increasingly common arrangement is for apprentices to spend the first year of their apprenticeship in college for a course in which further education is integrated with industrial training.

The pattern of certificates has for many years been: an Intermediate Certificate at the end of a course of 2 or 3 years; and a Final Certificate after an additional 2 years. More recently the terminology has in many schemes been changed to Craft Certificate and Advanced Certificate respectively. Above these levels a Full Technological Certificate is available in a number of subjects.

In 1965 over 16,000 Scottish candidates sat the Institute's examinations, chiefly the examinations in electrical engineering, mechanical engineering, and building crafts.

Operative. The operative, after a period of training which varies in length, is capable of carrying out specific operations which do not call for traditional craft skills. He is a semi-skilled or unskilled worker who may be able to operate a machine, and yet have little knowledge of the principles on which it works.

For operatives there is a range of courses designed to ensure proficiency in appropriate basic processes—for example in the iron and steel, chemical, and other industries. These courses, normally on a part-time basis, are mainly practical in content, and

TABLE 11

GENERAL PATTERN OF COURSES AND AWARDS

Level	Award	Entry requirements	Duration	Notes
Technologist	College Associateship or C.N.A.A. Degree	SCE 3 Higher and 2 Ordinary grade passes, or equivalent	4 years, full-time	Honours or ordinary degree standard. Complete or partial exemption from exams. of professional institutions
Technologist	College Diploma	SCE 2 Higher and 3 Ordinary grade passes, or equivalent	3–4 years, full-time or sandwich	Ordinary degree equivalent. Partial exemption from exams. of professional institutions
Technologist	Higher National Diploma	SCE 2 Higher and 3 Ordinary grade passes, or appropriate ONC or OND	3 years, full-time or sandwich	Partial exemption from exams. of professional institutions
Technician	Ordinary National Diploma	SCE 4 Ordinary grade passes	2 years, full-time	Entry to Higher National Certificate or Diploma

TABLE 11—*continued*

Level	Award	Entry requirements	Duration	Notes
Technician	Higher National Certificate	Appropriate ONC	2 years, part-time	With extra study, partial exemption from exams. of professional institutions; possible transfer to Associateship course
Technician	Ordinary National Certificate	SCE 3 Ordinary grade passes	2 years, part-time	Entry to HNC or HND course; possible entry to Associateship course
Technician or Craftsman	City and Guilds Full Technological Certificate	Advanced Craft or Final Certificate	1 or 2 years, part-time	
Craftsman	City and Guilds Advanced Craft or Final Certificate	Craft or Intermediate Certificate	2 or 3 years, part-time	Entry, in appropriate cases, to Full Technological Certificate course
Operative or Craftsman	City and Guilds Craft or Intermediate Certificate	Aged 16	2 or 3 years, part-time	Entry to Advanced Craft or Final Certificate course

many lead to certificates of the City and Guilds of London Institute. In some cases the course is held on the firm's premises, the education authority providing teaching and other assistance. Courses may last from 3 months up to 3 years, and some contain a substantial element of general education.

It may be useful to summarize the position with regard to levels of qualification, courses, and certificates awarded. This is done in Table 11.[10]

Pre-employment Courses

In addition to the courses for the four main categories as outlined above, there exists a variety of full-time pre-employment courses, normally of 1 year's duration, which are designed to prepare young school leavers for the careers they hope to follow.[11]

Pre-employment courses fall into two categories: pre-vocational courses, where the student's choice of occupation has already been determined and the emphasis is on vocational needs—for example commercial subjects, navigation, nursing; and pre-apprenticeship courses, in which students gain experience of different sections of an industry preparatory to making a final occupational choice—for example building and engineering.

These courses are intended for boys and girls who leave school at the minimum leaving age. They provide a bridge between school and employment, a preparation for the type of occupation the young people are likely to adopt and, usually, a continuation of general and social education.

Day Release

The provision of day release is an important element in the success of students following part-time courses in further education. The Crowther Report found that a student who secured day release was twice as likely to be successful in a National Certificate course as a student who had to rely on evening classes only.[12] However, day release facilities are not extensively used in Scotland.

In 1965, of the 15,000 or so students enrolled in National Certificate courses, 51% had day release and 2% block release; the remaining 47% attended evening classes only. Of all young persons under age 18 in insured employment, only $12\frac{1}{2}$% attend day release classes; the comparable figure for England is nearer 20%.

The Industrial Training Act, 1964, with its provision for the establishing of industrial training boards with responsibilities for determining the training and further education relevant to particular industries, is likely to lead to a closer integration of further education and industrial training, and to an increased demand for day release. Plans in England are for a doubling of the numbers of day release students by 1970.[13] A similar aim has been suggested for Scotland; but the Scottish figure of 100,000 was originally the target for 1965.[14]

Scottish Technical Education
Consultative Council

The 1956 White Paper on Technical Education[6] emphasized the importance of collaboration between educational and industrial interests in promoting new developments in technical education. After reviewing existing advisory machinery, the Secretary of State in 1959 appointed the Scottish Technical Education Consultative Council, consisting of representatives of industrial and educational organizations, with the following remit: "To secure the widest possible measure of consultation on vocational further education between employers, employees, and those responsible for its provision, and to advise on, and generally to promote, the development of such education."

This body replaced five Regional Advisory Councils for Technical Education which had been established in 1949. The Council has been active in many spheres of technical education, including day release and apprenticeship training. For example, the Council reached agreement with both sides of the engineering industry for the introduction in 1962 of an experimental apprenticeship scheme which provides for a 3-year course of full-time training—facilities being provided by Glasgow education authority—followed by 2 years in industry, to complete the normal 5-year apprenticeship.

Future work of the Council will entail close co-operation with the Scottish Committee of the Central Training Council, which was set up under the Industrial Training Act, 1964. This co-operation will have as its aim the twofold task of providing more and better training and technical education. The Consultative Council and the Scottish Committee issue the *STECC Newsletter*, a quarterly bulletin devoted to current developments in technical education and industrial training.

Teachers

A wide range of qualifications is accepted for teaching in further education, and teachers in this sphere are not required to have undertaken teacher-training. In 1965, of 2279 teachers employed full-time in colleges of further education, 1423 were certificated, and thus qualified to receive an additional payment of £80 per annum. Details of requirements for entry to training, certificates, and salary scales are given in Chapter 12.

A course of professional training is given at Jordanhill College of Education, Glasgow. It is a "mixed" course consisting of 2 months full-time study between May and July, supervised teaching in a college of further education for a session, and a further 2 months full-time training. The course may be taken by untrained teachers in service who are released by their education authorities, and by pre-service applicants drawn from industry and commerce who have been offered posts by education authorities. To facilitate recruitment and put potential teachers in touch with education authorities requiring staff, a Central Register is maintained by the Registrar for Further Education at Jordanhill.

In 1965 the Standing Committee on the Supply and Training of Teachers for Further Education recommended[15] that a single comprehensive training unit for teachers in further education should be developed at Jordanhill College of Education, where there is already a well-established Department of Further Education; that the existing "mixed" course should continue, and be offered three times a year, in order to aid the release of teachers by education authorities; that education authorities should be required to release untrained teachers to enter training not later than 3 years after appointment; and that education authorities should consider terminating the employment of teachers unable to complete training successfully. In this way the Committee sought to chart the way to an increased supply of trained teachers in further education up to 1980. Almost all these proposals were accepted by the Secretary of State in 1966.

Concern with the problems of teachers in further education was also shown by the publication in 1965 of a report on general conditions of service, staffing, and salary structure;[16] and by the formation in 1966 of an association of teachers in further education.

Commercial Education

Separate mention must be made of an important and expanding area of further education—that of commercial education. The body with wide responsibilities for such education is the Scottish Council for Commercial, Administrative and Professional Education, which was set up by the Secretary of State in 1961, and known until 1966 as the Scottish Council for Commercial Education. The Council includes representatives of relevant professional institutions, of education, and of industrial and commercial interests. Its objects are to keep under review the development of commercial education in Scotland, to devise courses, to conduct examinations and to award appropriate certificates.

The general pattern of courses and certificates in further education in commerce is shown in Table 12,[10] and the main "routes" are indicated in Fig. 6. The Junior Secretarial Certificate shown replaces the former Shorthand Typist and Clerk Typist Certificates.

In addition to the courses and certificates listed, there is a 1-year full-time course for university graduates leading to the

TABLE 12

S.C.C.A.P.E.: GENERAL PATTERN OF COURSES AND AWARDS

Award	Entry requirements	Duration	Notes
Scottish Certificate in Office Studies	3 years of secondary education	2 years, part-time	Entry to course for Scottish National Certificate in Business Studies, if in possession of 2 SCE Ordinary grade passes, or an endorsement award
Business Machine Operators Certificate	3 years of secondary education	2 years, part-time, or 1 year, full-time	
Junior Secretarial Certificate	3 years of secondary education	2 years, part-time, or 1 year, full-time	Entry to Secretarial Certificate course
Secretarial Certificate	SCE Ordinary grade English, or English I at Junior Secretarial Certificate level	2 years, part-time	Entry to Advanced Secretarial Certificate level
Advanced Secretarial Certificate	SCE Higher grade English, or English II at Secretarial Certificate level	2 years, part-time	

TABLE 12—*continued*

Award	Entry requirements	Duration	Notes
Scottish National Diploma in Business Studies	4 SCE Ordinary grade passes, including English, or an equivalent qualification	2 years, full-time	Entry to Scottish Advanced National Certificate in Business Studies. Exemptions at intermediate level from exams. of professional institutions
Scottish National Certificate in Business Studies	4 SCE Ordinary grade passes, including English, or an equivalent qualification	2 years, part-time	
Scottish Advanced National Certificate in Business Studies	Scottish National Certificate in Business Studies, or an equivalent qualification	2 years, part-time	

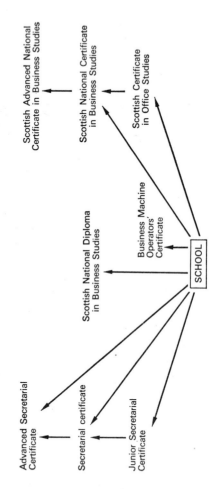

Fig. 6. Main Routes Through Further Education in Commerce

Diploma for Graduate Secretaries, and a 6-month full-time course for university graduates or those of comparable qualifications leading to the Diploma in Systems Analysis and Design.

As there are new developments in further education in commerce almost every year, the work of the Council is continually expanding. For example, examination entries in 1964–5 totalled almost 26,000, an increase of more than 4000 over the previous session.

The main provision of courses in commerce is in further education centres; this often means, in thinly populated areas, evening classes conducted in school premises. However, several new commercial colleges are being established in Scotland, the prototype being the Central College of Commerce and Distribution opened in Glasgow in 1962.

The School of Business and Administration in the University of Strathclyde—which includes the former Scottish College of Commerce—offers a B.A. degree specially designed for those preparing to be teachers of commerce; the Teacher's Diploma in Commerce and the corresponding Associateship, formerly awarded by the Scottish College of Commerce, are continued in the meantime. Several of the central institutions provide courses in commerce leading to a Teacher's Diploma in Commerce which is also acceptable for admission to a college of education for a course leading to the Teacher's Certificate (Secondary Education); in addition they offer a selection of courses which meet the requirements of the entrance regulations for training for the Teacher's Certificate (Further Education).

Trends in Vocational Further Education

Many of the trends in vocational further education have been implicit in what has been written above. It may be useful to summarize what appear to be some of the most important lines of development.

Already there have been notably successful attempts to rationalize the pattern of technical courses, and to integrate school work with the various branches of vocational further education. More teachers in secondary schools are now aware of the existence of these courses, their characteristics and standards; there is an increasing concern for the adequate guidance of pupils into appropriate courses; there has been the establishing of minimum standards of entry to National Certificate courses in terms of Ordinary grade passes in the SCE, and the introduction of more varied City and Guilds courses, twin lines of development which have acted to cut down the wastage which has hitherto been an unfortunate characteristic of vocational further education.

It seems likely that the late 1960's and early 1970's will see the provision in schools of courses more biased towards pupils' future occupations; a still closer linkage between school and further education; the efficient working of industrial training boards in connection with major industries; the increasing provision of courses for operatives, either in industry or in further education; the devising of courses, between the level of City and Guilds craft courses and National Certificate courses, specifically for technicians; an expansion of the provision of day release, block release, and "sandwich" courses—the latter actually pioneered in Scotland in the 1880's; an extension of the field of further education in commerce; an increasing provision of "liberal studies" in various courses of vocational further education.

One important line of development remains shrouded in some uncertainty—that of the junior or county college intended to give compulsory education on one day each week to all those not receiving education between the school-leaving age and the age of 18.[17] With the exception of this last, all the above developments are possible; that they are also desirable is not really in dispute.

NON-VOCATIONAL FURTHER EDUCATION: FORMAL

This is the sphere of adult education, in which sphere, although there has been of recent years an increasing tendency towards specialized courses, the emphasis is still primarily non-vocational. As the Advisory Council stated in 1952: "the function . . . is to enrich the lives of men and women and not to provide paper qualifications for gainful occupations."[18]

Education authorities have the duty to provide adult education courses, and in 1965 there were almost 30,000 enrolments in such subjects as English language and literature, foreign languages, social studies, philosophy, psychology, religious studies and music.[19] In their work in this sphere, education authorities often act in association with the extra-mural departments of the universities, and with voluntary bodies such as the Workers' Educational Association. For example, the Department of Extra-Mural Education at Glasgow University is involved with classes and courses in Glasgow and in ten counties in south-west Scotland, in accordance with agreements made with the relevant education authorities. The situation in practice is that education authorities co-operate with the University Extra-Mural Committees in the provision of adult education, and contribute towards the cost of the service. While large centres of population have the facilities to provide a variety of classes and courses, more rural and remote areas are limited in what can be arranged. One way of tackling this problem has been to appoint resident university tutors, who are peripatetic rather than resident, and engage in propagating, organizing, and teaching, adult education courses.

Some indication of the provision made by the extra-mural departments of the four older universities for the country as a whole is given in Table 13.[20]

The range of subjects provided by the extra-mural departments is extensive—for example archaeology, history, international affairs, social studies, philosophy, psychology, various sciences, English literature, modern languages, music, visual arts. Teaching techniques include lecturing, discussions, practical work and field studies where relevant. There is little place for didacticism in the approach to adult education, as tutors are faced with heterogeneous groups of mature, experienced adults with a variety of motives in seeking such education. Teaching schemes, however carefully prepared, have frequently to be modified and a premium is placed on experiment and flexibility.[21] In addition to normal

TABLE 13

PROVISION MADE BY EXTRA-MURAL DEPARTMENTS
OF SCOTTISH UNIVERSITIES, 1964–5

	Aberdeen	Edinburgh	Glasgow	St. Andrews	Total
No. of courses	31	273	380	70	754
No. of students	934	7032	9198	1882	19,046
No. of lecturers and tutors employed	63	188	443	121	815

classes, which usually meet on one evening a week for about 20 weeks, there are short extension courses on specialized topics, one-day and week-end schools, and summer schools in various locations.

Students in adult education come from a variety of social and educational backgrounds. The occupations followed by students enrolled in classes in the area served by Glasgow University Department of Extra-Mural Education in session 1964–5 were classified as: housewives, $17 \cdot 2\%$; manual, $4 \cdot 9\%$; non-manual (technical and supervisory), $35 \cdot 7\%$; professional, $33 \cdot 4\%$; not in paid work, $8 \cdot 8\%$.[22]

At the moment Scotland has only one college of residential adult education, at Newbattle Abbey, Midlothian, where students may take a 1-year full-time course of lectures and tutorials in such studies as literature, history, economics, philosophy, thereafter returning to their normal job, seeking a new career, or occasionally proceeding to undergraduate studies at a university. The college also provides short-term courses, lasting a week-end or perhaps a fortnight. There is a great need, especially in south-west Scotland, for a short-term residential college, and it is expected that a new residential centre will be established, probably not far from Glasgow.

Many of the developments in adult education have been actively encouraged by the Scottish Institute of Adult Education, founded in 1949. The Institute co-ordinates and promotes various lines of development, and its publication *Scottish Adult Education* provides a forum for discussion and information on subjects of interest to all concerned with adult education.

Like all branches of education, adult education is certain to expand in the future, for a variety of reasons: for example, the rapid advance of knowledge; the necessity for acquiring new skills, such as proficiency in a language; the increase in leisure time; perhaps even an inadequate supply of university places. Future developments may well include: the provision of an increased number of specialist courses, a trend already apparent;[23] development of the teaching of adults within industry; a move towards the provision of certificates of some kind to mark the satisfactory completion of courses; the increased use of television, perhaps on a "University of the Air" model, perhaps on a less ambitious scale; further provision of long-term and short-term residential courses; a continuation of the trend in subjects studied away from the politics and economics of the early WEA days, to the psychology, languages, and music of the affluent society.

NON-VOCATIONAL FURTHER EDUCATION: INFORMAL

This branch of further education includes those courses, provided mainly by education authorities, which are primarily for social and recreative purposes—courses in handicrafts, hobbies, country dancing and so on. There were over 120,000 enrolments in such courses in 1965. It is also the sphere of the Youth Service, to which this section of the chapter is devoted.

The Youth Service has developed over the years into a partnership involving voluntary organizations, the education authorities, and the central government.

Voluntary Organizations

Various voluntary organizations have been active in youth work for many years, some indeed since the nineteenth and early twentieth centuries—for example, the Boys' Brigade, the Boy Scouts Association, the Girl Guides Association. The basic aim of the voluntary organizations has been to provide for young people leisure-time activities which they will enjoy and which will be beneficial to them in their growth towards adulthood; hence the large number of organizations, each with its particular pattern of activities. There is evidence, however, that some of these activities are no longer so attractive to young people, and falling membership has led some of the traditional organizations to a reappraisal of their work in the light of the contemporary demands of young people. For example, the Haynes Report urged a new structure for the Boys' Brigade, changes in uniform, and a new awards system; and the Boy Scouts Association has now introduced such activities as skiing, pony trekking, canoeing, gliding and sub-aqua work.

At the present time twenty-nine voluntary organizations are in membership of the Scottish Standing Conference of Voluntary Youth Organizations, which considers matters of common interest to these organizations, and seeks to promote the work of the Youth Service in general. In 1965 the twenty-nine organizations were catering for nearly half a million young people spread over some 13,000 local units, staffed by ninety full-time leaders and 37,000 part-time leaders.

As their work is long-established and extensive, the voluntary organizations constitute the senior member of the partnership mentioned.

Education Authorities

Education authorities have the duty to provide adequate facilities for recreation and social and physical training, and this duty they carry out in two main ways: by assisting voluntary organizations and by providing facilities under their own control.

Assistance to voluntary organizations may be in the form of grants towards the provision or maintenance of premises, the provision of leaders or instructors, or permission to use school or other premises. For example, in 1965 about a third of the 13,000 voluntary units had the use of school premises.

Education authorities may themselves provide youth clubs, play centres, gymnasia, swimming baths, playing fields, etc.; they may employ organizers, leaders and instructors. Although only fifteen of the thirty-five education authorities make direct provision of facilities in this way, in 1965 these authorities operated 534 youth centres and clubs, with a membership of 44,000. The number of youth organizers, leaders, and specialist instructors employed by the authorities totalled 3718 of whom sixty-five were employed full-time.[24]

The machinery by means of which education authorities fulfil their obligations with regard to the Youth Service varies from county to county. Some authorities have established youth councils or committees—consisting of official representatives, delegates from the major voluntary youth organizations and others interested in youth work in the area—to advise them on Youth Service matters. In a number of areas there are also local youth panels or district youth committees which advise on the needs of youth in their districts.

Central Government

The third partner is the central government. National responsibility for social and recreational education is the responsibility of the Secretary of State operating through the Scottish Education Department. A branch of the Department deals specifically with this sphere. The work involves the oversight of the arrangements made by education authorities for the provision of facilities, the issue of circulars guiding national policy, and the setting up of committees or bodies to deal with aspects of informal further education.

The Department co-operates regularly with voluntary bodies. It gives direct aid to the national voluntary youth organizations by means of grants towards the costs of administration, organization and training carried out by their headquarters; and indirect aid, via the education authorities, to local units. It provides capital grants of up to 50% of approved cost for the adaptation of club premises and the building of new purpose-built centres.

In 1959 the Secretary of State appointed a Council, now called the Standing Consultative Council on Youth and Community Service, which has the function of promoting the further development of youth and community services, and of fostering co-operation among the statutory authorities and voluntary organizations concerned. The Council provides a valuable link between the central government and the Youth Service as a whole. Although it has no executive powers, and acts in a purely advisory and consultative capacity, the Council has made valuable contributions to youth work. It has organized conferences, conducted and guided publicity, arranged for research and field work, and made recommendations with regard to the training and terms of employment of youth leaders. It is generally referred to as the Kilbrandon Council, after its chairman, Lord Kilbrandon.

Youth Leaders

A major problem in youth work is that of ensuring an adequate supply of suitably qualified and trained leaders. Two reports of the Kilbrandon Council have proved helpful. The first,[25] on the training of part-time leaders, recommended greater co-operation among voluntary and statutory bodies in training at all levels, but particularly at local and regional levels. The second,[26] on the professional training of full-time youth leaders, recommended two types of course of initial training: a basic course of 2 years, and a special short course of two terms. As a result of this second report, Moray House College of Education instituted both courses in 1963, and Jordanhill College of Education instituted the 2-year course in 1964.

At present the pattern of training facilities in Scotland is as follows: at national level there are the full-time courses already mentioned at Moray House and Jordanhill Colleges of Education, and occasionally intensive courses sponsored by the Scottish Education Department and the Kilbrandon Council; at regional level there are courses arranged by regional training organizations which are representative of the statutory bodies and voluntary youth organizations; at local level there are courses provided by education authorities and by voluntary organizations for their own particular needs, and specialized courses of various kinds. In addition, facilities are provided by such servicing organizations as the Scottish Council of Physical Recreation.

In 1966, on the recommendation of the Kilbrandon Council, a board was set up to administer a scheme of national tests in leadership for part-time leaders in youth and community service. The board, which is composed of nominees of relevant bodies, also operates a national information service for the youth and community service in Scotland.

Comment

The history of the Youth Service since the Second World War has been one of boom in the period of widespread idealism which appears to affect all aspects of education immediately after a major war, succeeded by a slump in the 1950's, followed by a revival in the early 1960's. Two events were significantly associated with this revival: the setting up in 1959 of the Kilbrandon Council; and the publication in 1960 of the Albermarle Report.[27] This Report, widely welcomed by most educationists,[28] referred to England and Wales, but many of its features could be translated into a Scottish context—for example its analysis of the changing contemporary scene; its justification of the Youth Service; its expression of aims in terms of association, training, and challenge; its stress on the need for flexibility and variety in the Service; its underlining of the need for training courses for professional youth leaders, and for an imaginative building programme.

Subsequent developments throughout the 1960's have ensured that the provision of facilities for young people is more extensive than ever before; yet only one in every three adolescents takes advantage of this provision, a situation which has caused much soul-searching on the part of all concerned with the Youth Service in Scotland.

Future developments are likely to be along the following lines: an increase in the provision of more adventurous activities— there were 4600 entrants for the Duke of Edinburgh's Award in 1965; the attempt to modernize the image of the traditional uniformed organizations; increased co-operation between voluntary and statutory bodies in the general provision of facilities and activities; further stress on the need for the training of leaders; the more active involvement of education authorities in the direct provision of clubs and centres; the appointment to various secondary schools and colleges of further education of youth leaders or youth tutors, a development likely to be stimulated by the raising of the school-leaving age to 16 in 1970. Finally, there may well be an integration of provision of leisure-time occupations for "youth" with the provision of similar opportunities for the whole of the population. This appears to many to be the most practical way of developing the Youth Service, especially in new housing areas. In this case we may well see specially planned buildings with areas for social activities, quiet rooms for lectures, discussions and relaxation, craft rooms, coffee bar, floodlit outdoor areas—a concept of a centre far removed from the dingy draughty hall in which many youth organizations currently meet. The extended title of the Kilbrandon Council, covering youth *and* community service, may be a significant pointer in this direction.

REFERENCES AND NOTES

1. BURGESS, T., *A Guide to English Schools*, Penguin Books, 1964, p. 156.
2. Education (Scotland) Act, 1946, Section 1 (5). The current regulations governing further education in Scotland are: *The Further Education (Scotland) Regulations, 1959.* See also Scottish Education Department: Circular No. 405: *Further Education*, 31st Mar. 1959.
3. Scottish Education Department: *Further Education*. A Report of the Advisory Council on Education in Scotland, Cmd. 8454, Edinburgh, H.M.S.O., 1952, Chapter V.

4. WHITEHEAD, A. N., *The Aims of Education*, London, Macmillan, 1929, Chapter 4.
5. The Scottish system is thus simpler than the English, with its CAT's, Regional Colleges, Area Colleges, and Local Colleges.
6. *Technical Education*, Cmd. 9703, London, H.M.S.O., 1956.
7. For details of establishments and courses see Scottish Education Department: *Further Education in Scotland. Directory of Day Courses 1965–66*, June 1965. (Issued annually.)
8. For details see Scottish Education Department: Rules 1. *Arrangements and Conditions for the award of National Certificates and Diplomas*, Edinburgh, H.M.S.O., 1964, Appendix I.
9. *Ibid.*, Appendix II.
10. Table based on details contained in Scottish Education Department: *Further Education in Scotland. Directory of Day Courses 1965–66*.
11. For a concise account of the origin and development of such courses to that date see Scottish Education Department: *Education in Scotland in 1959*, Cmnd. 1018, Edinburgh, H.M.S.O., 1960, Chapter 2.
12. Ministry of Education: *15 to 18*, London, H.M.S.O., 1960, Vol. II, Part Three.
13. Department of Education and Science: *Day Release*, London, H.M.S.O., 1964.
14. Scottish Technical Education Consultative Council: *Sixth Report*, year ending 31st July 1965.
15. Scottish Education Department: *Future Recruitment and Training of Teachers for Further Education in Scotland*, Edinburgh, H.M.S.O., 1965.
16. Scottish Education Department: *Conditions of Service of Teachers in Further Education in Scotland*, Edinburgh, H.M.S.O., 1965.
17. For an early interpretation of the function of these institutions see Scottish Education Department: *Compulsory Day Continuation Classes*. Fourth Report of the Advisory Council on Education in Scotland, Edinburgh, H.M.S.O., 1943. For a more recent interpretation see Ministry of Education: *15 to 18*, London, H.M.S.O., 1959, Vol. I, Part Four.
18. Scottish Education Department: *Further Education. A Report of the Advisory Council on Education in Scotland*, Cmd. 8454, Edinburgh, H.M.S.O., 1952, Para. 236.
19. Scottish Education Department: *Education in Scotland in 1965*, Cmnd. 2914, Edinburgh, H.M.S.O., 1966, Table 14, p. 114.
20. Based on *Report of the Universities Council for Adult Education 1964–65*, Tables 1, 3, and 8.
21. For an interesting account of methods of approach and problems encountered see DEES, N. (ed.), *Approaches to Adult Education*, Oxford, Pergamon Press, 1965.
22. The University of Glasgow Extra-Mural Committee: *Annual Report 1964–65*, Appendix A, Table IV.
23. *Report of the Universities Council for Adult Education 1964–65*, p. 7.
24. Scottish Education Department: *Education in Scotland in 1965*, Cmnd. 2914, Edinburgh, H.M.S.O., 1966, p. 49.

25. Standing Consultative Council on Youth Service in Scotland: *The Training of Part-Time Leaders*, 1961. See also *Progressive Joint Training of Part-time Youth Leaders*, 1966.
26. Standing Consultative Council on Youth Service in Scotland: *Recommendations on the Long-term Provision of Professional Training for Youth Leaders*, 1962.
27. Ministry of Education: *The Youth Service in England and Wales*, Cmnd., 929, London, H.M.S.O., 1960.
28. For a provocative "anti-Albemarle" thesis, however, see MUSGROVE, F., *Youth and the Social Order*, London, Routledge & Kegan Paul, 1964.

In addition to the publications referred to above, useful information on technical education will be found in the following:

Scottish Education Department: *Technical Education.* A Report of the Advisory Council on Education in Scotland, Cmd. 6786, Edinburgh, H.M.S.O., 1946.

Scottish Education Department: *Technical Education in Scotland*, Edinburgh, H.M.S.O., 1953.

Scottish Education Department: *Technical Education in Scotland. The Pattern for the Future*, Cmnd. 1245, Edinburgh, H.M.S.O., 1961.

Each annual report of the Department has a chapter on current developments in the field of further education in general.

CHAPTER 11

The Universities

As THE development of universities was omitted from the first chapter on the historical development of the educational system, this chapter begins with a brief historical outline, before turning to an examination of the Scottish universities as they exist today.

HISTORICAL OUTLINE

Scots have always shown a particular concern for higher education, but from the twelfth to the early fifteenth centuries Scottish youths who wished to carry their education beyond the grammar or burgh school level had to go to Oxford, Cambridge, Paris, Bologna, and other continental universities.

In the fifteenth century, however, no fewer than three universities were founded in Scotland: St. Andrews in 1411, Glasgow in 1451, and Aberdeen (King's College) in 1494. To begin with, virtually only the Faculty of Arts flourished, the curriculum being arranged in the two divisions typical of all medieval universities: the Trivium, consisting of Grammar, Logic and Rhetoric; and the Quadrivium, comprising Arithmetic, Geometry, Music, and Astronomy. The student was examined for the degree of Bachelor of Arts in the middle of the third year, and for that of Master of Arts at the end of the fourth year. The "regenting system" operated, under which each student was assigned to a regent who took him through the whole course of studies up to graduation. With regard to curriculum, age of students, and discipline, the universities in their early days were more like secondary schools.

The scheme set forth in the *First Book of Discipline* envisaged the universities as forming the coping-stone of a national system of education. An 8-year course was planned for students from ages 16 to 24, 3 years to be devoted to studies in Arts, and 5 years to professional studies in Medicine, Law, or Divinity. The internal organization of the universities was considered in some detail, and although the scheme for a national system of education did not materialize, the proposals made, plus the general impact of the Reformation, had some effect on the universities. For example, Andrew Melville abolished the regenting system and remodelled the teaching in various ways, first of all at Glasgow University, where he was Principal from 1574 to 1580, and later at St. Andrews.

Edinburgh University was established by Royal Charter in 1582 on the initiative of the Town Council. It was thus not an independent institution, like the other three universities, but in respect of such aspects as curriculum and appointment of professors was subject to the municipality. This situation led to various conflicts but it was not until the passing of the Universities (Scotland) Act, 1858, that Edinburgh University obtained a constitution similar to those of the other three universities.

Marischal College, Aberdeen, was founded in 1593, and although various efforts were subsequently made to bring Marischal College and King's College under the same authority, the union of the two into the University of Aberdeen was not brought about until 1860, as a consequence of the passing of the Universities (Scotland) Act, 1858.

In the seventeenth and eighteenth centuries, a 4-year course leading to the award of the M.A. degree was the common pattern in all the universities, the curriculum consisting of Greek, Logic, Moral Philosophy and Natural Philosophy. There was also teaching in Theology, Medicine and Law. The regenting system, which had been reintroduced, was the accepted system of the seventeenth century, but throughout the eighteenth century regents were replaced by specialist professors, a move which progressively raised the standard of teaching. Lectures were given in

Latin, and students were expected to converse in Latin, as late as the eighteenth century. Another striking feature of university life was the extreme youth of many of the students; it was not uncommon for a student to matriculate at age 13 or 14, and graduate at age 17 or 18.

In the nineteenth century the development of the universities was largely determined by the reports of several Royal Commissions and two important Acts of Parliament. The reports of 1831 and 1858 led to the passing of the Universities (Scotland) Act, 1858, which introduced major changes in the constitution, administration and teaching of all the universities. For example, it instituted in each university a University Court, defined the powers of the existing Senatus Academicus in each university, and introduced to each a new advisory body, the General Council. An executive commission set up by the Act was empowered, among other things, to draw up uniform conditions for courses of study and the award of degrees. As a consequence, regulations were made for degrees in Arts, Law, and Medicine, and the basis was laid for developments in Divinity. For example, in Arts the curriculum was prescribed for the 4-year course for the ordinary degree of M.A., and graduation with honours was introduced.

The report of the Royal Commission which sat from 1876–8 served as a basis for the Universities (Scotland) Act, 1889, which remodelled the constitution of the Scottish universities. As this Act has largely governed the workings of the four older universities in the twentieth century, the composition and functions of the University Court, Senatus Academicus, and General Council are described in some detail in the next section of this chapter.

The 1889 Act also set up an executive commission with powers to deal with a variety of matters, including the granting of degrees and the institution of new degrees. In Arts, regulations for the ordinary degree of M.A. were altered to allow an increased choice of subjects, and the normal length of the course was reduced to three sessions; the choice of honours groups was widened, and three grades of honours introduced. New Faculties of Science were created in all the universities, although the pattern of graduation at ordinary and honours levels of the B.Sc. degree was not instituted until about 1921. In Medicine, the course was extended from 4 to 5 years, and the pattern of M.B., Ch.B. established.

As a result of ordinances of the commissioners, University College, Dundee, which had been opened in 1883, was affiliated to and made part of St. Andrews University in 1897; and from 1892 women were admitted to graduation in any faculty of a university, at the discretion of the University Court, on practically the same terms as men.

In the twentieth century various factors have influenced university development: the greatly increased demand for higher education; the general expansion of knowledge; the creation of completely new branches of study; the national need for scientists and technologists; and so on. As a consequence, new buildings have been built, new chairs founded, new departments formed, new subjects introduced. New degrees have been instituted and changes in existing requirements have been made. Not surprisingly, the existing provision of university education proved inadequate. Two former central institutions, the Royal College of Science and Technology, Glasgow, and the Heriot-Watt College, Edinburgh, were raised to university status, the former in 1964 as Strathclyde University, the latter in 1966 as the Heriot-Watt University. A completely new foundation, the University of Stirling, receives its first students in 1967; and Queen's College, Dundee, becomes the separate University of Dundee, also in 1967.

Thus Scotland, having had four universities for the best part of four centuries, finds herself, in a space of four years, with eight.

INTERNAL GOVERNMENT AND ADMINISTRATION

The older Scottish universities derive their constitution from the Universities (Scotland) Acts of 1858 and 1889, amended by the Universities (Scotland) Act, 1966. Although there are variations in detail the basic system of government is the same for all four universities. What follows describes the position at Glasgow University.

The Chancellor, who is elected for life by the General Council, is the titular head of the university. His functions, however, are entirely ceremonial and advisory. The Rector, who is elected by the undergraduates, serves a 3-year period of office. He is traditionally an important national figure, often in politics, and as Rector is mainly concerned with representing the students on the University Court. The Principal and Vice-Chancellor, who is appointed by the Crown, is the most important and powerful figure in the university, being responsible for shaping and guiding policy. He participates in the main governing bodies of the university—for example, he is president of the Senate and *ex officio* member of the University Court and General Council.

The University Court consists of nineteen members: the Rector; the Principal; the Lord Provost of Glasgow; one assessor nominated by the Chancellor, one by the Rector, and one by the Lord Provost, Magistrates, and Town Council of Glasgow; four assessors elected by the General Council, and six elected from among its members by the Senate, of whom at least two are readers or lecturers; up to three persons, co-opted by the University Court, of whom not more than one may hold an appointment in the university.[1] The University Court, as the supreme governing body, administers the whole property and revenue of the university, and has extensive powers, exercisable by ordinance or by resolution, with regard to all major matters affecting the university.[2] Much of the work of the Court is carried out by specialist sub-committees.

The Senate consists of the Principal, all the professors, and certain readers and lecturers. The 1966 Act provided for an increased representation of non-professorial staff: not less than one-third of the Senate now consists of readers and lecturers elected by the readers and lecturers of the university.[3] The Senate regulates and superintends the teaching and discipline of the university. As the Senate is a large and somewhat unwieldy body, a great deal of its work is carried out by various committees.

The Faculties function as committees of the Senate, which remits business to them for consideration.

The General Council consists of the Chancellor, the members of the University Court, the Senate, readers and lecturers who have held their appointments for at least 1 year, and all the graduates of the university. The functions of the General Council are almost entirely advisory; it has the right to consider all questions affecting the well-being and prosperity of the university, and to make representations on such questions to the University Court. The General Council acts through two statutory half-yearly meetings, and through three main committees.[4]

Mention must also be made of the Students' Representative Council, the official means of communication between students and the university authorities. The SRC, which consists of student representatives elected at the beginning of each session, furthers the educational interests of students, promotes their social life, and through its committees operates various student services.

Reference was made above to the making of ordinances by the University Court. The 1858 and 1889 Acts required that legislation by ordinance of any of the four older universities be submitted to the Courts of the other three, then to the Privy Council and to Parliament. Thus the procedure for founding a chair, or carrying out any major changes in curricula, was rather slow and clumsy. The Robbins Committee was strongly critical of this situation, and recommended that the Universities (Scotland) Act, 1889 should be repealed, and the constitutions of the four older universities correspondingly amended.[5] The government eventually decided on amendment rather than repeal of the 1889 Act, and the Universities (Scotland) Act, 1966, removed the requirement of submitting draft ordinances to the Courts of the other three older universities, and provided that much of the business formerly done by ordinance would henceforth be executed by resolution of the Court after internal consultation. The Act also empowered each of the four universities to apply for a charter making fresh provision for its constitution; after any of the universities secures such a charter, the Universities (Scotland) Acts will cease to apply to it.

These Acts do not apply to the newer universities, which have their own charters, and regulate their own affairs, subject to a certain amount of oversight by the Privy Council.

UNIVERSITY AUTONOMY AND GOVERNMENT CONTROL

Universities are independent institutions and have a large measure of control over their own affairs. However, since university education is of importance to the nation's economy, and since public money constitutes over 80 % of university revenue, the government has a substantial interest in university finance and development. The machinery for giving effect to this interest without impairing university autonomy is the University Grants Committee, established in 1919.

The Committee consists of a full-time chairman, a deputy chairman, and twenty other members appointed by the Secretary of State for Education and Science. Most of the members of the Committee are actively engaged in university teaching or research; the rest are drawn from other forms of education, from industry, and from research establishments. The Committee's terms of reference are, broadly: to inquire into the financial needs of university education in Great Britain; to advise the government as to the application of any grant made by Parliament towards meeting these needs; to collect, examine, and make available information relating to university education throughout the United Kingdom; to assist the preparation and execution of plans for the development of the universities in order to ensure that they are fully adequate to national needs.

With regard to university finance, the Committee has a twofold task: to advise the Treasury on the total money to be made available to the universities; and to allocate the total provision among the universities.

Government grants to universities are of two kinds, recurrent and non-recurrent. Non-recurrent grants are given on an annual basis for capital development, and are allocated by the UGC to specific building projects. The value of the building programme as a whole is controlled by the Treasury, after consultation with the Committee. Total non-recurrent grants to the universities amounted in 1957–8 to £10·7 million; in 1964–5 to £62 million, including £7·3 million to Scottish universities.

Recurrent grants, which are in the main block grants in aid of general university expenditure, are calculated for periods of five academic financial years, usually on a rising scale for each year of the quinquennium. The procedure is for the Committee to undertake a programme of visitations to the universities to discuss with them their needs for the coming quinquennium. After each university has submitted to the Committee particulars of its quinquennial estimates and development plans, the Committee submits its recommendations to the Chancellor of the Exchequer. Thereafter the government decides on the total amount of the recurrent grant for each of the 5 years, and the Committee allocates to each university a share of the total. Total recurrent grants made available amounted in 1957–8 to £34 million; in 1964–5 to £89·6 million, including £13·6 million to Scottish universities.[6]

The government, by retaining responsibility for the overall level of grants, can therefore determine the overall extent of university development; it can also, in conformity with academic advice, influence the direction of development. But since, in the case of non-recurrent grants, the UGC bases its advice to the government on estimates submitted by individual universities, each university has considerable control over the extent and direction of its development. Moreover, the fact that recurrent grants are in the main block grants, and once received are allocated internally at the discretion of individual universities, ensures for each university a considerable measure of autonomy in carrying out its work.

Thus the UGC serves as a "buffer" device between government and university, and plays a vital part in effecting a compromise between the potentially conflicting requirements of government control and university autonomy. This autonomy is further safeguarded by the fact that, within this financial framework, the universities are free to determine the content of curricula, the methods of teaching employed, the balance between teaching and research, the standard of the degrees awarded, and so on. They have also autonomy with regard to the selection of students and, in general, the appointment of staff.[7]

ENTRANCE REQUIREMENTS

Entry to one of the four ancient universities is governed by a standard minimum set of Entrance Requirements prescribed by the Scottish Universities Entrance Board, which was set up in 1918, and has its headquarters in St. Andrews. Each of the four universities is represented on the Board, and each student entering upon a degree course at any of these universities must possess the Board's Certificate of Attestation of Academic Fitness.

The regulations of the Entrance Board are contained in "Announcements" published by the Board annually on 1st February. The present requirements, in terms of the Scottish Certificate of Education, are for four passes on the Higher grade, or three passes on the Higher grade provided two are at Credit standard (60%), or one is at Very Good standard (70%). The subjects which are accepted as qualifying for the Certificate of Attestation of Academic Fitness are arranged in groups, and there are stipulations with regard to the groups from which the passes must be drawn. Rules are laid down for holders of other certificates, for example the English General Certificate of Education and certificates awarded by certain foreign examining bodies. The Board also conducts its own Preliminary Examinations, and candidates who attain the appropriate standards qualify for the Certificate of Attestation of Academic Fitness.

It must be stressed that the Board's Certificate does not guarantee acceptance by any Scottish university, since admission is determined by individual Faculty requirements, and also by the number of places available; in recent years the shortage of university places has led to competition in which the gap between the Entrance Requirements of the Board and actual entry conditions has widened considerably.

This situation, plus the fact that the new universities—Strathclyde, Heriot-Watt, and Stirling—set their own entrance standards, has led to considerable criticism of the Entrance Board and speculation as to its future. To date the Board has performed three functions of fundamental importance: it has laid down minimum entrance requirements; it has passed all applicants through a preliminary screening process, thus simplifying the task of selection for the universities; and it has assessed the equivalence to Scottish requirements of the qualifications held by students from overseas, building up in the process invaluable records of precedents which individual universities could not easily replace. It would seem unwise to dispense entirely with a body which performs such useful functions; whether or not it will be possible to create a new Entrance Board, representative of the eight Scottish universities, and with functions acceptable to all, remains to be seen.

COURSES

The traditional faculties of the four older universities are those of Arts, Science, Medicine, Law and Divinity. In some cases additional faculties have been established—for example Engineering and Social Science. Within most faculties a variety of courses is provided, and recent years have seen the introduction of new subjects and new groupings of subjects, a process which is likely to be accelerated as a result of developments in the four new universities.

Courses for degrees in Arts and Science are normally of 3 years' duration for an ordinary degree, and 4 years (sometimes 5) for an honours degree. Courses for degrees in Medicine normally last for 6 years, Dentistry 5 years, and Veterinary Science 5 years. All the universities offer courses leading to various higher degrees, and an important feature of Scottish university education is the continuing increase in the numbers of post-graduate students, especially in Science.

One of the most distinctive features of the Scottish university system when compared with the English is the 3-year course for the ordinary degree of M.A. or B.Sc. The pattern of these courses —generally of five subjects, two of which are studied for two sessions—reflects the traditional Scottish preference for a broad general education. The ordinary degree has retained much of its old prestige in Scotland; it is still the first choice of over 30% of Arts faculty entrants. This is in marked contrast to the position in England where the pass degree is the first choice of only about 5% of students.

The Scottish emphasis on breadth is further reflected in the fact that students who intend to take an honours degree are required to take classes additional to their honours subjects in the first 2 years. This again contrasts with the situation in England where honours students are usually engaged from their first year on courses involving a high degree of specialization, often in a single subject. Such specialization, following on the more specialized work of English sixth forms, means that students in English universities reach the same honours standard in 3 years that Scottish students reach in four.

The new universities have introduced changes in the typical Scottish degree structure. For example at Strathclyde University the first degree in Arts is a B.A., the curriculum for the ordinary degree in the School of Arts and Social Studies consisting of thirteen classes, of which four from one subject group form the first principal subject, and two from another subject group form the second principal subject. The curriculum for the honours B.A. degree comprises the curriculum for the ordinary degree plus four honours classes, which may be devoted entirely to the student's first principal subject, or divided equally between his two principal subjects.

At Stirling University the courses to be provided will lead, whatever the area of study, to the degree of B.A., ordinary or honours, and honours degrees will be awarded in single and in combined subjects. The intention is to concentrate to begin with on the arts, the basic sciences, and the social sciences, and to provide for combinations of subjects which cut across conventional divisions between the arts and the sciences. An honours course in Technological Economics is planned to combine studies in social science, scientific principles, mathematics, and case studies in applied science, with a view to equipping graduates for careers in industry and the public service. It is also proposed to provide a course which will combine academic studies, the study of education, and practical teacher training, and will thus lead to an honours degree plus a professional qualification as a teacher.

These and various other developments have been warmly welcomed in Scotland. It must be admitted, however, that Scottish universities tend on the whole to be conservative, and that there has been comparatively little of the bold experimentation which has characterized many of the courses provided by some of the newer universities in England.

METHODS OF TEACHING

University teaching is generally conducted by means of lectures, discussion periods, and practical classes. Discussion periods are of two main types: tutorials, which are usually for one to four students, and seminars, which are usually attended by more than four students. Students in Scottish universities have long suspected that they were provided with more lectures and practical classes, and fewer discussion periods than university students south of the border, and that in general they worked longer hours and received less guidance in their work. Appendix Two of the Robbins Report confirmed their suspicions.[8]

The average hours of teaching received by undergraduates in Scottish universities is 17 per week; of this total just over $9\frac{1}{2}$ hours are spent in lectures, just under $1\frac{1}{2}$ hours in discussion periods, $5\frac{1}{2}$ hours in practical classes, and $\frac{1}{2}$ hour in other periods. The average hours of teaching received by British undergraduates as a whole is $14 \cdot 8$ per week, of which 8 are spent in lectures, over $1\frac{1}{2}$ in discussion periods, $4\frac{1}{2}$ in practical classes, and $\frac{1}{2}$ hour in other periods.

Nearly three-quarters of all students at Scottish universities would like to have changes made in the amount of time they spend receiving different types of teaching: 40% would like more seminars and 53% would like more tutorials. Surprisingly, only 14% would like fewer lectures—and 8% would like more.[9] In spite of this clear demand for more seminars and tutorials, when asked if they would want this if it meant a reduction in the number and range of lectures offered, over 50% of the students in Scottish universities said they would not.[10] Thus the lecture, traditionally entrenched in Scottish university teaching, is generally acceptable to students. The frequent criticisms recorded are usually criticisms of poor lectures or bad lecturing.[11]

It should be noted in passing that the mass lecture audience is the exception; only 13% of lectures given in Scottish universities are to audiences of 100 students or more, and almost half of all lectures are to audiences of under 20.

The Hale Committee makes the point that "the main purpose of a university education, apart from the acquisition of know-ledge, should be to teach the student to work on his own and think for himself".[12] The problem is to ensure that the methods of teaching employed contribute to the attainment of these ends. Many departments in Scottish universities are not at all complacent about their teaching methods, and at the present time thought is being given to such diverse aspects as lecturing technique, the balance between lectures and discussion periods, methods of handling tutorial and seminar groups, the use of closed-circuit television, and the possibilities of programmed learning.

STAFF

It may be useful to begin with some basic facts about university teachers. There were just under 5000 full-time university teachers in British universities in 1938–9, 11,000 in 1954–5, and over 17,000 in 1964–5. Of the 1964–5 total, 2979 were in Scottish universities.[13]

The various grades of university teachers, and the percentage of teachers in each grade in Scottish universities are as follows (Great Britain figures are in brackets): Professors: 11% (12%); Readers: 3% (6%); Senior Lecturers: 18% (13%); Lecturers: 50% (47%); Assistant Lecturers: 13% (10%); Demonstrators: 1% (2%); Research staff: 2% (4%); Others: 1% (6%).[14]

Unlike school teaching, university teaching is predominantly a male profession. Only 10% of all university teachers are women —the figure in Scotland is as low as 7%—and only 2% of all professors are women.[15]

University teachers are highly qualified academically. Of those with first degrees, 81% have an honours degree of a British university, and of those who took honours, 59% have first-class degrees. The figure for Scotland is 65%, which is second only to Oxford and Cambridge, where 76% of the staff with honours degrees have first-class honours.[16]

The Robbins Committee estimated that the number of university teachers which will be required in Britain will be 26,000 by 1973–4, and over 42,000 by 1980–1.[17] In order to attract such numbers of suitably qualified staff, adequate salaries and conditions of service are necessary. The salaries of university teachers are established by the government in consultation with the UGC, present scales for non-medical teachers being as follows:

Professors	Minimum £3570. Maximum £4990.
Readers	A range of scales with varying maxima up to £3415.
Senior Lecturers	A range of scales with varying maxima up to £3415.
Lecturers	£1470–£2630.
Assistant Lecturers	£1105–£1340.

Perhaps more important than salary are such factors as promotion prospects; adequate accommodation, library facilities, and equipment; the availability of technical and clerical assistance; and the provision of funds for research. It would appear to be shortcomings in these areas which act as determinants in the much-publicized "brain drain" to North America and elsewhere.

One aspect of working conditions, for students as well as teachers, is the student/staff ratio. In Scottish universities this is just over 8:1, slightly less favourable than that for British universities as a whole. Yet the improvement in Scottish universities has been relatively great; in 1938–9 the ratio for Britain was 10:1, that for Scotland 14:1.[18]

The two main functions of a university teacher are those of teaching and research. In the survey conducted for the Robbins and Hale Committees, university teachers were asked to classify their own professional work during a fortnight in February, 1962.[19] In the case of Scottish university teachers, 34% of their professional working time was spent on teaching, 27% on research, 12% on private study, 9% on administration, 12% on other work within the university, and 6% on work outside the university. These figures were close to those for British university teachers as a whole. Thus during term university teachers spend on average a third of their working time on teaching, including preparation and correction of students' work, and just under a third on research.

On the relationship between teaching and research the Robbins Committee commented: "There is no borderline between teaching and research; they are complementary and overlapping activities."[20] This is so, but the question of emphasis arises, and the fact that promotion depends on research and publications, rather than on teaching ability, may well determine where the university teacher's interests lie. Certainly few are trained to teach; in the survey mentioned above only 7% had had a course of professional teacher-training; but 58% of all university staff—65% in Scotland—considered that newly appointed staff should receive some form of organized instruction or guidance on how to teach.[21]

STUDENTS

The number of full-time students in Scottish universities rose from 10,000 in 1938–9 to 14,000 in 1954–5, and to over 25,000 in 1964–5. The Robbins Committee estimated that the total number of places needed in Scottish universities will be 40,000 by 1973–4, and 55,000 by 1980–1.[22]

The 25,283 students attending Scottish universities in 1964–5 were distributed among the universities as follows:[23] Aberdeen: 3241; Edinburgh: 7563; Glasgow: 6902; Strathclyde: 4107; St. Andrews (including Queen's College, Dundee): 3470. Of the total number of students, 45% were studying arts or social studies, 21% pure science, 16% applied science, 12% medicine, 2·5% dentistry, 2% veterinary science, and 1·5% agriculture and forestry.[24]

The social class composition of the university population is of interest, because of the suggestion sometimes made that Scottish universities are "more working class" than English universities, that is, that they contain a greater proportion of students with working class backgrounds. It is difficult to get evidence to substantiate this claim; indeed the Robbins Committee quotes figures which show that a quarter of all undergraduates in Scottish universities come from the families of manual workers, and this proportion is exactly that for British undergraduates as a whole. The main deviations from the average are in Wales, where the proportion of students from working class backgrounds was found to be as high as 40%, and in Oxford and Cambridge, where the proportions were only 13% and 9% respectively.[25]

The Undergraduate Survey for the Robbins Committee provided some interesting information about the school backgrounds of university undergraduates, highlighting the relative position with regard to independent schools north and south of the border. In Scottish universities, 65% of students come from public (that is, education authority) schools, 19% from grant-aided schools, and 16% from independent schools. The corresponding figures for England and Wales are 62%, 14%, and 24%, those for Oxford and Cambridge being 30%, 17%, and 53%.[26]

Both social class and school background may well affect preparation for university life, and the transition from school to university has given cause for concern in Scotland, as elsewhere. As yet, only a few education authorities have been experimenting with schemes to prepare final-year pupils for the changes involved.[27] The Hale Committee reported the results of a survey conducted in the United Kingdom in autumn 1961 to ascertain whether new students obtained "instruction or advice on the nature of university work, and generally on how to be a university student".[28] Forty-seven per cent of the men and 62% of the women received advice at school, usually from school staff. At some universities new students are invited, often through the Students' Union, to come up to the university for advice before formal enrolment. Forty-nine per cent said they had been offered such an opportunity, but only 27% in Scotland.

With regard to supervision during their first degree course, the Undergraduate Survey for the Robbins Committee revealed that 72% of undergraduates at Scottish universities had at least one official supervisor of their work, a figure comparable to that for all British undergraduates. However, only 8% of Scottish undergraduates met their supervisor once a fortnight or more often; the figure for all British undergraduates was 42%, and for those at Oxford and Cambridge 95%. In addition, 40% of all undergraduates were allocated to someone, other than the academic supervisor, for advice on personal matters, the proportion varying from 68% at Oxford and Cambridge to 25% in Scotland.[29]

Thus with regard to guidance about coming to university, academic supervision, and advice on personal matters, Scottish students appear to fare less well than students in British universities in general.

Closely tied to these issues is the problem of "wastage", the term used to describe students who leave university without obtaining a degree. The wastage rate for students in arts, science, and technology is about 14%, and tends to be higher in technology than in science, and in science than in arts. The wastage rate also varies considerably from one university to another.[30]

The reasons for wastage are complex, and blame has been attached to university teachers, the students themselves, the courses provided, the methods of teaching employed, and so on. The UGC adopted the main categories of academic, personal, and disciplinary reasons, and over 80% of all who leave without achieving success do so for academic reasons. In view of the fact that about 50% of all wastage occurs in the first year at the university, there is a particular moral for the schools in this statement by a Scottish educationist: "Today's student frequently suffers from an inability to adapt to the new freedom of the university after the authoritarian atmosphere to which he has been accustomed for at least 12 years."[31]

As indicated by many of the figures given in this chapter, the key word in present-day higher education is "expansion". This affects all aspects of university life: the number of universities, the size of universities, numbers of students and staff, the courses provided, and even methods of teaching. Expansion may also affect the quality of work done, and, in spite of the comforting words of the Robbins Committee about the "pool of ability",[32] many in university circles see the main task facing the universities as that of ensuring that quality is not sacrificed in the interest of quantity. This is one area of the educational system in which the traditional Scottish emphasis on academic excellence is surely not misplaced.

REFERENCES AND NOTES

1. Universities (Scotland) Act, 1966, Section 2 and Schedule 1.
2. *Ibid.*, Sections 3–6 and Schedule 2.
3. *Ibid.*, Section 7.
4. *Ibid.* Sections 9 and 10 contain certain changes affecting General Councils.
5. Committee on Higher Education: *Higher Education*. Report of the Committee appointed by the Prime Minister under the Chairmanship of Lord Robbins 1961–63, mnd. C2154, London, H.M.S.O., 1963, Para. 690. This report, of enormous importance for British higher education, will be quoted frequently in this chapter. Referred to below as *Robbins Report*.
6. UGC: *Returns from Universities and University Colleges in receipt of Exchequer Grant*. Academic Year 1964–1965, Cmnd. 3106, London, H.M.S.O., 1966, Table 13, p. 47.

7. For a consideration of the constituents of academic freedom see *Robbins Report*, Paras. 711–24.
8. *Robbins Report*, Appendix Two (B), Part IV, Section 1.
9. *Ibid.*, Appendix Two (B), p. 262, Table 9, and p. 264, Table 10.
10. *Ibid.*, Appendix Two (B), p. 265, Table 11.
11. See, for example, the memoranda from the National Union of Students and the Scottish Union of Students to the Hale Committee. UGC: Report of the Committee on *University Teaching Methods*, London, H.M.S.O., 1964, Appendixes III and IV.
12. *Ibid.*, Para. 249.
13. UGC: *Returns from Universities and University Colleges in receipt of Exchequer Grant*. Academic Year 1964–1965, Cmnd. 3106, London, H.M.S.O., 1966, Table 9, p. 36.
14. *Robbins Report*, Appendix Three, p. 16, Table 11.
15. *Ibid.*, Appendix Three, p. 172, Annex G, Table G.1.
16. *Ibid.*, Appendix Three, p. 20, Table 16.
17. *Ibid.*, Appendix Three, p. 135, Table 3.
18. *Ibid.*, Appendix Three, p. 7, Table 4.
19. *Ibid.*, Appendix Three, Part I, Section 10 gives full details.
20. *Ibid.*, Para. 557.
21. *Ibid.*, Appendix Three, p. 88.
22. *Ibid.*, p. 160, Table 44.
23. UGC: *Returns from Universities and University Colleges in receipt of Exchequer Grant*. Academic Year 1964–1965, Cmnd. 3106, London, H.M.S.O., 1966, Table 4, pp. 20–1.
24. *Ibid.*, Table 5, p. 25.
25. *Robbins Report*, Appendix Two (B), p. 429, Annex C, Table C.2.
26. *Ibid.*, Appendix Two (B), p. 9, Table 11.
27. For an interesting example see CRAIGIE, J., From school to university, *Scottish Educational Journal*, 24th July 1964.
28. UGC: Report of the Committee on *University Teaching Methods*, London, H.M.S.O., 1964, Appendixes V and VI.
29. *Robbins Report*, Appendix Two (B), p. 269, Table 15, and p. 273, Table 18.
30. *Ibid.*, Appendix Two (A), pp. 127–9, and Tables 3, 4, and 5.
31. MACKINTOSH, M., *Education in Scotland Yesterday and Today*, Glasgow, Robert Gibson & Sons, 1962, p. 182.
32. *Robbins Report*, Paras. 137–46.

CHAPTER 12

Teachers

ALTHOUGH the parish dominies of the seventeenth to nineteenth centuries are frequently thought of as dedicated and efficient men, this was by no means always the case. As late as 1848 Professor Fleming could say, at the Free Church Assembly, that he had known people "taken from the plough and the loom and pitchforked into a parish school"; and this entry to the school was in the role of teacher, not pupil. It is a long way from this situation to the present close concern of the teaching profession with academic qualifications, professional training, salary and status. The history of this development in Scotland is a fascinating study, but outwith the scope of this book.[1] This chapter deals with the present situation.

THE TRAINING OF TEACHERS

The Training System*

The system of management and administration of teacher-training in Scotland is governed by regulations made by the Secretary of State. The current regulations are *The Teachers (Training Authorities) (Scotland) Regulations, 1958*, and amendments.

Colleges of Education. Training is carried out in ten colleges of education:

Aberdeen College of Education, Aberdeen.

Dundee College of Education, Dundee.

* See page 258, Addendum 1.

Jordanhill College of Education, Glasgow.
Moray House College of Education, Edinburgh.
Notre Dame College of Education, Glasgow.
Craiglockhart College of Education, Edinburgh.
Dunfermline College of Physical Education, Edinburgh.
Callendar Park College of Education, Falkirk.
Craigie College of Education, Ayr.
Hamilton College of Education, Hamilton.

Notre Dame and Craiglockhart Colleges of Education are for Roman Catholic women only; Dunfermline College is for women teachers of physical education, men teachers of physical education being trained in the Scottish School of Physical Education at Jordanhill; Callendar Park, Craigie, and Hamilton Colleges of Education are for non-graduate women teachers only.

Governing Bodies. The 1958 Regulations brought about a considerable devolution of responsibility throughout the training system, giving managers of the colleges more independence, Principals increased powers, and teaching staffs a greater say in the content of courses and in the running of the colleges.

Each college of education now has a governing body composed of representatives of relevant education authorities, universities, teachers, churches, and the Secretary of State, the number of governors varying with the college concerned. A future development in this sphere may well be the appointment of representatives of college staffs to governing bodies. Governors normally hold office for 3 years.

Each governing body exercises a general control over the college of education and everything connected with it. For example, a governing body has functions with regard to the provision of courses; the appointment of Principal and staff; the promotion of research work; the award of diplomas and certificates to students who have successfully completed college courses. Although this is the legal position, in actual fact various functions of a governing body devolve upon the Principal and the administrative or academic staff of the college. It is the Principal who is responsible for the whole organization and discipline of the college, including such matters as the admission of candidates qualified to take the various courses provided, the suspension of any staff member or any student guilty of serious misconduct, the termination of the course of study of any student whose progress is unsatisfactory.

Board of Studies. Each college has a board of studies composed of members of the teaching staff. The function of the board of studies is to advise and assist the Principal with regard to such matters as the content of courses, co-ordination of studies, maintenance of standards, discipline of the students, and other aspects of college life.

Scottish Council for the Training of Teachers. The governing bodies are the fundamental bodies in the training system. From them is built up the Scottish Council for the Training of Teachers, the Regulations ensuring the representation on the Scottish Council of the various interests represented on the governing bodies.[2] The Scottish Council serves as an advisory and co-ordinating body for the whole field of teacher-training in Scotland. It advises the Secretary of State on matters of major importance in teacher-training and, although not concerned with the routine day-to-day administration of the colleges of education, it advises governing bodies with regard to new developments or improvements thought desirable. The Council also has certain specific functions, as detailed in Part IV of the 1958 Regulations.

A standing committee of the Scottish Council deals with the problems of alternative entry qualifications to training, and applications for the exceptional award of teaching certificates or endorsements. A further standing committee, that of the Principals of Colleges of Education, gives general guidance and advice to the Secretary of State and governing bodies.

The Scottish Council has some notable achievements to its credit, particularly the swift establishment of three new colleges of education. It is, however, to be dissolved in the near future, when a few of its functions will be transferred to the new General Teaching Council to be described later, and certain other functions may devolve upon the governing bodies.

Finance of the Training System. Present expenditure of the training authorities is nearly five million pounds per annum. Over half of this expenditure is met by grants payable by the Secretary of State, and just over a quarter by contributions from education authorities, each authority contributing a sum proportioned to the number of certificated teachers in its service. The balance of the expenditure is met from fees and other sources.*

Entry Requirements and Certificates†

The training of teachers in Scotland is at present governed by *The Teachers (Education, Training and Certification) (Scotland) Regulations, 1965*, which came into operation on 1st April, 1965. These Regulations replaced the 1931 Regulations[3] which had become complex, having been amended ten times up to 1962.

Under the new Regulations, three Certificates may be awarded: the Teacher's Certificate (Primary Education); the Teacher's Certificate (Secondary Education); the Teacher's Certificate (Further Education).

For entry to courses leading to the award of Certificates, candidates are required to have certain basic educational qualifications, usually expressed in terms of passes in examinations held at the end of courses of secondary education, plus, for some courses, the possession of an approved diploma, associateship, or degree, with or without honours. Exact details are given in Schedule 1 to the 1965 Regulations, and in the Scottish Education

* See page 258, Addendum 1.
† See page 259, Addendum 2.

Department's *Memorandum on Entry Requirements and Courses, 1966.* What follows is an outline of the general position.

The Teacher's Certificate (Primary Education). There is a course of three sessions for women who usually come straight from school to college. For such students the normal entry requirement in terms of the Scottish Certificate of Education is of passes in at least four subjects on the Higher grade; or in at least three subjects on the Higher grade and in two other subjects on the Ordinary grade; or in at least two subjects on the Higher grade and in four other subjects on the Ordinary grade. These passes must include a pass in English on the Higher grade and a pass in arithmetic or in mathematics. Entry requirements are also expressed in terms of passes in other examinations, for example the University Preliminary Examinations, or the English General Certificate of Education.

There is a course of one session for men and women who already hold a degree of a university in the United Kingdom, or an associateship of a central institution awarded with honours, or an associateship or diploma of a central institution together with an educational qualification as described in the previous paragraph.

There is a course of one session, and in some cases of one term or equivalent for men and women who hold a Teacher's Certificate (Secondary Education) together with an educational qualification as described in the first paragraph.

Where a candidate does not satisfy the prescribed requirements, the Scottish Council determines whether or not the qualifications possessed are acceptable as an appropriate alternative.

The Teacher's Certificate (Secondary Education). There is a course of one session open to men and women holding an approved diploma, associateship, or degree, with or without honours, on condition that the award held attests to the successful study of a subject or combination of subjects which qualifies the holder to teach the subject(s) in a secondary school. This means in practice that ordinary graduates are normally required to have obtained passes in two graduating courses in any subject in which they seek a qualification. Honours graduates may also acquire a subsidiary qualification in subjects other than their honours subjects, if they hold certain relevant degree passes. It is possible for an original award to be appropriately supplemented by a course of study approved by the Scottish Council.

Unless the academic or technical qualification is a university degree or an associateship of a central institution awarded with honours, it must be supported by a general educational requirement expressed in terms of passes in examinations held at the end of courses of secondary education. This applies, for example, to candidates for the Certificate in art; music; commerce; speech and drama; engineering and related subjects; agriculture, horticulture, rural economy; homecraft; nautical subjects. Although successful candidates are all awarded the Teacher's Certificate (Secondary Education), there are usually separate courses for honours graduates, ordinary graduates, and holders of awards in the above subjects.

There are courses of one, two, and three sessions for candidates for the Certificate in technical subjects, and courses of three sessions for men and women leading to the award of the Certificate in physical education. Each course has its own particular pattern of entry requirements.[4]

The Teacher's Certificate (*Further Education*). The course consists of 2 months' full-time study, followed by a session of supervised teaching employment in further education, and completed by a further 2 months' full-time study.

The course is open to men and women who hold a degree of a Scottish university, an associateship or diploma of a central institution, a diploma of a college of education, a Higher National Diploma, a Higher National Certificate, an Advanced Certificate of the Scottish Council for Commercial, Administrative and Professional Education, or a Certificate of the City and Guilds of London Institute, on condition that the qualification attests to the successful study of a subject or subjects which qualifies the holder to teach the subject(s) in a further education centre. Each candidate must possess such experience in industry or commerce as in the opinion of the Scottish Council is necessary for the teaching of his subject(s); and, unless he holds an associateship with honours of a central institution, or a degree of a university in the United Kingdom, he must hold passes on the Ordinary grade of the Scottish Certificate of Education in English and in either mathematics or such other subjects approved as appropriate.[5]

Each candidate who successfully completes a course of training is awarded a provisional certificate by the Secretary of State on the recommendation of the relevant governing body. The Scottish Council deals with applications for the exceptional award of a provisional certificate from persons who for some reason do not satisfy the requirements of the Regulations.[6]

The holder of a provisional certificate is on probation for 2 years. After each year of service the headmaster of the school in which he is employed submits to the Secretary of State a report on the manner in which the holder has discharged his duties, and on his promise of success as a teacher. The probationer will also be visited by one of H.M. Inspectors. At the end of 2 years the holder applies to the Secretary of State for the award of a certificate in final form, and on the basis of the reports he has received the Secretary of State awards the certificate, or extends the period of probation, or withdraws the provisional certificate.

Certificated teachers who satisfy relevant requirements may have certain special qualifications which are awarded to them entered on the certificate by means of an endorsement. At the present time special qualification may enable the teacher to act as: a principal teacher of a nursery school (women only); an infant mistress (women only); a teacher of one or more categories of pupils requiring special educational treatment; a teacher of backward pupils in secondary schools or departments.

It will be gathered from the above outline that in Scotland great emphasis is laid on qualifications and professional training. There are in general no non-graduate men teachers of general subjects in primary schools; all teachers of academic subjects in secondary schools must be graduates; and all graduates must have a course of professional training. The situation is thus quite different from that which obtains in England.*

Courses

In keeping with the general movement towards devolution already mentioned, the content of courses is now determined by the Principal of the college of education with the advice of the board of studies and with the approval of the governing body; the detailed prescriptions of content in the 1931 Regulations were seen as inconsistent with the greater measure of autonomy in academic matters accorded to the colleges in 1959.

Content varies from course to course, but normally all pre-service training includes supervised teaching practice in schools in accordance with the subject interests of the students; tuition and demonstration in teaching method; and work in such areas as Education, Psychology, Physical Education, Health Education, Religious Education, Speech Training. In addition to such content common to most courses, particular courses have additional relevant subjects of study. A course such as the three-session course for women has to be planned to cater for both the continuation of the general education of the students, and their professional preparation as primary school teachers.

The 1960's constitute a decade of interesting developments in Scottish teacher-training. Experiments are being conducted in areas as diverse as group teaching practice, the use of closed-circuit television, the initial teaching alphabet, forms of cumulative assessment, programmed learning, and the extension of seminar and group tutorial work as a counter-balance to mass lecturing techniques.

* See page 259, Addendum 2.

One of the most important lines of development is that of in-service training. Colleges of education have for many years run vacation courses, week-end courses, and courses of varying length for certificated teachers seeking a further certificate or endorsement; but the rapidity of educational change is likely to cause a considerable expansion of courses of in-service training. Jordanhill is planned to be the main centre for this work, and it may well be that developments in this sphere will cause modifications in the present system of pre-service training.

Two recent developments are of such significance as to merit separate mention: the institution of a 4-year course leading to a B.Ed. degree of a neighbouring university; and the proposal to institute a 4-year course leading to an Associateship of a college of education.

The official impetus to the B.Ed. degree stems from the Robbins Report of 1963, which states: " . . . we recommend that the Colleges of Education should develop courses of 4 years' duration leading to a degree, and that these courses should be of a balanced, concurrent nature, liberal in content and approach, although directed towards the professional work that lies ahead."[7]

The first B.Ed. on such lines in Scotland was instituted in 1965 by Aberdeen University in close co-operation with Aberdeen College of Education. The course is open to men and women holding a Certificate of Fitness of the Scottish Universities Entrance Board. The students matriculate as students both of the university and of the college, and take, concurrently with their degree studies, a course for the Teacher's Certificate (Primary Education) or the Teacher's Certificate (Secondary Education), the combined course lasting 4 years.

The content of the courses and general administration are dealt with by a Board of Studies composed of representatives of the university and college, and college lecturers teaching these courses are recognized for this purpose by the university.

One of the features of the new degree is its grouping of subjects in three categories: "academic" (English, languages, history, geography, Biblical studies, mathematics, various sciences);

"professional" (education and educational psychology); and "practical" (art and crafts, music, physical education, dramatic art). All courses are available on an Ordinary Standard, and some on an Advanced Standard. Every candidate for the degree must pass in seven courses, including at least two academic, at least one practical, and both professional. He must also pass at least one course at Advanced Standard. In this arrangement we see the effect of the traditional pattern of the "ordinary" degree of the Scottish Arts faculty, though the provision for practical subjects at the ordinary level is an innovation. Teaching practice in the first year is in primary schools, so that a decision to take the primary or secondary certificate is postponed till second year.

As the Principal of the college writes:

> Here at last is what Scottish teachers, writers, and educational associations have been demanding for well over a century—a first degree which is genuinely professional. In the four years of his combined course the candidate will spend more than half his time in the direct study of education—its philosophy, psychology and sociology, its teaching methods and practice—much of this at university ordinary level. He may, if he wishes, continue his educational studies to advanced level, and then to a master's degree.[8]

Edinburgh University, in co-operation with Moray House College of Education, introduced a new B.Ed. degree in 1966, as did Glasgow University in co-operation with Jordanhill College of Education. Limitations of space prevent description of these courses, each of which differs in interesting ways from the course provided at Aberdeen. At Dundee the introduction of a B.Ed. degree has been unavoidably delayed by the promise of university status to Queen's College.

The proposal to institute B.Ed. degrees has been generally welcomed both within and outside the teaching profession; not so the suggestion to institute a 4-year course leading to an Associateship of the colleges of education. The proposal was made to the Scottish Council for the Training of Teachers by its Committee of Principals. The Principals recommended the introduction of a 4-year associateship open to men and women with educational qualifications less than those required for a Certificate of Fitness to enter a university. The argument was that such a qualification would produce teachers for primary schools, for the non-academic pupils in secondary schools, and also sub-specialists in practical subjects for either primary or secondary schools.

There were three main aims behind the Principals' proposals: to increase the supply of teachers, especially men teachers, in order to provide for the raising of the school-leaving age in 1970; to provide a different kind of training in order to produce the kind of teachers required for the new courses being planned for non-certificate pupils in secondary schools; and to provide male non-graduate teachers for primary schools. Of these aims, the second was the most compelling.

The teachers' organizations in general expressed disapproval of the idea of an associateship; the Educational Institute of Scotland, for example, was concerned about the lowering of entry qualifications to training, and the influx of non-graduate men to the profession. The Scottish Council, faced with a difficult situation, advised the Secretary of State to proceed with the institution of associateships. At the time of writing the Secretary of State has made no official pronouncement, so that the future of the associateship is uncertain.

SUPPLY, RECRUITMENT, AND DISTRIBUTION

Supply and Demand

In 1965 there were 40,929 certificated teachers employed full-time in public and grant-aided educational establishments. This figure includes re-employed retired teachers over 70 years of age. Of the total, 94% were employed in primary and secondary schools, $4·2\%$ in further education centres and central institutions, $1·5\%$ in colleges of education, and $0·3\%$ in administration. Forty-five per cent of the total were university graduates.

The total number of certificated teachers in service increased by over 5000 in the decade 1955–64. Percentage increases between 1959 and 1964 are shown in Table 14.[9]

TABLE 14

TEACHERS AND STUDENTS: INCREASE IN NUMBERS
BETWEEN 1959 AND 1964

	A	B
College-trained women	3·4	78·2
Honours graduates	4·4	13·4
Ordinary graduates	7·1	30·2
Teachers of practical and aesthetic subjects	13·6	34·5
Total	6·5	49·6

Col. A: percentage increase in numbers of teachers in service.
Col. B: percentage increase in numbers of students entering training.

In spite of the increases noted in Table 14, the demand for teachers has continued to outstrip supply.[10] The shortage of some 3700 in 1965 was expected to fall gradually in the late 'sixties but to rise to one of around 6000 in 1970, with the raising of the school-leaving age to 16. To reduce class sizes to the maxima at present prescribed in England and Wales would require an additional 3000 teachers.

The continuing shortage of teachers has had various undesirable consequences in the schools: over-large classes; "doubling-up" of two classes under one teacher; part-time education for some pupils; and the employment of uncertificated teachers, of which there were 2826 in September 1965, 623 of them having qualifications officially described as "seriously below standard".

The first entry in column A and the first entry in column B of Table 14 highlight the familiar feature of "wastage" through marriage of college-trained women. Of the women who completed training between 1960 and 1964, 26% were no longer in service by October 1964, and a further 17% were married but still teaching at that date. If "wastage" through marriage creates problems of shortage, it is nevertheless true that it is the return to teaching of married women which keeps the schools going; in 1965 married women constituted almost a quarter of the entire teaching force.

Pattern of Shortage

It is not only the overall shortage, but the pattern of shortage which causes concern; some areas are worse off than others. A Working Party set up by the Secretary of State in 1957 devised a scheme of voluntary restraint in recruitment on the part of the better-staffed education authorities. Although this scheme had a certain amount of success, more active measures were thought necessary. Proposals for a salary incentive to operate in schools in certain defined areas of Glasgow and three neighbouring counties proved unacceptable, however, and in February 1965 a committee was set up "to consider measures to secure a more equitable distribution of teachers and to make recommendations". The recommendations, now published, centre round the payment of an additional £100 per annum to teachers in schools designated, according to certain stated criteria, as "schools of temporary shortage", plus the payment in some cases of travelling allowances to teachers in such schools.[11] These proposals are at present under consideration.

The pattern of shortage in terms of qualification likewise causes concern; some categories of teacher are scarcer than others. In 1964, when the overall deficiency was 9%, the most serious shortages were in music (27%), commerce (21%), homecraft (21%), and mathematics (20%). The situation in mathematics is critical; as far back as 1960 about 60% of serving teachers with honours degrees in mathematics were over 50 years of age. It has been suggested that the simple remedy is to award higher salaries to teachers of mathematics, but such a move would certainly meet the united resistance of teachers in general.

The Special Recruitment Scheme

One of the most successful attempts to provide additional teachers has been the Special Recruitment Scheme, which provides financial assistance to late entrants to the profession from other walks of life. The scheme is open to both men and women who satisfy certain requirements. Grants are paid to enable them to take various courses which lead eventually to teaching. It should be noted that this is purely a financial scheme; it does not offer alternative methods of securing recognition as a teacher; there is no "dilution" either of the academic demands or of the course of professional training. The total number completing training under the Scheme, from 1951 to the end of 1965, was 4730.

Suggested Remedies

Various reasons may be given for the shortage of teachers in Scotland. Teachers themselves usually suggest: inadequate pay, low status, poor working conditions, extra-curricular duties, and competition from industry. Not all of these stand up to factual investigation. For example, in spite of fierce competition for educated manpower, teaching is still getting a sizeable proportion of graduates. A study[12] based on Glasgow University showed that over the years 1958–62, 57% of all Glasgow Arts graduates and 40% of all Glasgow Science graduates entered teacher-training. The study claimed that salary was not a major deterrent, and that various factors held by the students to be deterrents revealed a lack of knowledge of such aspects as the work of colleges of education, promotion prospects, and working conditions.

From this and similar evidence it would seem that, in the absence of salary scales which would be obviously and positively attractive, the developments noted below are most likely to go furthest towards meeting the teacher shortage in Scotland.

1. Improved publicity for teaching as a profession—for example, the purposes and content of teacher-training

courses; salary scales in teaching as compared with industry; promotion prospects; general conditions of work; opportunities available for experimental work and research.

2. Provision, especially for graduates, of facilities for "trial runs", under suitably supervised conditions, before a final decision is made to take up teaching.

3. Payment equivalent to the first year's salary for graduates taking the training year.

4. Widespread publicity for the Special Recruitment Scheme.

5. Flexibility with regard to arrangements to facilitate the return to the profession of married women—for example, by arranging for part-time teaching, and/or providing nursery school places for their children.

6. The introduction of a 4-year Associateship course as described earlier in this chapter, and/or the admission of men to the 3-year course for women at colleges of education.*

With regard to other suggestions, it seems clear that the introduction of B.Ed. degrees is unlikely to increase numbers, though if the degree adds lustre to the profession it may have the side-effect of stimulating recruitment; and the payment of salary plus pension to re-employed retired teachers must surely be urged rather as a matter of justice to the individuals concerned than as a very satisfactory method of increasing the supply of qualified teachers.

Even if all these measures are adopted, it is highly probable that there will still be a shortage of teachers. The possibility of reducing maximum class sizes, introducing compulsory part-time education for those who have left school and are under age 18, and in general forging ahead with what are considered desirable developments in education, will almost inevitably result in demand for teachers outstripping supply for the next decade or two.

* At the time of writing, this latter move has just been recommended to the Secretary of State for Scotland by the General Teaching Council.

SALARIES AND SUPERANNUATION

Salary Negotiations: The Scottish Joint Council

Teachers' salaries are prescribed by Regulations made by the Secretary of State. Before making such Regulations the Secretary of State must have regard to recommendations made to him by the Scottish Joint Council for Teachers' Salaries, a body representative of teachers and their employers, the education authorities.

The Scottish Joint Council is the successor to the National Joint Council. In an action raised by certain members of the Scottish Schoolmasters Association in the Court of Session in Edinburgh in December 1963, it was ruled that, since the teachers' representatives on the National Joint Council were all nominated by only one of the teachers' professional organizations, the Educational Institute of Scotland, the Council was not properly constituted in terms of Section 83(4) of the Education (Scotland) Act, 1962.

The new Scottish Joint Council was constituted by the Secretary of State in March 1964. The constitution provided for the appointment to the Council of two teachers nominated by the Scottish Secondary Teachers' Association, and one teacher nominated by the Scottish Schoolmasters Association. Before the year was out, the Scottish Schoolmasters Association was excluded by the Secretary of State from membership of the Council because the Association refused to observe the code of practice with regard to the confidentiality of the Council's proceedings.

The Council consists of a Chairman and thirty other members appointed by the Secretary of State: eighteen of these are teacher members, sixteen of them nominated by the Educational Institute of Scotland, and two by the Scottish Secondary Teachers' Association; twelve are authority members, eight of them nominated by the Association of County Councils in Scotland, and four by the Scottish Counties of Cities Association. In addition there are eight assessors, two appointed by the Secretary of State, three by the Association of Directors of Education in Scotland, and three by the local authority associations.

No recommendations with regard to salaries may be made by the Council unless arrived at with the approval of a majority of all the teacher members and a majority of all the authority members. Procedure is laid down for action in the event of disagreement between these majorities.

It should be stressed that the Scottish Joint Council only makes recommendations to the Secretary of State. He can, and frequently does, alter the recommended salary scales. There is thus reason for the charge that the Council is not a genuine negotiating body at all, and the three main teachers' organizations are united in their dissatisfaction with the present machinery. Discontent reached a new pitch in January 1966, when the Secretary of State substituted salary increases averaging approximately 13% for the Scottish Joint Council's recommendations of nearly 15%. The present machinery is being reviewed, and it seems likely that any new system will involve the Secretary of State at an earlier stage of negotiations.

Salary Scales

Current salary scales, operative from 1st April 1966, are prescribed in *The Teachers' Salaries (Scotland) Regulations, 1966*. Scales for the main categories of teachers in primary and secondary schools are given in Table 15, which also includes a comparison with the scales laid down from 1st July 1961 and 1st April 1963.

Certain responsibility allowances are paid as additions to basic salary scales. Examples of total maximum salaries for teachers in certain promoted posts in primary and secondary schools are given in Table 16.

Separate salary scales are prescribed for teachers in further education, though the same principle of basic scale plus responsibility allowances operates. Basic scales only are shown in Table 17.

Comparisons are frequently drawn, usually by teachers, between salaries in teaching and in other professions. The aim of the exercise is usually to show that teachers are relatively under-paid when compared with doctors, dentists, and lawyers. Such comparisons are difficult to make fairly, and the final result must be a value judgement. What is factually established, however, is that Scottish teachers are better off in the mid-sixties than at any time since the Second World War. Figures published in 1965[13] show how the basic salaries of graduate teachers changed in relation to the cost-of-living index in each of the years 1945–64. With 1945 taken as the base year, and actual salaries adjusted for changes in the approximate purchasing power of the pound based on the consumer price index for the year, the figures show a steady fall to 1950, a static phase to 1956, and a fairly steady rise to 1964, by which time the honours graduate's basic scale had increased at the maximum by 40%, that of the ordinary graduate in secondary schools by 28%, and that of the ordinary graduate in primary schools by 21%.

Nevertheless, despite these genuine increases in real earnings, teachers in Scotland, as in most other countries, believe themselves underpaid considering the importance of the work they do.

Superannuation: Main Scheme

Teachers in Scotland have a contributory superannuation scheme. Each teacher contributes 6% of his salary, and his employer, the education authority, contributes 8%.

The age of compulsory retirement is 70, but a teacher who has attained the age of 60 and has been employed in the requisite class of service for 30 years, qualifies for a retiring allowance. In the case of a teacher who is or has been a married woman, the qualifying period is reduced by the number of completed years, not exceeding 10 years, during which she was, while married, absent from teaching service. The retiring allowance consists of a pension and a "lump sum". The pension is calculated at the rate of one-eightieth of pensionable salary, and the lump sum at the rate of three-eightieths of pensionable salary, for each year of first class service. The maximum number of years of service which

TABLE 15
SALARY SCALES

Basic scales	1st July 1961	1st April 1963	1st April 1966
	£	£	£
SCALE 1 1st or 2nd class honours graduates in secondary schools	840–1600	900–1750	1020–1980
SCALE 2 3rd class honours graduates in secondary schools	810–1600	870–1750	980–1980
SCALE 3 (a) Ordinary graduates in secondary schools (b) Technical graduates or holders of certain technical diplomas (c) Teachers of art (d) Certain teachers of commerce or of music with higher qualifications	770–1330	820–1470	930–1660
SCALE 4 (a) Ordinary graduates in primary schools (b) Teachers of technical subjects with certain supplementary qualifications (c) Women teachers of homecraft (Group III Diploma)	680–1240	730–1370	830–1550

TABLE 15—*continued*

Basic scales	1st July 1961	1st April 1963	1st April 1966
SCALE 5 (a) Teachers of physical education (b) Certain teachers of technical subjects	615–1240	665–1370	750–1550
SCALE 6 (a) Women primary teachers, college trained, 4 years (b) Teachers of music with two approved qualifications (c) Teachers of horticulture or of speech and drama (d) Certain teachers of technical subjects	625–1110	675–1275	760–1440
SCALE 7 (a) Women primary teachers, college trained, 3 years (b) Teachers of music with one approved qualification (c) Women teachers of homecraft (Group I or II Diploma) (d) Teachers of technical subjects (with no additional qualifications)	560–1070	600–1190	680–1340
SCALE 8 Teachers holding certain lesser qualifications	550–900	590–990	670–1120
SCALE 9 Certain uncertificated teachers of technical subjects	530–835	570–920	640–1040

TABLE 16

SALARIES IN CERTAIN PROMOTED POSTS

	1st July 1961	1st April 1963	1st April 1966
	£	£	£
Head teacher of senior secondary school			
with over 1000 secondary pupils	3185	3450	3900
with 300 primary + 300 secondary	2505	2685	3035
Head teacher of junior secondary school			
with over 1000 secondary pupils	2740	2975	3365
with 300 primary + 300 secondary	2315	2525	2855
Head teacher of primary school			
with over 1000 pupils	2040	2220	2510
with 700 pupils	1890	2070	2340
with 300 pupils	1640	1795	2030
Principal teacher of a subject in a large senior secondary school	2050	2275	2575
Special assistant teacher in a senior secondary school	1690	1850	2095
Principal teacher of a subject in a large junior secondary school	1835	2025	2290

TABLE 17

SALARY SCALES IN FURTHER EDUCATION

Basic scales	1st July 1961	1st April 1963	1st April 1966
	£	£	£
GRADE I or GROUP IA 1st or 2nd class honours graduates or other teachers doing advanced work	960–1750	1020–1920	1150–2170
GROUP IB 3rd class honours graduates doing intermediate work	910–1750	970–1920	1100–2170
GRADE II or GROUP II Ordinary graduates or equivalent or non-graduate teachers doing intermediate work	785–1420	835–1560	940–1760
GRADE III or GROUP III Non-graduate teachers (including Diploma holders)	685–1290	735–1420	830–1600

may be taken into account is 45. The "pensionable salary" is the average salary of the last 5 years. For example, a teacher who retires after 40 years of service, with a pensionable salary of £1800 per annum, qualifies for a lump sum of £2700 and a pension of £900 per annum.

At the age of 60 or thereafter a teacher in good health may surrender part of the pension granted or to be granted to him in order to provide either a pension for his wife or other dependant after his own death, or an annuity during the joint lives of himself and his wife, plus a pension for his widow. It is also possible for a teacher to surrender the whole or a part of his lump sum in exchange for an additional pension of an equivalent actuarial value.

The scheme also provides for the following: to a teacher who becomes incapable through infirmity of mind or body of serving efficiently as a teacher, a disablement allowance if he has more than 10 years' service, a disablement gratuity if he has more than one but less than 10 years' service; to the personal representatives of a teacher who dies after completing not less than 5 years' service, a death gratuity.

Full details of these and other provisions are given in the relevant statutory instruments.[14]

Although the teachers' superannuation scheme is in general adequate, it is by no means uniquely attractive. In other walks of life a few schemes are non-contributory, or demand smaller percentage contributions from salary. Moreover, there is a general tendency to plan for a pension of around two-thirds of salary, whereas most teachers retire with a pension equal to half, often just under half, of their pensionable salary.

Superannuation: Widows' and Children's Scheme; Dependants' Scheme

The Report of a Working Party on Widows' Pensions[15] bore fruit in the Regulations[16] which brought into operation, from 1st April 1965, the first pensions scheme in Britain for the widows, children, and other dependants of teachers.

Participation in the Widows' and Children's Scheme was made compulsory for all new male entrants to the profession, but serving teachers could opt out. For those who participate the rate of contribution is 2% of salary, in addition to the 6% contribution under the main superannuation scheme. With income tax relief, the additional contribution is reduced to an average net contribution of $1\cdot4\%$ of salary. Serving teachers with less than 10 years' service were required to pay for all of it; those with 10 or more year's service were required to pay for at least 10 years, and could opt to pay for as much more of their service as they wanted. Such service can be paid for, either by way of an additional percentage contribution from salary, or by surrender of a portion of the lump sum payable on retirement, or by a combination of these methods.

In the case of a teacher with 10 or more years of reckonable service the position is as follows: if such a teacher dies in retirement, his widow is eligible for a widow's pension equal to one-third of the pension which was being paid to the teacher under the main superannuation scheme; if such a teacher dies while still in service, his widow is eligible for a widow's pension equal to one-third of the main scheme pension which the teacher would have received if he had retired on health grounds on the day of his death. If the widow's pension as thus calculated is less than £115 per annum, a minimum award of £115 a year is made. It should be noted that this fraction, one-third, is only applicable in cases where all the teacher's past service is reckonable under the scheme; if he had only "bought in" a fraction of his past service, the widow's pension would be that fraction of one-third of the main scheme pension.

Where the contributor is survived by a widow and children, children's pensions are payable at the rate of £60 for one eligible child, £110 for two, £160 for three, and £210 for four or more eligible children. Where the contributor is not survived by a widow, but is survived by children, the annual rates of children's pensions are £85 for one eligible child, £105 for two, £245 for three, and £325 for four or more eligible children.

If a contributor dies before completing 10 years' service, but after completing 3 years' service, his widow may, under certain circumstances, qualify for a widowed mother's pension, or a widow's short-service pension.

Participation in the Dependants' Scheme, which is open to both men and women, is entirely voluntary. Under this scheme women teachers may provide pensions, for example, for dependent parents or an invalid husband; and men teachers may provide for parents or dependent relatives other than their widows or children. Details with regard to nominees, contributions and benefits are given in the Regulations.[17]

Both the Widows' and Children's Scheme and the Dependants' Scheme are administered by a Board of Management which exercises powers vested in it by the 1965 Regulations. The Secretary of State is responsible for the general administration of the Schemes, and the costs of administration are met by the Secretary of State and the education authorities.

Thus one of the oldest and most eagerly sought aims of the teaching profession, a pensions scheme for the widows, children, and other dependants of teachers was eventually realized in 1965. Although the original aim of the profession to have the additional percentage contributions shared between teachers and employers was not realised, there is no doubt that the scheme eventually evolved is comparable with schemes available in other sectors of the public service.

PROFESSIONAL ORGANIZATIONS

The three main professional organizations for Scottish teachers are the Educational Institute of Scotland, the Scottish Secondary Teachers' Association, and the Scottish Schoolmasters Association.

Educational Institute of Scotland (EIS)

Although various attempts at organization among Scottish teachers were made in the eighteenth century, the most useful starting-point is 1847, when the EIS was founded for the purpose of promoting sound learning and of advancing the interests of Scottish education. These remain the aims of the Institute; its present structure is outlined below.

The business of the Institute is conducted by a Council, which works mainly through committees. There is an Executive Committee, an Education Committee, a Finance Committee, a Salaries Committee, a Law and Tenure Committee, and various other committees. It is the Executive Committee which transacts the business of the Institute between meetings of the Council, and a Parliamentary Sub-Committee performs the important task of watching over all legislative proposals affecting Scottish education or the interests of teachers, and brings the Institute's views before Members of Parliament and government departments.

Members are grouped in Local Associations, which regulate and transact the business of the Institute within their respective areas. A further grouping is in terms of Education Districts: teachers in primary schools, secondary schools, special schools, and further education centres are organized in separate Education Districts for the purpose of considering relevant questions of curricula, techniques of teaching, conditions of service, and so on.

The whole business of the Institute is reviewed by the Annual General Meeting, which consists of members of Council and delegates from all the Local Associations.

Although various aspects of Institute policy come under attack, especially from rival professional organizations, there is little doubt that the Institute has been of considerable value to Scottish education in general, and there is no doubt at all that it has benefited many individual members of the profession in particular. Its recommendations are usually carefully considered by the Secretary of State and the Scottish Education Department; it produces a weekly publication, *The Scottish Educational Journal*; it has international affiliations and close contacts with the principal English associations; it offers its members legal cover and advice, special terms for insurances, a house purchase scheme, and a confidential trading scheme. In 1965 over 30,000 teachers were members of the EIS.

Scottish Secondary Teachers' Association (SSTA)

The SSTA was constituted as a separate Association in January 1946, in order to safeguard the interests of secondary school teachers who felt that, as a minority group in the EIS, their views received insufficient attention. Such teachers were concerned, moreover, about the adoption by the EIS at that time of a "common maximum" salary policy, the policy that all teachers, regardless of qualifications, should eventually reach the same maximum basic salary. A cardinal feature of SSTA policy has been its insistence on differential salary scales.

The SSTA is open to all qualified teachers in all secondary schools and in further education, and its constitution provides for equality of representation of teachers of various categories at Congress, Council, and Executive. Membership of the SSTA is incompatible with membership of the EIS.

The affairs of the Association are administered by the Council which works through committees—for example, an Executive Committee, a Finance Committee, a Salaries Committee, an Education Committee, and a Law Panel.

For the purpose of electing members to Council, representatives to Congress, and nominating members for the Salaries Committee, schools are grouped into thirteen territorial regions, and a fourteenth region through which Roman Catholic teachers are represented. Subject panels, which meet in five different centres throughout Scotland, enable teachers to discuss problems of curricula, SCE examination papers, and other topics concerning their own subjects.

The supreme authority of the Association is Congress, an annual meeting of the Office-bearers, members of Council, and six representatives from each of the fourteen regions.

The SSTA has grown in stature over the years. Committees have produced reports on various aspects of Scottish education; it provides for its members legal protection, insurance and other benefits. In 1965 over 3700 teachers were members of the SSTA.

The Scottish Schoolmasters Association (SSA)

The SSA, founded in 1933 to advance the interests of school-masters within the EIS, broke away from the Institute for the express purpose of safeguarding and promoting those interests.

The organization of the SSA is in many respects similar to that of the other Associations, the business of the Association being conducted by a Council working through committees, members being grouped into local branches, the supreme authority of the Association being the Annual General Meeting. The SSA has various arrangements with the English National Association of Schoolmasters; for example, Class B members of the SSA are entitled to full benefits of membership of the NAS. In 1965 over 2700 teachers were members of the SSA.

During a middle stage of its development the Association acquired a reputation for being militantly anti-feminist—for example, it staunchly opposed the policy of equal pay for men and women teachers. More recently this militancy has been directed to the problem of salaries in general. As already described, it was a legal action brought by members of the SSA which led to the replacement of the National Joint Council by the Scottish Joint Council; and it was the subsequent attitude of the Association to the issue of secrecy with regard to the deliberations of the Scottish Joint Council which highlighted the urgent need to establish adequate salary-negotiating machinery.

From time to time tentative suggestions are made about "professional unity", the implication being that it would be desirable to have all teachers in one professional organization. In this way, it is claimed, a united front could be presented on such matters as salaries and conditions of service. It was, however, the inadequacy of one organization for a profession with a wide variety of qualifications and professional interests which led to the establishing of other associations, and—although this is an open question—it is probably true that Scottish teachers gain more than they lose by the existing situation.

PROFESSIONAL STATUS

The status of teachers in Scotland, as in many other countries, is not as high as teachers themselves would like it to be, and not as high as that of other professions demanding similar education and training. Many reasons have been put forward to account for this situation: salary level; absence of "mystique" such as that found in medicine and law; lack of control of professional matters; the existence of various levels of qualification within the profession; the attitude of successive governments to education—and so on. Though the reasons for the situation may be complex, it is certainly the case that an important factor determining the status of any profession is the amount of control of their own affairs allowed to the members of that profession. In this connection there have been significant advances in Scottish education in the 1960's.

In May 1961, following strikes and threats of strikes by Scottish teachers, the Secretary of State set up four working parties on matters relevant to the standing of the teaching profession. As a result of developments consequent on the publication of the four reports[18] teachers have attained the following: a Liaison Committee, representative of the main teachers' organizations, the Association of Directors of Education in Scotland, and the Scottish Education Department, to provide an opportunity for discussion of questions concerning curricula, examinations, and school organization; legislation[19] to allow teachers to serve as appointed members on education committees; legislation[20] which has made possible the establishing of the scheme for the provision of pensions for teachers' widows; proposals for improvements with regard to conditions of tenure, consultation between education authorities and teachers, and the possible involvement of teachers in selection boards dealing with promotion.

The most important development, however, was the appointing by the Secretary of State, also in 1961, of a committee under the chairmanship of Lord Wheatley, to review the arrangements for the award and withdrawal of certificates of competency to teach. The committee's report, published in 1963,[21] made recommendations which aimed at conferring on the teaching profession a considerable degree of autonomy. Welcomed by teachers, government, and the interested public, this report led directly to the passing of the Teaching Council (Scotland) Act, 1965, which, by establishing a General Teaching Council, gave the Scottish teaching profession a measure of self-government believed to be the first of its kind in the world.

The General Teaching Council, set up in 1966, consists of forty-four members. Twenty-five elected members represent teachers employed in schools, further education centres, and colleges of education; fifteen appointed members represent local authorities, directors of education, the universities, central institutions, the Church of Scotland and the Roman Catholic Church; and four members are nominated by the Secretary of State. Members hold office for four years.

The main functions of the Council are the making of recommendations to the Secretary of State with regard to conditions which individuals must satisfy in order to be recommended by the governing body of a college of education to the Council for registration; and the establishing of a register of teachers. Registration will replace certification by the Secretary of State. The Council also makes recommendations to the Secretary of State with regard to the supply of teachers, but matters of salary and conditions of service remain the province of the Scottish Joint Council or its successor.

With regard to professional discipline, the Council sets up, from its own members, an Investigating Committee and a Disciplinary Committee; the Disciplinary Committee has the power to direct that an application for registration be refused, or that a name be removed from the register—for example, if the person concerned has been convicted of a criminal offence, or has been guilty of infamous conduct in a professional respect.

The Council must keep itself informed as to the general content and arrangement of courses provided in colleges of education.

To this end the Council may appoint persons to visit colleges of education and to report to the Council, which may make recommendations on the basis of such reports to the relevant governing bodies.

It should be noted that the Council has not been given complete control over standards of admission to the profession. Although the Secretary of State must have regard to the Council's recommendations, he may still overrule the Council; in such a case, however, he would have to make public the Council's recommendations, and his reasons for rejecting them.

These changes, all of which are expected to be completed by 1st April 1967, constitute a landmark in the history of Scottish education in general, and in the development of the status of the teaching profession in particular. The establishing of the General Teaching Council, increasing consultation between teachers, education authorities, and the Scottish Education Department, higher salaries, pensions for teachers' widows, even the employment of auxiliaries to relieve teachers of routine chores in schools —all these play a part in raising the standing of the profession in the eyes of the general public, and, perhaps as important, in the eyes of the teachers themselves.

ADDENDA

As this book goes through the press, certain changes are taking place with regard to teacher training.

1. *The Teachers* (*Colleges of Education*) (*Scotland*) *Regulations 1967* replace *The Teachers* (*Training Authorities*) (*Scotland*) *Regulations, 1958*. The new Regulations provide for the dissolution of the Scottish Council for the Training of Teachers, so that colleges now have no standing national body based on their own governing bodies to speak and act on their behalf. However, governing bodies are empowered jointly to appoint a committee for consultation on matters of common interest, and the Principals of the colleges are likely to continue to meet and function as an effective and powerful group. Other changes provided for by the

new Regulations include: the inclusion in the governing body of each college of the principal, vice-principal, and a small number of members of the teaching staff; the extension of the period of office of governing bodies from three years to four; and the discontinuance of contributions by education authorities to the financing of the colleges.

2. *The Teachers* (*Education, Training and Registration*) (*Scotland*) *Regulations 1967*, at present in draft form, will replace *The Teachers* (*Education, Training and Certification*) (*Scotland*) *Regulations 1965*. The new Regulations express without change of substance the provisions of the 1965 Regulations so that the same conditions shall apply for the registration of teachers by the General Teaching Council as have applied for the certification of teachers by the Secretary of State. The three Certificates are renamed Qualifications, so that candidates for registration are required to secure a Teaching Qualification (Primary Education), a Teaching Qualification (Secondary Education), or a Teaching Qualification (Further Education). The special qualifications available under the 1965 Regulations as endorsements on Certificates are in future to take the form of college of education awards.

The Regulations also provide for the admission of men on the same footing as women to the three year course for primary school teachers, a development recommended by the General Teaching Council and accepted by the Secretary of State.

The Regulations amend *The Schools* (*Scotland*) *Code, 1956, The Teachers* (*Superannuation*) (*Scotland*) *Regulations, 1957*, and *The Teachers' Salaries* (*Scotland*) *Regulations 1966* to take account of the changes necessitated by the introduction of the new nomenclature and arrangements. The consequences of these amendments, and particularly the fact that existing teachers will have to register to maintain their present rights in relation to permanent appointment and salary scales, are currently the subject of debate in the teachers' professional organizations. As a result the making of the Regulations in their final form has been delayed.

REFERENCES AND NOTES

1. See CRUICKSHANK, M., *The History of the Training of Teachers in Scotland.* To be published by the University of London Press in the series of volumes sponsored by the Scottish Council for Research in Education.

2. For exact details of the composition of the Scottish Council see *The Teachers (Training Authorities) (Scotland) Regulations, 1958*, Second Schedule.

3. *The Regulations for the Preliminary Education, Training and Certification of Teachers for Various Grades of Schools (Scotland) 1931.*

4. For full details of standard qualifications, supplementary courses, and appropriate alternative qualifications for the Teacher's Certificate (Secondary Education) see Scottish Education Department: *Memorandum on Entry Requirements and Courses 1966*, Edinburgh, H.M.S.O., 1966, Appendix A.

5. *Ibid.*, Paras. 14 and 15. Appendix B has full details of standard qualifications required for the Teacher's Certificate (Further Education), and appropriate alternative qualifications accepted.

6. For procedure see *The Teachers (Education, Training and Certification) (Scotland) Regulations, 1965*, Regulation 8.

7. Committee on Higher Education: *Higher Education*, Cmnd. 2154, London, H.M.S.O., 1963, Para. 363.

8. SCOTLAND, JAMES, Bachelor of Education. First moves in Scotland, *Times Educational Supplement*, 18th June 1965.

9. "Open" talks on supply, *Scottish Educational Journal*, 15th Oct. 1965.

10. A Departmental Committee on the Supply of Teachers in Scotland, appointed in May 1950, submitted four reports. The fourth report in December 1961 made tentative forecasts to 1970 and 1975.

11. Scottish Education Department: *Measures to Secure a more Equitable Distribution of Teachers in Scotland*, Edinburgh, H.M.S.O., 1966, Paras. 56–69.

12. University of Glasgow Appointments Committee: *Report of Sub-Committee on Recruitment to School Teaching*, 1963.

13. Index of Teachers' Earnings, *Scottish Educational Journal*, 23rd July 1965.

14 *The Teachers (Superannuation) (Scotland) Regulations, 1957*, and amendments. *The Teachers (Superannuation) (Scotland) Rules, 1965.*

15. Scottish Education Department: *Pensions for Teachers' Widows*, Edinburgh, H.M.S.O., 1962.

16. *The Teachers (Superannuation) (Family Benefits) (Scotland) Regulations, 1965.*

17. *Ibid.*, Part IV.

18. Scottish Education Department: (1) *Consultation on Educational Matters.* (2) *Relations between Education Authorities and Teachers.* (3) *Appointment of Teachers to Education Committees.* (4) *Pensions for Teachers' Widows.* Edinburgh, H.M.S.O., 1962.

19. Education (Scotland) Act, 1963, Section 4.

20. *Ibid.*, Section 3.

21. Scottish Education Department: *The Teaching Profession in Scotland*, Cmnd. 2066, Edinburgh, H.M.S.O., 1963.

Concluding Comment

THIS book has sought to present a factual outline, together with a certain amount of evaluation, of the Scottish educational system. The attempt has also been made to suggest what future trends are likely to be. While it would be tedious to summarize what has been said earlier, it is perhaps worthwhile to highlight briefly the most important directions of development.

The winds of change which began to blow on Scottish education in the mid-1950's have never since been less than moderate in strength, and have affected virtually every aspect of the educational system. Their direction has been broadly determined by official action in the form of various reports issued between 1955 and 1965.

In 1955 *Junior Secondary Education* laid the basis for the planning of non-academic courses of secondary education, and suggested guiding principles for the selection of curriculum content and the choice of methods of teaching. In 1959 the *Report of the Working Party on the Curriculum of the Senior Secondary School* led to far-reaching changes in the curriculum and examination structure of secondary schools providing certificate courses. In 1962 *New Ways in Junior Secondary Education* assessed developments in 3-year secondary courses to that date, and indicated where further progress was desirable. In 1963 the report *From School to Further Education* went further, recommending the inclusion in non-certificate courses of more obvious vocational elements, and stressing the need for forging links between school and further education. In the same year the report of the Robbins Committee on *Higher Education* indicated the need for a vast expansion in the sphere of education in universities, institutions of advanced further education, and colleges of education, and provided a mass of factual information on the basis of which policy decisions could be made. Finally, in 1965 the memorandum *Primary Education in Scotland* charted the way ahead for primary schools in terms of a more integrated curriculum and more stimulating and progressive teaching techniques.

Action which has been taken on the lines suggested by these reports has indicated what future developments may be expected in Scottish education. Unless there is a complete change of policy with regard to the building of nursery schools, there is likely to be little progress in the provision of nursery education at least until the later 1970's, when the problems arising from the raising of the school-leaving age to 16 in 1970 have been wholly or partly solved. Even then nursery provision is likely to suffer in favour of fresh demands on resources from other areas of the educational system.

In primary education there is certain to be less slavish adherence to the traditional policy of drilling in the three R's, an attempt to provide a broader, more integrated and more interesting curriculum, a more widespread adoption of group work, project and activity methods, and the development of a more relaxed, informal relationship between teacher and taught. Transfer tests at the end of primary education are likely to loom less large, or to disappear, thus removing the distorting and narrowing effect they have tended to have on the primary curriculum.

Secondary education will develop along comprehensive lines. Small secondary schools in the more remote areas are likely to be closed in accordance with the trend towards centralization. Large schools will be expected to provide a "common" first year for all pupils, and to offer a wide range of subjects and combinations of subjects for academic and non-academic pupils, and an increased number of extra-curricular activities. More and more children are likely to remain at school beyond the statutory leaving age, to sit the Scottish Certificate of Education examinations at Ordinary and/or Higher grades, and to continue their education at institutions of further or higher education.

The expansion of further education, already considerable, will certainly continue, with an increasing provision of day release, block release, and sandwich courses. A new partnership between industry and education is likely to develop gradually as a result of the Industrial Training Act, 1964.

Colleges of education will be required to train teachers for the changing situation outlined above, and there may well be a demand for training for the purpose of teaching broader age groups of children, and new combinations of subjects. There will be a considerable expansion of the facilities for in-service training and refresher courses. The B.Ed. degree is likely to be well established in the major colleges before 1970, and a four-year associateship course may eventually be introduced.

In the universities, the emphasis to begin with will be on expansion in an effort to ensure that all applicants with the requisite entrance qualifications get a university place. New courses will be developed, and existing courses modified, in order to meet the needs arising from changes in economic, social, and industrial conditions. Experiments are likely with unusual combinations of subjects and with new teaching techniques. In all these areas much is expected of the newer universities.

As the speed of educational change increases, as improved methods and techniques are advocated, and as ever larger sums of money are spent on education, the need becomes greater for decision-making in education to be soundly based, wherever possible, on research findings. The Scottish Council for Research in Education, established as long ago as 1928, has to its credit an impressive list of over fifty publications, and is at present concerned with research projects covering a variety of topics. It is to be hoped that the future will see an increased allocation of funds for the purposes of educational research, and the more efficient translation of research findings into action on the classroom floor.

In the light of the above and other developments described in previous chapters, it is probably no longer true to say that Scottish education, when compared with English education, is "marking time or even falling behind". It is true that Scottish education is unlikely to regain its pre-eminence of former centuries, but there is little doubt that any decline has been halted, and perhaps some ground has been regained. As a result, the general prospect in Scottish education at the present is brighter, and the possibility of achieving desirable developments is greater, than at any time in the past 30 years. Whether or not full use is made of the various opportunities for progress which now present themselves is a judgement which the future will make.

Index